Robert Howes was born and brought up in Bristol.
Secretary of the Westminster CHE (Campaign for Homose...
group from 1978 to 1980, and a telephone volunteer and befriender for
London Friend and Cambridge Friend between 1981 and 1992. He has
been a member of Gay West since 1985.

GAY WEST

Civil Society, Community and LGBT History
in Bristol and Bath 1970 to 2010

Robert Howes

SilverWood

Published in paperback in 2011 by SilverWood Books, Bristol, BS1 4HJ
www.silverwoodbooks.co.uk

ISBN 978-1-906236-75-5

British Library Cataloguing in Publication Data
A CIP catalogue record for this book is available from the British Library

Set in Sabon by SilverWood Books
Printed in England on paper certified as being from responsible sources

To my late parents for their love and support

Table of Contents

Preface

I should like to thank the many people who have contributed to this work, particularly those who have given me interviews, either face to face or by telephone. The information they have provided has given an invaluable additional dimension to the documentation, suggesting new leads and clarifying aspects which are sometimes obscure in the written sources. Interviewees have also helped greatly by putting me in touch with their friends, providing a practical example of the value of friendship networks. I have included names in the text with the written consent of the persons concerned or when they are a matter of public record (e.g. newspaper articles published with the interviewee's consent). Many other people have been involved in the LGBT movement and the fact that they are not named here is in no way intended to diminish their contribution.

The research for this book was carried out with the knowledge and co-operation of Gay West, who have also given permission for me to quote from their documentation. I am most grateful to the Chairman, Paul Green, for his support with this project. This is not an official history, however, and the final responsibility for the text and the opinions expressed in it remains mine.

Sources of Documentation

Besides my own collection of the Gay West newsletter, I have used the documentation sources listed in the footnotes and I am most grateful to their owners and archivists for allowing me access and giving me permission to cite them. Many of the documents cited are in Gay West's own archive, currently held by the Membership Secretary, Martin Reeves, who kindly allowed me to consult the contents at my leisure. I should particularly like to thank Charlie Beaton for access to his personal archive and to Andy Foyle and Chris Leigh for their advice. I gratefully acknowledge permission given by the Campaign for Homosexual Equality to cite the documentation held in the Hall Carpenter Archive in the London School of Economics. I am also much indebted to Sue Donnelly, the LSE archivist, and her staff for their help.

The book collection of the LSE Library and the newspaper cuttings in the Lesbian and Gay Newsmedia Archive (LAGNA) have also been of immense assistance in writing this book.

List of Interviewees

Diesel Balaam	26 July 2008
Vince Baughan	19 May 2008
Charlie Beaton	9 September 2009
	14 February 2010
	2 May 2010
John Bescoby	20 July 2007
Stephen Bradford	6 July 2008
Donald Branch	4 August 2009
Chris Brown	15 March 2010
Edward (Eddie) Cherrie	5 February 2010 (by telephone)
Nigel Collins	24 August 2009
Steve Cossey	24 July 2009
Ernie Everest	31 March 2008
Andy Foyle	28 April 2008
Roland Gonzalez Attwell	28 July 2007 (by telephone)
	23 August 2010 (by telephone)
Manuel Gosano	11 April 2008
Paul Green	2 August 2008
Peggy Hancock	6 June 2011
	Plus various conversations
John Hesketh	26 November 2011
Gerry Hunt	11 August 2008
Bob Illingworth	13 December 2009
Bob Johnson	12 August 2009
Norman Lapper	13 December 2009
Chris Leigh	4 August 2009
Ken Little	21 August 2009
John Martin	16 August 2008
Angela Needham	30 November 2009 (by telephone)
Bob Osborne	6 July 2008
John Pritchett	3 June 2007
	23 November 2009
Rachel	16 December 2009 (by telephone)
	20 December 2009 (by telephone)
Sid Roberts	21 July 2009
Philip Smith	16 August 2008

Kerry Sutton-Spence   10 January 2010 (by telephone)
Keith Thomas   13 December 2009
Julian Vagg   19 May 2008
James W   21 October 2008
Dale Wakefield   19 January 2010
Berkeley Wilde   19 March 2010

A number of other people gave me information on condition of anonymity. I am grateful to all the above for their help with this project.

1

Setting the Scene

This book is a study of LGBT (lesbian, gay, bisexual and transgender) activism in the Bristol and Bath region, describing the development of the LGBT movement in the area over a period of forty years, with a particular focus on the Gay West group. Gay West is a voluntary self-help organisation which provides social and support facilities for LGBT people. Through its predecessor organisations, CHE (Campaign for Homosexual Equality) Bristol and Bath Gay Awareness Group/Bath CHE, Gay West can trace its origins back to April 1970 and so is one of the oldest LGBT organisations with a continuous existence in the country, covering most of the period since the decriminalisation of male homosexuality in 1967. The book sets this group in its historical and geographical context, showing how its development has reflected changes in the social and political environment at both the national and local levels.

The book also describes the development of the commercial LGBT scene in Bristol and Bath. In attempting to sketch the sites and facilities used by gay men and lesbians since the 1960s, I seek to show how groups such as Gay West have co-existed alongside the continuing gay subculture and commercial scene, and have at the same time helped to expand the range of sites available to LGBT people. Gay West has generally sought meeting places outside the recognised gay scene and tried to use, albeit on a temporary basis, facilities regularly frequented by the general community for social or business purposes. A major argument of this book is that in searching for and using physical spaces which are regarded as fully legitimate and acceptable by the general community, Gay West has helped to situate the needs and wishes of LGBT people on the same level as those of mainstream society. This search has sometimes been strongly contested and in asserting the legitimacy of LGBT social activities, Gay West has contributed to the creation of space for LGBT people in civil society. In short, it argues that the search for physical space has also created a moral and social space, and indirectly a lever for political advance and acknowledgement.

While some of this history is specific to this organisation and this area, much else has undoubtedly been replicated in other towns and cities across England and Wales (Scotland has a rather different history). The following pages are therefore intended to serve as a case study, with the aim of throwing light on the development of the LGBT movement outside the large metropolitan centres. In particular, the book looks at a number of areas to which historians have so far given relatively little attention.

Firstly, the LGBT movement in the UK has been dominated by the left-discourse of gay liberation, left-wing groups have been the most energetic in political activism and the main legislative reforms have been achieved under Labour governments. The Left has undoubtedly had a major direct influence on the LGBT movement and this has been reflected in the attention which historians have given to the movement's revolutionary, liberationist wing. Nevertheless, there was also a significant reformist side taking an assimilationist approach. A principal aim of this book is to examine how reformist discourses, which can be characterised as liberal, conservative or apolitical, have been deployed and what happens when they encounter prejudice and homophobia.

Secondly, most published work discusses the LGBT movement at the national level or focuses on life in the major concentrations of LGBT populations, particularly London, Brighton and Manchester. Much less has been written about other British cities and yet anyone who went on the London Lesbian and Gay Pride marches of the 1970s and 1980s cannot fail to have been struck by the number of banners carried by local groups and gaysocs (university LGBT societies) from cities and towns across the country, or noticed how the listings carried by *Gay News* and other gay guides bore witness to the existence of LGBT life outside the main urban areas. What happens in the provinces is important because not all LGBT people can or wish to move to the large urban centres. Furthermore, although in the UK major political decisions are made in London, the great majority of MPs who contribute to this process represent constituencies outside the capital and give particular attention to the views presented to them by their constituents. The LGBT History Month and a number of Lottery Heritage funded projects are now beginning to direct attention to history at the regional or local area. This work hopes to contribute to this trend by focusing on LGBT history in a region which is not known as a major lesbian and gay centre but which nevertheless has a rich LGBT history waiting to be uncovered.

Thirdly, much of the published history and analysis on British

LGBT life has concentrated on political groups and movements, culture (the press, television, literature, art, cinema, popular music, etc.), social life and oral history. Little attention has been given until recently to self-help organisations working in the voluntary sector, yet these have been some of the longest-lasting LGBT institutions, providing information (e.g. Lesbian and Gay Switchboards), befriending and counselling (e.g. Friend), social facilities (e.g. Kenric, Gay Outdoor Club) and religious services (e.g. Lesbian and Gay Christian Movement, Metropolitan Community Church).[1] This book looks at the voluntary sector, charting how one LGBT self-help organisation has constituted and run itself over the years.

Finally, this work is also a tale of two cities, Bristol and Bath. Although only some 12 miles apart, they are very different in terms of their economic and social history, and each retains a distinctive character. This difference is reflected in the differing course of development of the local LGBT movement in the two cities. To some extent, this reflects the personalities and the political outlook of the activists involved in the local movement but it also depends on the political culture of the particular locality. The book sets out the physical, social and political context in which the LGBT movement worked. It contrasts some of the alternative choices open to lesbian and gay activists working at the local level and how they have been affected by the local political culture.

LGBT history is marked by long periods of silence, where documentation is absent because male homosexuality was illegal. Even since decriminalisation in 1967, there are many gaps in the record. LGBT organisations have a high turn-over rate and collective memories are short. Research for this project has revealed a striking example: since 1993, Gay West has been holding its Saturday coffee shop in the same building where the Bath Gay Awareness Group held its first public meetings in 1973, without anyone realising because the people involved had completely changed. This book is not intended to be a comprehensive history of Gay Bristol or Gay Bath – a work written from the perspective of the women's movement or the commercial scene would look very different. Nevertheless, it aims to recover some of this collective memory and I hope that it will encourage further research into other aspects of LGBT history in the area.

Gay West as an organisation is notable for its longevity, where so many others have come and gone. With its predecessors, it covers almost the entire period when male homosexuality has been legal in Britain. In his study of changing sexual behaviour and attitudes in postwar Britain, *The World We Have Won*, Jeffrey Weeks shows how the position of LGBT people has also changed over the last 60 years.[2] As another recent study shows, there are now three generations of gay men, as well as women,

15

each with different experiences, who have lived through the years of gay liberation.[3] The long history of Gay West acts as a thread, providing a point of reference to the changes in the political situation, social attitudes and intellectual concepts around same-sex relations over the last forty years.

Theoretical Framework

In 1994 a Gay West activist exhorted his fellow members: "homosexual sex between men over 21, and now 18, did not become legal because 35 men in Bristol drank tea, ate biscuits and talked about the weather. Also, no matter how good your Victoria sponge is, you wont [sic] achieve equality before the law for gays by serving it to your friends. Such things happened, and are happening, because people were, and are, prepared to campaign."[4] On one level, the writer is perfectly correct. The great works of political philosophy are rather short on recipes for Victoria sponge cake. But even philosophers need physical and social sustenance. The tension between campaigning, or political activism, and social activities forms a recurrent feature of the history of Gay West and its predecessors. Activists wanted the group to act as a vehicle for pressing political decision-makers for better conditions for gay people but found that socialising was the main attraction for the majority of the members, who were essential for the group's continued viability and claims to representativeness. This book tries to unpack some of the assumptions in the above quotation. It argues that, in the context of the LGBT movement as a whole, social activities were complementary to political activism rather than its antithesis, as it sometimes seemed. The mundane activities of everyday sociability also had political implications.

Firstly, for the sake of historical accuracy, it is necessary to carry out a certain amount of finessing to the quotation. The group of men referred to also included women (although always in a minority), the majority of the meetings were held in Bath rather than Bristol and they generally drank coffee rather than tea. Most importantly, however, they did this openly. The idea of a group of gay men and women sitting round in the middle of Bath drinking coffee does not sound much like a revolutionary act. But the fact that for over twenty-five years such a group has been meeting regularly in a public place in the centre of a British city, openly advertising its status and presence, and even on occasion receiving the police as its guests (rather than the other way around) *is* something new. Indeed, nothing like it has happened before in over a thousand years of British history. Bath, of course, is not the only British city where this has happened and, indeed, it is part of a trend which has swept across the western world. Rather than argue for the uniqueness of this phenomenon, therefore, this book seeks to analyse the history of Gay West as a representative microcosm of what has happened across the country during the last half-century, albeit noting that many incidents were specific to this particular group.

In 1955, Peter Wildeblood began the account of his recent trial by stating openly that he was a homosexual. He noted that he could say this because his private life had been made public by the newspapers and he was in the rare position of having nothing left to hide.[5] This trial and other equally notorious ones in the mid-1950s helped to trigger the setting-up of the Wolfenden Committee, whose recommendations set in train the lengthy process of law reform. And yet fifty years later – not a long span in human history – the serving Prime Minister and leaders of the main opposition parties were giving interviews to a gay magazine in order to appeal to the "gay vote", with only minimal press comment.[6] The legislative reforms promoted by the New Labour government in the early 2000s were bitterly resisted by opponents in the House of Lords, most organised religious groups are still hostile to homosexual equality and horrific examples of homophobic violence still occur. Nevertheless, the changes seem to have been accepted by British society at large and have been incorporated into the mainstream. In particular, there was little sense that they were the fads of a metropolitan elite foisted upon an unwilling country. These developments represent an enormous change in attitudes towards LGBT people in less than a life-span, a change which has had its effects in the provinces as much as in London.

This work draws on the theoretical insights of academic work in the areas of social movements, community, civil society, identity and space. Gay West is part of the lesbian and gay movement, which is itself one of the new social movements which have had a major impact on society, politics and culture across the western world since the 1960s. In the UK, modern social movements began with the Campaign for Nuclear Disarmament (CND) in the late 1950s and include the peace, anti-racism, women's and environmental movements.[7] In his study of social movements in Britain, Paul Byrne makes a distinction between protest campaigns, protest movements and social movements. Protest campaigns are centred upon a single issue, and of limited durability. Protest movements are seeking political changes, alterations to specific areas of public policy, while social movements are as interested in cultural as political change.[8] The LGBT movement in general has included elements of all three, with the battle against Section 28 epitomising a protest campaign and the lengthy political struggle for law reform to ensure equality representing a protest movement while at the same time the changes in the way lesbians and gay men see themselves and are seen by others is an example of the cultural change pursued by a social movement. All three elements are reflected in the history of Gay West and its predecessors.

Three other aspects of social movement theory are particularly relevant to the present study. Tarrow notes the cyclical nature of social movements, with "cycles of contention" marked by periods of mobilisation, followed by demobilisation.[9] D'Emilio noted in the Afterword to the second edition of his pioneering study of the American gay movement:

> There are moments when events, circumstances, and personalities combine to spark a great deal of change in a compressed period of time. These moments of leaping ahead are always accomplished through some combination of militant collective action and radical visionary outlook. But in between are longer stretches of just creeping along. They display less drama and excitement; the kind of change that occurs often escapes notice at the time. But the work of these eras is critically important nonetheless.[10]

Melucci refers to social movements' "double existence within the invisible networks of civil society and in the temporary mobilizations through which they become publicly visible".[11]

The lesbian and gay movement in the Bristol area generally reflected the trend of the national movement, which saw a period of intense activity in the early 1970s, followed by a decline in the mid-1970s and early 1980s, with another period of mobilisation in the later 1980s. To a casual outside observer, the LGBT movement would only become visible during protest campaigns such as the Gay News blasphemy trial in 1976–79 and Section 28 in 1987–88 or during the annual Pride marches and festivals. In reality, the movement continued between these events and this work shows that the LGBT movement has existed continuously in the Bristol area since 1970. Melucci warns against the tendency to judge collective action in terms of its impact on the political system because this weakens understanding of the independent processes at work within social movements.[12] Stephen M. Engel, in his comparison of the American and British gay and lesbian movements in the light of social movement theory, also emphasises the importance of the cultural dimension.[13] This work will discuss the political repercussions of the LGBT movement in the west but will show how political activity, while important, is only part of the picture.

In his classic sociological text, *Community and Civil Society*, Ferdinand Tönnies makes a distinction between, on the one hand, community [Gemeinschaft], which is a living organism based on family, neighbourhood and friendship, and is expressed in custom or religious feeling, and on the other hand, civil society or association [Gesellschaft], which is a mechanical creation, based on legal systems, policy and public opinion.[14] Community carries a warm sense of belonging and integration and is regularly invoked by both the Left and the Right.[15] As an ideal, it expresses a virtually universal longing for humane social existence at the most basic level.[16] Identity-based social movements such as the LGBT movement have used the concept of community to mobilise their constituents, to generate feelings of self-worth, purposiveness and activism in their participants and to win concrete gains in terms of rights, services and participation in government machinery.[17] Lesbian and gay organisations, and now increasingly public bodies and the media, frequently refer to the "gay community" and indeed Gay West's official subtitle (for historical reasons) is "Bath Gay Community Organisation".

Community is, however, a problematic concept for LGBT people, as a number of critics have pointed out. The concept of community has been the subject of much theoretical debate, particularly in the context of globalisation and neo-liberalism. Communitarians such as Amitai Etzioni have developed a critique of liberal individualism, which has itself been criticised for its implicit conservatism.[18] Feminists like Marilyn Friedman point to the exclusion and suppression of non-group members, especially those defined by ethnicity and sexual orientation, which characterise many communities.[19] Young lesbians and gays who have been thrown out by their families or those ostracised by neighbours and workmates can testify to the negative aspects of community feeling, fuelled by homophobia. Furthermore, while identity may be presented as a bond between community members, this is often not the case because communal participants are not identical and many of those to whom an identity is attached do not take part in communal activities.[20] In response to these problems, theorists such as Friedman and others have developed a distinction between communities of fate (those we are born into, based on ethnicity, nationality, religion or class) and communities of choice (those we make a conscious decision to join, such as the women's or LGBT movement).[21] Consequently, the ideal of community cannot be taken as an automatic good without, as Iris Marion Young points out, a critical reassessment to accommodate a politics of difference.[22] Nevertheless, in a British context, Mike Homfray has argued that communitarianism can be compatible with gay and lesbian equality.[23]

The other side of Tönnies's dichotomy is civil society. This concept can be traced back to John Locke, Adam Ferguson and other writers of the Scottish Enlightenment, as well as Hegel, but it took on a new lease of life in the 1970s and 1980s when it was invoked by the opponents of the totalitarian communist regimes of Eastern Europe and the military dictatorships in Latin America. Although it has been largely replaced in these areas by the triumph of liberal democracy and market economics, civil society has since become an important tool of international donor agencies in their attempts to secure better governance in developing countries.

Civil society is a loose concept and has been defined in different ways but it is now generally agreed to comprise that section of society which is not directly involved either in government or the state, on the one hand, nor in the market or economy, on the other. Frank Prochaska defines civil society as a separate sphere or half-way house formed of free associations standing between the state and society, which mitigate the atomising effects of both bureaucratic government and the market. As a buffer between the government and the citizenry, civil society promotes a moral environment in which individual rights and civic virtues, essential to social well-being, may be expressed.[24] In practical terms, civil society usually refers to the voluntary sector, charities and non-governmental organisations (NGOs). Prochaska also notes that the wish to protect one's community or to express one's aspirations through charitable work has long held an appeal. Charitable association is a promising way for various minorities who are culturally vulnerable or politically isolated to forge a relationship with the wider society.

The growing interest in civil society is related to the concept of human rights, which has been one of the main drivers towards LGBT equality since the 1980s. Vieira and DuPree flag up five ways in which civil society contributes towards human rights: 1) it provides a sphere of action for all social groups; 2) it makes injustice public; 3) it protects private spaces from state and market incursion; 4) it intervenes and interacts directly with legal and political systems; and 5) it drives social innovation.[25] During the 1980s and 1990s, the concept of human rights was extended to include sexual orientation.[26]

Questions of identity loom large in the academic literature, ranging from the use of labelling theory and stigma to describe closet homosexuals in the 1960s to the multiple identities inhabited today.[27] Discussions of identity have covered the differences between the gay world and the straight world, divisions within the gay world based on the classic sociological concepts of gender, class and ethnicity, and the kaleidoscope of self-categorisations associated with sexual diversity, including the different political groupings of lesbians (gay women, radical feminists, lesbian-separatists), bisexuals, transgenders (transvestites, transsexuals), HIV positive people and people with AIDS (PWAs), queers, couples and civil partners, drag queens, clones, SM adepts, bears and so on.

The question of identity is not static or just a private matter but is a dynamic process which has political and social ramifications as well. As Craig Calhoun explains, the links between civil society and the public sphere of social movements, like the LGBT movement, are largely based on identity. Identity formation needs to be approached as part of the process of public life, not something that can be settled beforehand in a private sphere. Recognising the diversity of identities which people bring from their manifold involvements in civil society is an issue of democratic inclusiveness.[28]

The fifth theoretical focus is the use of space. During the 1990s, academics began to explore the relationship between physical space and sexuality, concentrating on the means by which LGBT people have temporarily colonised geographical sites for sexual purposes or socialising. Historians have recovered the hidden history of major world cities, such as New York, Rio de Janeiro and London, recording the places where gay men and women lived, socialised, formed friendship networks and engaged in sexual relations.[29] Geographers have looked at LGBT use of space in more theoretical ways, mapping residential areas, bars and cruising areas as well as charting the rise of the pink economy through consumption patterns and the development of gay villages.[30]

Of Sodomitic Societies and Buggery Clubs

Modern concepts of civil society were developed in the context of dictatorship and it may seem a bit far-fetched to compare the situation of gays in Britain with totalitarianism. Indeed the parallel should not be taken too far but it is worth considering the implications of the definition of civil society offered by Jean Cohen and Andrew Arato as:

> a normative model of a societal realm different from the state and the economy and having the following components: (1) *Plurality*: families, informal groups, and voluntary associations whose plurality and autonomy allow for a variety of forms of life; (2) *Publicity*: institutions of culture and communication; (3) *Privacy*: a domain of individual self-development and moral choice; and (4) *Legality*: structures of general laws and basic rights needed to demarcate plurality, privacy, and publicity from at least the state and, tendentially, the economy.[31]

If we use this as a template to assess the situation when the 1967 Sexual Offences Act decriminalising male homosexuality in England and Wales was passed, we can see that the comparison is not altogether fanciful. Taking the last item – legality – first, until 1967 the law criminalised all male homosexual acts, in private as well as public. Although, in practice, the police rarely invaded private homes, the law in theory denied all privacy to gay men and, in particular, laid them open to blackmail. The ramifications of the law also denied gay men the benefits of publicity and plurality. Unless claiming life-long celibacy, gay men could not identify themselves as such without admitting to being criminals and so could not form openly-gay associations (groups, clubs) or cultural institutions (magazines, newsletters), without laying themselves open to the risk of criminal prosecution. Gay men lived in a climate of fear of exposure. The only people to escape from this threat were those who, like Peter Wildeblood, had already been ruined or who, like Quentin Crisp, were prepared to lead a marginalised and dangerous life. The great majority of gay men avoided detection and many people have happy memories of the parties and personal friendships of the period but careless correspondence or an ill-judged smile could spell disaster. As Patrick Higgins points out, the civil rights of homosexuals who fell into the grasp of the judicial system were routinely abused by police and judiciary alike.[32] Consequently, while the law acted as a form of social control rather than outright repression, its effect was to create an atmosphere of insecurity, with the ever-present possibility of arrest or blackmail.

The furtiveness and sense of insecurity engendered by illegality is vividly conveyed in this excerpt from the memoirs of James Kirkup, author of the poem which provoked the *Gay News* blasphemy trial. While teaching at Bath Academy of Art in Corsham in the mid-1950s, he picked up "an elderly, rubicund gent" in a public toilet in nearby Chippenham.

> It transpired that my gent had to catch a bus to Bath, the one that passes through Corsham, so we got on the same bus and went upstairs, where there were many empty seats, and indulged in mutual masturbation all the way to my stop. I had an orgasm round about Pickwick, and it was only then that I noticed our local plain-clothes officer was sitting on the opposite side of the bus, a few seats in front of us. We had covered ourselves carefully with coats when the conductor came upstairs to take our fares, and tried to cover our passion with stony faces and nonchalant cigarettes. [After arriving home] I got a sickly feeling of nagging anxiety: I was sure that the plain-clothes dick had spotted what my companion and I were up to under our raincoats. [...] I was overcome by waves of nausea and agonies of doubt and fear, and for the next few days I lived in terror of hearing a knock on the door and seeing a detective in our stone porch.[33]

Lest this vision of the Stasi travelling on the Chippenham bus seem like unfounded paranoia, it is worth recalling a famous case which occurred in Bath some fifteen years earlier during the Second World War. When the Blitz started in London, the leading theatrical photographer Angus McBean moved to Bath and set up a studio and flat in Kingston House, Pierrepont Street. He soon became the centre of a circle of gay servicemen and other young men. Early in the morning of 23 November 1941, the Bath police raided the flat and arrested the 37–year old Mcbean and a 16–year old who was staying with him. In searching the flat, the police found a diary and letters which led them to several of McBean's friends. They were arrested, their homes searched and further diaries and letters found, which resulted in almost twenty men being questioned.

McBean stood trial at Winchester Assizes in March 1942, together with five others, all in their teens or twenties, and pleaded guilty. The judge, Lord Chief Justice Caldecote, at the time Lord Chief Justice of England, rather undermined the majesty of the law by farting while he passed sentence but he did not allow this moment of human frailty to reduce the severity of the law. McBean was sentenced to four years hard labour (twice as long as Oscar Wilde, as he later remarked) and twelve months imprisonment to run concurrently, while the other defendants received shorter custodial sentences. One man was convicted on the basis of a series of love letters he had written to another of the defendants. While the investigations were going on, one man committed suicide and another died when the car he was driving ran off the road, probably deliberately. The case achieved considerable notoriety and was reported in both the local press and the *News of the World*.[34]

According to one historian, it was another spate of prosecutions in Somerset which provided the impetus for setting up the Homosexual Law Reform Society (HLRS), the lobby group which pressed for the implementation of the Wolfenden Committee report's recommendations on the legalisation of male homosexual relations.[35] In January 1958, R.D. Reid, a former Taunton headmaster who had himself been convicted of a homosexual offence before the war, wrote a letter of protest to the *Spectator*.[36] This was followed by a letter to the *Times* organised by Tony Dyson and signed by prominent political and intellectual figures, calling on the government to implement Wolfenden's recommendations.[37] This in turn led on to the creation of the HLRS.

The main argument used by those advocating reform of the criminal law in the 1960s was its corrosive effects in promoting blackmail, an argument dramatised in the film *Victim*, starring Dirk Bogarde, which was released in 1961. When Lord Arran's bill was first introduced into the House of Lords in 1965, supporters such as Lady Gaitskell and the Marquess of Queensberry used reasoned arguments to press the need for change. Making his maiden speech, the Marquess of Queensberry, great-grandson of Oscar Wilde's nemesis, said: "I do not believe that our laws on this subject, as they relate to adults, are in any way a solution. They have, if anything, helped to produce a nasty, furtive, underworld that is bad for society and bad for the homosexual."[38]

The opponents of law reform found it difficult to combat the blackmail argument but were particularly concerned that relaxation of the legal penalties would lead to greater acceptance of homosexual behaviour. They appealed to deeper gut emotions. Lord Kilmuir, who, as Sir David Maxwell Fyfe, had been Home Secretary at the time of the series of notorious trials which led to the setting-up of the Wolfenden Committee in 1954, warned: "I believe that the result would be, and must be, after 432 years [of homosexual behaviour being a criminal offence], that if people find that the view is changed, then, in the eyes of many of them, this behaviour will have a respectability that it never had before. I also believe that many of those who now keep silent and discreet about their desires will feel free to proselytise [...] I have in mind the proselytisation which goes out from sodomitic societies and buggery clubs, which everybody knows exists."[39] Lord Goddard, Caldecote's successor as Lord Chief Justice of England, agreed: "If this Bill goes through, so that buggery is no longer a criminal offence provided it is done in private and with no boys concerned, then it will be a charter for these buggers' clubs. They will be able to spring up all over the place."[40] He recalled how on circuit in Suffolk he had once had 16 people in the dock at the same time: "None of these men would have been guilty of a criminal offence at all if this Bill had gone through."

The Gay and Lesbian Movement at National Level

The tenacious battle fought by opponents in Parliament meant that the 1967 Sexual Offences Act as passed was only a partial measure of reform. It decriminalised male homosexual relations in private in England and Wales but did not apply in Scotland and Northern Ireland or to the Armed Forces and the Merchant Navy. The age of consent was fixed at 21 and a very narrow definition of privacy adopted. The Act left the other legal measures regulating homosexual behaviour in public unchanged and even raised the maximum penalty for gross indecency involving a man under 21.[41] Although it relieved gay men of the worst fears of blackmail and prosecution, allowing space for activism, it also represented a reformulation of the mechanisms of social control.

One of the first priorities of the fledgling gay movement of the early 1970s was to consolidate and extend the limited gains of the 1967 Act. When the gay movement began to expand beyond the confines of the subculture and become more visible, there was a backlash from some state authorities, who attempted to maintain the restricted boundaries originally envisaged even by some of the Act's parliamentary supporters, i.e. the decriminalisation of homosexual behaviour in private. As gay men in particular became more open and self-confident, this narrow interpretation of the law ran into conflict with a primary gay requirement for sociability, i.e. the opportunity to meet other gay men for social or sexual purposes. For years after the 1967 Act had become law, the police and the legal establishment fought a long rearguard action to contain and as far as possible repress the increased visibility of gay men. At the legal level, this was encapsulated in the controversial ruling of the Law Lords in 1972 upholding the conviction of the alternative magazine *International Times (IT)* for publishing contact ads for gay men, which attempted to roll back the decision of Parliament by arguing that there was a material difference between merely exempting certain conduct from criminal penalties and making it lawful in the full sense.[42] On the ground it was manifest in the aggressive policing of gay men gathering outside gay pubs such as the Coleherne in Earls Court, a sharp rise in the number of prosecutions for indecency, frequent seizures of gay soft-porn magazines and eventually an attempt to close the Gay's the Word bookshop by prosecuting its owners for the stock they imported from abroad.[43]

For another two decades, the LGBT movement and the gay press had to struggle to justify themselves as members of civil society and legitimise their presence in the public sphere. The deficiencies of the 1967 Act meant that further law reform would be the main focus of activism and would effectively characterise the LGBT movement in the UK.[44] This was not necessarily pre-ordained. Lesbians also faced much social prejudice and discrimination but their main problem was invisibility rather than illegality. Consequently, their first priority was to mark their presence in the public sphere by launching a magazine, *Arena Three*, in 1964. The social group Kenric was started in 1965 by lesbians who had split away from *Arena Three*.[45] Both were more concerned with social isolation than legal matters. Countries where homosexuality was not illegal also have different histories. In Brazil, for example, sociability was responsible for initiating the LGBT movement. In 1963, a group of middle-class gay men who organised private drag shows modelled on beauty queen contests started publishing a monthly mimeographed magazine called *Snob*, which discussed their group's activities in terms drawn from the gossip columns of society magazines.

In the early 1970s, the LGBT movement in Britain was divided between assimilationist and liberationist groups. For two years after the passing of the 1967 Act, nothing much happened but British gay activists began to organise in 1969, the year of the Stonewall Riot in New York. The campaign for parliamentary law reform in the early- and mid- 1960s was driven by the London-based Homosexual Law Reform Society. After the passing of the 1967 Act, the HLRS largely went into abeyance and was eclipsed by the separate Manchester-based North-Western Homosexual Law Reform Committee, which became the Committee for Homosexual Equality (CHE) in 1969 and Campaign for Homosexual Equality in 1971. From the second half of 1969 CHE began to set up local groups in London and other cities and towns in England and Wales. Its membership expanded rapidly in the early 1970s, reaching a peak of around 5,000 in the mid-1970s.[46] CHE was the nearest thing to a mass political organisation which the LGBT community in Britain has experienced. It had an essentially reformist outlook, pressing for further law reform in the areas omitted by the 1967 Act but also highlighting the many forms of social discrimination which male and female homosexuals still faced. CHE had a pyramid structure, with a National Council, National Executive and a national office, initially in Manchester and later in London, plus groups at the local level. It held a number of national conferences, of which the one held at Malvern in 1974 remained famous for the good feeling it engendered. Although CHE ran a number of national campaigns, particularly in the area of education, its complicated hierarchical structure and emphasis on procedural matters gained it a reputation for bureaucracy and ineffectiveness. Besides their role of mobilising activists, however, the meetings of the local groups also fulfilled a social function, allowing gay men and women to meet in a benign environment, free from police attention and the pressures of the commercial scene.

The Gay Liberation Front (GLF) sprang from the experience of the American gay liberation movement and the Stonewall Riot of 1969, as well as the counterculture and the radical New Left of the 1960s. It held its first meeting in the London School of Economics on 13 October 1970 and GLF groups were soon formed in the provinces, particularly in colleges and universities. GLF adopted a revolutionary, almost millenarian position, rejecting reformist lobbying tactics in favour of direct action, favouring the outrageous over the respectable and demanding respect for gay rights. It popularised slogans such as "Gay power", "Gay pride" and "Gay is good, gay is angry". Probably its most influential slogan was "The personal is the political": GLF's ideology affected every aspect of its supporters' lives, particularly its emphasis on coming out, or assuming one's homosexuality openly and proudly. GLF was relatively short-lived, beginning to fragment within two years of its beginnings and effectively disappearing by 1974. Nevertheless, its radical vision energised sexual politics and profoundly affected many gay people's outlooks, giving it a lasting influence on the future development of the LGBT movement.[47]

There was a fair amount of rivalry and hostility between CHE and

GLF but there was also some overlap and people attended meetings of both movements. After the demise of GLF, CHE remained as the main political organisation representing gays throughout the 1970s. CHE did not support any political party, although many of its activists were Liberals. Acting on the assumption that MPs would again be given a free vote, it concentrated on trying to build parliamentary support for further law reform, with the aim of remedying the main deficiencies of the 1967 Act. Public opinion, however, became increasingly hostile to sexual liberation and radical movements during the late 1970s and as the Conservative government elected in 1979 consolidated its hold on power during the 1980s, lesbian and gay activists found themselves fighting a series of defensive battles against encroachments on civil liberties. Between 1967 and 1987, the only major legislative changes were the extension of the existing provisions of the 1967 Act to Scotland (in 1980) and Northern Ireland (in 1982).

Once the euphoria of the early 1970s had passed, the lesbian and gay movement faced an uphill struggle, marked by much frustration and frequent disappointments. Yet, paradoxically, during these years, the gay press grew and flourished, the commercial scene consolidated itself and expanded, and the gay presence in culture jumped the walls of coded fiction, plays and films, and began to permeate popular culture, from pop music to television. The following chapters concentrate on an analysis of the development of the lesbian and gay movement at a local level, centred on the Gay West group, but the events described were played out against a backdrop of increasingly open (although often hostile) debate about LGBT issues in the national press, radio, television and latterly, the internet, and a cultural discourse in film, theatre, art, music, soap operas and fashion, as well as in academia.

The rest of the book is organised chronologically and thematically. Chapters 2 and 3 describe the economic, social and political context, the gay subculture and the development of the LGBT movement during the 1970s in Bristol and Bath respectively. The chapters include detailed histories of Gay West's predecessor organisations, CHE Bristol and Bath Gay Awareness Group/Bath CHE. Chapter 4 recounts Gay West's creation as part of National CHE's restructuring and analyses the way it has been organised internally as a voluntary group. Chapter 5 deals with questions of identity, looking at how Gay West helped people come out and develop a LGBT identity, its external relations with other LGBT organisations and activities, and the way in which it responded to diversity within its own membership, notably over the role of women and different age cohorts. Chapter 6 discusses the nexus of politics, the market and civil society during the 1980s and early 1990s, examining specific cases involving LGBT issues and the different political parties at the local level. It also looks at Gay West's relationship with the commercial gay scene and its insertion in local civil society and the public sphere through its relations with other voluntary organisations and the media. Chapter 7 shows how the group reacted to the two major events of the 1980s, the AIDS crisis and Section 28, with sometimes unexpected results. Chapter 8 looks at the changing environment of the 1990s and 2000s and the way in which developments in the commercial scene and LGBT movement in Bristol impacted on the group. Finally, Chapter 9 takes two case studies – the saga of Gay West discos and the police liaison initiative – and reflects on the strengths and limitations of the civil society model in relation to political activism. It then returns to the question of community to discuss the extent to which Gay West has lived up to its subtitle of "gay community organisation" and what general conclusions can be drawn from the idea of community in this context.

2

Bristol in the 1970s

Economic and Political Background

Bristol traces its origins back to the Middle Ages. Until the first half of the 18th century, it was the second port in England after London and vied with Norwich as the second city. It owed its position to its pre-eminence in maritime trade, reflected in the saying "All ship-shape and Bristol fashion", and it continued to prosper throughout the 18th century. The inconvenient fact that much of this prosperity derived from the transatlantic slave trade and sugar plantations in the West Indies continues to haunt the city. Bristol developed a diversified industrial economy based on tobacco, printing and packaging, chocolate and aerospace during the 19th and early 20th centuries but these manufacturing industries began to decline as the postwar boom came to an end. The city underwent considerable economic restructuring in the 1970s and 1980s, with an increase in banking and financial services, and today has a mixed industrial and service economy, with its two universities filling an important role.[48]

Bristol's unemployment rate was above the national average during the 1970s but, although it nearly doubled during the early 1980s, it remained below the national average after 1979. Bristol's diversified economy was not decimated during the 1980s in the way that many northern industrial cities suffered and, despite pockets of poverty, the region as a whole remained relatively prosperous. The city has a population of around 430,000, with one million living in the wider region. There is now a substantial black and ethnic minority population, drawn from many parts of the world, which in 2007 comprised 11.9% of the city's population (in line with the national average).

As well as its commercial and industrial heritage, Bristol also has a strong tradition of dissent. In 1831, large parts of the city centre were burnt down in three days of riots sparked off by popular unrest over the

Reform Act and in 1980, Bristol was the first British city to explode into rioting in the inner city area of St. Paul's.[49] Generally, however, dissent has been less violent. Quakers and Wesleyan Methodists had a strong presence in the coal-mining areas surrounding the city in the 18th century. Trade unions were a powerful force in local industrial relations, especially around the docks, from the later 19th century, although suffering a decline in the 1980s.[50] Bristol was one of the leading provincial centres of the suffragette movement and first-wave feminism in the 19th century.[51]

From 1945 until the 1980s, Bristol's electoral politics were split between Labour and Conservative. The first Labour MPs were elected in 1923 and at least one Bristol seat has been held by Labour ever since. Labour has won at least half the city's seats in all the general elections since 1970, except 1983 and 1987. Local politics were dominated by the split between Labour and anti-Labour forces for much of the mid-20th century. For most of the period from 1972 until 2003, the Labour Party remained the largest party and controlled the City Council. As a result of the political realignments of the mid-1980s, the number of Liberal Democrat councillors gradually increased and Bristol politics became increasingly split three ways between Labour, Conservative and Liberal Democrat.

As a result of local government reorganisation in 1974, Bristol lost its county status and many of its powers to the newly-created Avon County Council, which had regional planning responsibility for the area covering Bristol, Bath and the surrounding suburban and rural areas. Avon was relatively balanced politically: the Conservatives were in control between 1974 and 1981, while Labour held the largest number of seats from 1982 until Avon was abolished in 1996, with rising Liberal Democrat numbers in the 1990s.

Consequently, when the gay movement started in Bristol in 1970 it found itself in a complex environment. Economically, it was a period of rapid restructuring, which, while painful, was tending to increase the region's longer-term prosperity. Politically, Labour was a major force in city politics but did not hold a monolithic grip on power. There was a tradition of working class politics, moderate trade unionism and local, generally peaceful, dissent. The city's business elite to some extent held aloof from politics and preferred to work through informal networks and links with political figures. The creation of Avon County Council in 1974 added a new arena for political activity, one with wider horizons, which initially was to prove more open to gay interests. Two other new factors which were trying to break through the cultural consensus in the late 1960s and early 1970s were middle-class protest, particularly against the council's plan to build a ring of motorways through the inner suburbs, and the development of the women's movement, with the Bristol Women's Liberation Group publishing the magazine *Enough*.[52]

The Gay Subculture in Bristol

The gay subculture had existed long before the emergence of the new politicised gay movement.[53] In Britain prior to 1967, a semi-clandestine gay subculture provided some possibilities for gay men and women to meet, socialise and find sexual partners. In London, there were numerous facilities available to homosexual men, ranging from theatres, pubs, cafes and private clubs to the Biograph picture house and the Brigade of Guards.[54] For lesbians, there was the Gateways club and the social events organised by the *Arena Three* magazine. In provincial cities, such as Bristol, the facilities were much more limited, consisting mainly of public toilets (known in gay slang as "cottages"), cruising areas, a few gay pubs and late-night coffee-bars, and private parties. Some of these places had a long history, while others were gay for only a short time before police action or a change of management policy forced people to move on. It is beyond the scope of this work to attempt to trace all places in the Bristol area which have been frequented by gays at different times. It therefore concentrates on outlining the main sites used by gay men and women from the 1950s onwards and which provide the backdrop to the development of the organised LGBT movement.

Prior to decriminalisation, any gay man wishing to make contact with others faced the problem of knowing where to go, given the lack of published information before the beginnings of the gay press in the late 1960s. Access to pubs and parties was generally restricted to those already familiar with the gay subculture, except for certain pubs which had obtained widespread notoriety in their local area. In these cases, however, anyone seen entering or leaving the premises risked being labelled and stigmatised. Public toilets, on the other hand, offered the apparent security of anonymity and were widely known to be meeting places for homosexuals because of publicity given in the press to court cases and popular folklore. Graffiti and messages written on the walls indicated to the uninitiated which were likely to be the most promising locations.

Consequently, in provincial cities where little else existed, public toilets were the main place where gay men met. The frequent references to cottaging in oral accounts indicate its pervasiveness before 1967 and it continued unabated afterwards.[55] While the primary purpose was usually sexual, sometimes social contacts were also made, introducing newcomers to gay pubs and private social networks. The use of public areas for sex by gay men, has long been controversial, both in LGBT circles and among the general public.[56] Men using these areas ran the risk of arrest, blackmail or physical assault, sometimes leading to social ruin if their names were reported in the press. Gay critics of cottaging argued that it reflected badly on the LGBT community and was no longer necessary once legal facilities became available, while defenders argued that it was part of gay culture and still served a real need for some people.

A large number of public toilets in Bristol were regularly frequented by gay men. A map provided by an interviewee shows over thirty locations spread right around the city, from Horfield in the north to Bishopsworth in the south and the Portway in the west to Fishponds in the east. This geographical spread across the city contrasts with the concentration of female prostitution in the Portland Square-City Road area. Although in the official mind homosexuality was traditionally associated with prostitution, as evident in the remit of the Wolfenden Committee, this seems to derive from the special situation of London's West End and applied less to Bristol, although both groups shared some city centre pubs. Men would sometimes spend an evening cottaging, moving from one lavatory to another in search of partners. Generally, they used the cottages as meeting places, preferring to go off to secluded locations or take partners home rather than have sex actually in the cottage. Different cottages would be busy at different times of the day, with the period when people were going home from work being a favourite time. The cottages most frequently mentioned by interviewees and in court cases were in Anchor Road near the Cathedral, at Cumberland Basin in Hotwells, on Blackboy Hill, on the Centre, at Lawrence Hill, by the Arches in Cheltenham Road, and underground by Bristol Bridge and near the Grosvenor Hotel at Temple Meads. The ingenuity of gay men in using these locations is a testimony to their powers of resistance but also a reminder of the marginalisation of homosexuals before the 1970s.

Cruising for sexual partners in open-air areas has a long history in countries with warmer climates and more tolerant attitudes. In Bristol, the Downs have long had a reputation as an area for heterosexual sex, with complaints about female prostitutes recorded in 1884.[57] According to some reports, the Downs have been used by gay men for cruising at least from the 1950s; it may initially have started as a spillover from the cottage near the Water Tower and later gravitated towards the Avon Gorge. By the 1990s, the area was quite notorious.[58] Another cruising area, located nearby on the Portway at Shirehampton, was the subject of press campaigns in the 1980s. The increasing availability of cars in the post-war years opened up new possibilities in the surrounding countryside, with cruising areas developing at Tormarton near Junction 18 of the M4 and at the top of Tog Hill. The latter area has even been graced on occasion by the presence of a former cabinet minister.[59] The cottaging/cruising scene is a moveable feast and, as the police remarked in 1995, they would chase men away from one site, only to find them at another when they arrived there.[60]

Pubs were a major feature of the clandestine gay subculture and some subsequently made the transition into the legal commercial scene. Today's gay pubs consciously set out to attract LGBT customers and so usually employ gay staff and display rainbow flags and notices to inform potential customers of the fact. In the days of the clandestine subculture, the use of pubs for socialising by gay men depended on the attitude of the landlord. Some landlords welcomed gay customers or tolerated their presence for financial reasons but this welcome was usually contingent. Any pub which became too notorious risked losing its licence when it came up before the magistrates for renewal and so the licensing regulations effectively obliged landlords to police their own premises.[61] Gay pubs did not advertise themselves as such and usually became known through word of mouth between gays. One of the major obstacles to people just coming out was actually discovering which pubs to go to in order to meet other gays.

The effects of this precarious mix of clandestinity and conditional toleration can be seen in the anecdotes told by a Bristol barmaid who was popular with gay men and attracted a gay clientele to the pubs where she worked in the 1950s and 1960s.[62] For years Peggy worked in the Radnor Hotel in Bristol but when it closed in the mid-1960s, she had to find another job. Three landlords gave her instant dismissal because they did not like the gays who followed her. However, when she moved to the Ship in Redcliffe Hill, the landlord did not object because he valued the trade she brought. This ambivalence could produce incongruous results, particularly as times began to change in the 1970s. When *Gay News* started publishing its gay guide in 1975, the *Bristol Evening Post* contacted the licencees of the local pubs mentioned, several of whom denied that they had a gay clientele, one quite vehemently. Their attitude was criticised by LGBT activists but it was presumably an automatic response to the old fear of trouble or losing their licences if their pub became known as a "haunt of homosexuals".[63]

It seems that in most cases the police turned a blind eye and several pubs in the St. Nicholas Market area in the heart of the mediaeval city were patronised by a gay clientele. The longest-established was the Radnor Hotel at 30 St. Nicholas St., which was known as a gay pub before the Second World War and possibly as far back as the 1890s. The Radnor was very social, many of its customers knew each other and there were lots of parties, in the pub or in people's homes. According to the barmaid mentioned above, they used to hold private parties in the pub after it closed and the local policeman would knock on the door, take off his helmet and

The Radnor Hotel, Bristol, derelict in August 2009. Photo: Robert Howes.

come in for a drink. He used to protect the gay customers from trouble from straight men and tell them to pass on warnings when there was going to be a blitz on the cottages, saying that he preferred to know where the gays were. Although the police regularly took action against cottaging (i.e. public sex), the pub was never raided, suggesting that the police preferred a policy of control to outright suppression.

The Radnor closed in the mid-1960s when the owner went bankrupt, and its gay customers moved to the Old Duke opposite the Llandoger Trow for 2–3 years. The Radnor then re-opened and was later renamed the Porcupine, retaining some gay customers in the evenings. In May 1973, the Elephant opened as a gay pub a short distance away at 20 St. Nicholas St. It was run by a flamboyant gay man and his parents. When *Gay News* visited Bristol in summer 1976 on the first of their forays into the provinces, they found that the Elephant was the current favourite pub, with a friendly crowd. "Red shaded lamps, red plush benches on a comfortably worn carpet, add to the snugness of the bars." The Radnor, on the other hand, was described as "a pub with a gay past but a dwindling gay present", with gay women being the last to desert it.[64] The landlord tried to turn it into an evening bar for businessmen and in March 1987, as the Porcupine, it was reported as no longer welcoming gay people.[65]

For most of the 1970s and 1980s, the Elephant was the main gay pub in Bristol but there were others. The Ship in Park Row was run by two gay men from the early to mid-1970s and catered mainly for gay men.[66] A number of other pubs were also briefly patronised by gays without becoming totally gay pubs, such as the Greyhound in Clifton and the Garricks Head in the city centre.[67] The scene had its characters, including Sapphire, a large camp black man, and Mrs Truscott, an old lady who used to be bought drinks by customers in the Ship.[68]

During the later 1950s, a number of coffee-bars around Park St., such as the Calypso and the Manhattan, used to be taken over by gays after the pubs closed in the evening.[69] The first gay club to open was the Moulin Rouge at 72 Worral Road, Clifton, which appears to have started in the late 1960s; by February 1973, it was listed as an outlet for *Gay News*. It had an unusual location in a quiet residential street and was originally a swimming pool and so had a large sunken dance floor. For a while it was highly successful, attracting between 600–700 gay men and lesbians at weekends and being described as the largest club in the west. As newer clubs opened near the city centre, the Moulin Rouge was largely deserted by gays. Lesbians continued to go there but in February 1976 a fight broke out when a straight man started arguing with some women who were attending a lesbian conference, resulting in one woman being taken to hospital.

A few gay men and transvestites were still using the Moulin Rouge when the *Gay News* team visited in summer 1976 but there was a further assault involving a woman later in the year. Radical lesbians organised a boycott, demanding that the club under its present management be closed and that suitable premises be made available by the Council for a gay club. It lost its music licence in October that year following complaints from the police and local residents. Rumours surrounded the club linking it to the criminal underworld. [70]

A number of new clubs opened in the mid-1970s. Bristols at 4 Broad Quay on the Centre was originally a straight club but after a successful experiment with a gay evening on Tuesdays became totally gay with a big party on New Year's Eve 1974/75. It had a friendly atmosphere and welcomed gay women. [71] The Kings Club at 17 Prince Street opened in February 1975, with many of the staff coming from the Moulin Rouge. It was described by the *Gay News* team in 1976 as "a club worth visiting for its own sake [...] Kings boasts three floors – on the ground floor there's a good-sized pub-like bar; on floor one, a dimly lit bar takes up one end with the disco/dance floor (plus light show) down the other. A door off the disco floor leads to a comfortable upstairs lounge bar where lighting is brighter and people gather to talk". [72] These two clubs were relatively short-lived.

The Oasis at 12/14 Park Row, which opened around 1976, "is less lavishly appointed – one long bar switches its way through partitioned sitting areas. Dancing, on a well-sprung floor, is to the beat of a juke-box rather than a DJ". [73] Customers had to knock on the door to gain entry. By 1979, it was advertising itself as "Men only", which caused some resentment among activists, but it remained the main club through the 1980s. [74] Its owner regularly held benefits for gay voluntary organisations. Club 49 at 20 Christmas Steps, which opened around 1977, was mixed but patronised by lesbians, despite some problems with the doorman. [75] There was also the Top Deck Drinking Club at the same address. Both these clubs lasted until the 1990s. Chantelles at 135 Whiteladies Road started as a club for women and friends around 1977 but ran into trouble when straight men started going to it. [76] This address nevertheless continued to offer club and restaurant facilities for women for several years under different names. In 1982, it was known as Pierrot's. [77]

A characteristic of the club scene was that many opened, enjoyed popularity for a short while and then disappeared. Cinderellas at 40 Park Street which started in early 1982 was an example of this trend and others followed. Some achieved a certain notoriety, such as the BQ Bar Club for women, held on Thursday evenings in the British Queen pub, which was located in the inner city district of St. Pauls. [78] This was very popular despite the rough location but the pub was eventually burnt down. Another common feature over the years was clubs and discos which only ran once a week or once a month, either in commercial clubs or other facilities such as community centres. This was particularly the case of clubs catering for lesbians, such as Hint of Pink, Lick at Lakota and the Lesbian Lilac Cafe (in St. Werburgh's Community Centre) in the early 1990s.

There were also a number of restaurants which advertised in the gay media. The longest-running was Michael's at 129 Hotwell Road, which lasted from the mid-1970s to around 1993/94. It was run entirely by gay people and according to *Gay News* "not only is the food superlative but the ambience [...] altogether delightful". Michael's regularly gave donations towards LGBT causes and participated in the gay festivals. On the fringe of the commercial gay scene in the mid-1970s was a sauna in Portman Square, St. Pauls, described as sleazy and falling to bits, but which managed to avoid being raided by the police (as was common elsewhere at that time).[79]

The commercial gay scene in Bristol moved around the city over time. Originally concentrated in the historic centre of the city near the old docks, it extended in the 1960s to the student and bedsitter district of Clifton with the opening of the Moulin Rouge club. Most of the pubs and clubs, which opened between the 1970s and the mid-1990s, such as the Ship, Oasis, Kings, Club 49, Griffin, Queen's Shilling (later Queenshilling) and Pineapple, were on or near the Centre (the former Tramways Centre, built over the covered-in River Frome) and interspersed with the entertainment venues serving the city's straight population. In the later 1990s and 2000s, a whole range of new pubs and clubs opened in the Old Market area, about a mile from the Centre on the other side of the inner ring-road. This area had long been run down and suffering from urban blight and the process appears to have been driven by property interests rather than any Council policy. In the 2000s, the entrepreneurs began to market the area as a gay village in a conscious attempt to reproduce the success of Manchester's gay village. The result was that by 2010 Bristol's gay scene was concentrated in the Old Market/West Street area, with another cluster of commercial establishments located about a mile away between the Centre and the University.

The scene meant different things to different people. To a working-class man in his late twenties who was just coming out in the early 1980s, it was exciting and democratic. He met a wide range of new people and broadened his cultural horizons.[80] To a Bristolian of the next generation, returning to his native city in the early 1990s after being an activist in Australia and London, it appeared to be "going to sleep".[81] Many people lived their entire gay lives on the commercial scene but others found it an alienating experience or tired of it after the first flush of excitement. It was these people who generally found their way to LGBT groups.

Lesbian and Gay Movement

The debates and discussions which were going on in London in the early 1970s soon spread to the rest of the country. During the 1970s Bristol developed a lively alternative lesbian and gay movement based on voluntary organisations, including a number of political groups, a switchboard, a gay centre, a gay pride festival and a gay women's magazine that had national significance.

CHE Bristol in the Early 1970s

The first local group to be founded was CHE Bristol, which held its first meeting in April 1970.[82] This appears to have been the result of an advertisement placed in the local press by the Campaign for Homosexual Equality, which, starting in the second half of 1969, began to encourage the creation of local committees outside its original base in the North-West of England. This led to the establishment of groups in London, the East and West Midlands and Bristol, and eventually throughout England and Wales.[83] Initially, CHE Bristol's meetings took place fortnightly on Saturdays at the flat of one of its members. They were attended by an average of 18 members and consisted of a short business meeting, after which they took on a semi-social atmosphere. The group was run by an elected committee, consisting of a chairman, secretary, treasurer, press officer, convenor and deputy convenor. By January 1972 CHE had 73 members in Bristol, the largest number outside London, and for a while during late 1972 and spring 1973 there were two CHE groups in the city.[84] The local paper published a sympathetic article on the group in May 1972.[85]

In autumn 1972, the group started a mimeographed newsletter, initially called *Chews*, then *Chewssheet*, which appeared approximately every two months. It contained a mixture of editorial, news and comment about CHE locally and nationally, a programme of forthcoming events and earnest articles on subjects such as "Sex for Pleasure", "Why am I homosexual????", "A question – 'Am I mature?'", "The ingredients of an 'affair'" and "Homosexuality – a Part of Nature's Plan?", as well as a column by a woman member signed 'Maggie'. In mid-1974, it changed its name and then appeared under a number of variations of *CHE Bristol Newsletter*. The group's activities comprised a mixture of guest speakers, discussions, social events, pub nights and outings, as well as hosting visits by other CHE groups. Most of the meetings were held in committee members' homes but the group made use of the Friends Meeting House in

Horfield for a couple of months in autumn 1973 and St. Mary's Church House, Tyndall's Park Road in early 1975. In 1973, the group also set up a befriending service called Confidential Friend, which ran for a year or so.[86]

A questionnaire sent to members of the group at the end of 1973 revealed that 70% were also members of National CHE, the average age was 41 and 15% were women. The newsletter gives no detailed membership figures for this early period but claimed a total membership in the region of 100 in April/May 1974 and referred to 70 newsletters being sent out in July 1974 (not all to members). The renewal rate in January 1974 was 56%, down from 63% the previous year. Turnover in the group's funds for 1973–74 was £126, with most money spent on postage.[87]

In summer 1973, the newsletter appealed for more members to become involved in political activity or campaigning.[88] Members of the group sent questionnaires to some of the candidates in the 1973 Avon County elections. When the first of two General Elections was suddenly called in early 1974, the group sent questionnaires to all the candidates in Bristol and surrounding areas, with a covering letter stating the CHE case. "With specific exceptions, the Labour & Liberal candidates answered sympathetically, and promised support, whilst the Conservatives were not really disposed to committing themselves."[89]

Bristol CHE in the early 1970s largely conformed to the staid respectable stereotype of CHE. The Convenor during 1972–73 characterised the goals which he had set for the group as "recognition as a responsible body by the 'Establishment' organisations" and cited good relations with the Samaritans, Bristol Council of Social Services and the Departments of Health and Social Service of Bristol Corporation as proof of success.[90] He also had strong views on the running of CHE nationally and endorsed a motion opposing the recognition by CHE of "Awareness Groups", which included GLF people as well as CHE members.[91] This motion (which would have excluded Bath Gay Awareness Group) was opposed by other CHE groups, such as Reading Gay Alliance.[92] The antipathy felt by some CHE members towards the flamboyant behaviour of GLF was evident when in October 1972 members of CHE Bristol and the Bath Gay Awareness Group appeared on Harlech TV's *Now It's Your Say* programme on Gay Liberation, together with a group of Rad Fems from the London Notting Hill commune, the most radical wing of GLF. A male member of CHE Bristol who watched the broadcast wrote a lengthy denunciation of the "limp wristed, lisping, fabricated faggots" and "irresponsible morons" of GLF, contrasting them with the "representatives of C.H.E. who I am proud to say dressed and conducted themselves in a dignified manner and who spoke with intelligence and continuity".[93]

Gay Britain

BRISTOL

The first in a series of reports on gay life in Great Britain

Bristol was built upon seven hills and drew its strength from shipping (wine, spice and slaves), the Anglican church and Nonconformity. Two centuries ago it was the second largest city in England; it now ranks as number nine but is still the capital of the West Country, set deep in the Somerset hills.

Light and airy, 'Bristle' is not spectacularly beautiful upon first sight but it is a comfortable, unshowy place with Georgian squares, terraces and courts, bookshops, theatres, health food and crafts shops and good places to eat. Although some of its suburbs are depressing, the centre of Bristol seems to have escaped the worst of 20th century town planning—the shops are individual in style and there are few high rise buildings. Gay News took the two hour train journey from London to find out how Bristol's 25,000 gay people (the total population is around half a million) fit into the city which prides itself upon its tolerance and encouragement of the individual and its successful juggling of the radical with the reactionary.

Upon arrival

Go to Bristol armed with addresses of clubs, pubs and organisations plus a map of the city (A-Z Street Atlas, 45p, recommended), especially if you arrive after 6pm. Gay Bristol is not very evident at first. You will not find Gay News in any book shop except Maynards (next door to the Hippodrome Theatre) and not only does the public library not stock the paper but their notice board does not include any posters for either CHE or Gay Switchboard. Gay Switchboard is not listed in the telephone directory, though you will find it listed in the monthly community paper Bristol Voice, and the Evening Post has advertised it under: 'Gay Women ring . . .'. We saw a new pamphlet called Bristol's Pubs which rather sniffily mentions that St Nicholas Street pubs (home of The Elephant and the Radnor Hotel) will soon be completely taken over by gay patrons.

Advice and Counselling

IF YOU PHONE the Citizens Advice Bureau in Bristol, ask for homosexuals.

We tried asking for information about "gay organisations" and the man we spoke to looked

Nigel Collins, Charlie Beaton (Bristol CHE), Jean Watson with Rebel, Anne Smith, Jay Purnell, Don Branch and, kneeling, Dale Wakefield (Bristol Gay Switchboard) at the end of a gay car rally from Bristol to Midsomer Norton organised by Switchboard and the Women's Group.

university and polytechnic attitudes towards gays. "Both constitutions now state that there must be no discrimination against gay people." But few students have come out to any degree. The university Gay Soc only attracts about 12 people a month and GLF contains only 3 people including Tim. "GLF may rise again," says Tim, "I hope it will. It's never properly functioned since the early 70s before CHE rose as a group. The Gay Soc is mainly social because the majority of students who come to meetings have had very little contact with the gay scene let alone the gay movement. But we've got a large pink banner with Avon Gay Students on it and I'm optimistic that next year will be better. The general information network is better now—the university refers people to Switchboard straight away. And recently a Catholic student who tried to pass a motion preventing sabbatical union officers from participating in gay politics, was booed out of the meeting by heterosexual students.

"There is still a definite lack of a radical men group in Bristol and I've been very annoyed by the lack of support among gay Poly students. But in my next two years I'm hoping to change this situation."

Pubs and Clubs

CURRENT favourite with the gay pub set is The Elephant, a Courage House in St Nicholas Street, opposite the fish market.

Like any gay pub there are cliques—little groups of regulars who know everything about one another from their mothers' maiden names to, well, everything. But, as John from Clifton remarked, "down here, the cliques are a lot more difficult to get out of than to get into."

And The Elephant crowd is certainly friendlier than most. Landlord Jack sees to that, offering visitors a warm welcome to his maroon and purple pub. Red shaded lamps, red plush benches on a comfortable worn carpet, add to the snugness of the bars. Customers sit at, or stand round, tables on ornate legs (some of the legs have been salvaged from old Singer sewing machines, allowing patrons to drink and treadle at the same time). Food's good if you steer clear of the cellophane rolls and stick to fresh seafood offerings.

"Of course, it's packed on Saturday nights," said nattily-attired Adrian. "It's the best pub at the moment. But it's like a morgue the rest of the week."

Not quite fair. Business was still pretty brisk on Sunday night, though hot couples were well represented, and the gay crowd was well down in numbers.

Not a stone's throw, just a few yards down St Nicholas Street from The Elephant, is a pub with a gay past but a dwindling gay present. Gay women seem to be the last to

many nights on Switchboard, she also is the mainstay of the Women's Centre and of ... magazine which she edits with a ...

Avon and Somerset countryside recently Membership is a fairly healthy 47 and ...

During the winter of 1973–74, CHE Bristol went through a crisis, with arguments over the future of the group, exchanges of frostily formal correspondence and all the appearances of a power struggle. The committee was restructured and in April 1974 the convenor resigned, complaining that he had been "deposed".[94] A founder member later remarked that "The pursuit of politics and power to the virtual exclusion of all else nearly killed CHE Bristol in 1974."[95] Trevor Locke, a student activist, took over as chairman and the new committee made an effort to put on more events, noting in July 1974 that "The June Programme has been a gratifying success, and gives us all hope and confidence for the future of the group."[96] The group maintained a full programme of events until early 1975, but when Locke resigned to concentrate on his studies, it seems to have gone into decline.

Other Lesbian and Gay Groups

CHE Bristol was joined soon after its foundation by other gay groups, with the University serving as an important focus. Student activism at the University of Bristol owed much to the efforts of Trevor Locke. Initially Locke proposed setting up a University of Bristol Gay Liberation Front and issued a newsheet manifesto on 1 December 1971 which ended with the GLF slogan "Gay is good, proud and beautiful". The first meeting was scheduled to be held on 9 December and the University of Bristol Gay Liberation Front Society was launched at an inaugural general meeting on 15 December 1971, at which the attendance gradually grew from four to eleven at the end of the evening.[97] A year later, however, the society voted to change its name to Gay Students Society. Locke reported the decision

> to reject its G.L.F. orientation in favour of a more C.H.E.-type approach. [...] It was not felt, at the AGM that the ideas of the Gay Liberation Manifesto were wrong but that they had proved themselves to be out of keeping with the conservative attitudes of the kind of students who study at Our University. By adopting a CHE style of approach we hope to be able to get through to a larger cross-section of gay students than we did last session.[98]

The group had 2 paid-up members in January 1972 and 13 in October 1973.[99] In 1973 Locke was elected President of the University's Student Union and persuaded the Student Union to support the NUS gay rights policy in full.[100] The first National Gay Rights Conference organised by the NUS was held at the University of Bristol on 20 October 1973.[101] The Gay Students Society or Gaysoc worked with the Bristol Gay Awareness Group and CHE Bristol and also doubled as the CHE Bristol Youth Group.[102]

The more radical vision offered by the Gay Liberation Front also attracted support in the city. Bristol Gay Awareness Group was listed in *Gay News* as a GLF group in September 1972 and held their first disco in the Dug Out club in 1973.[103] In autumn 1973 four members of the group began to make plans to set up a telephone befriending and advice service for isolated homosexuals on the lines of London Icebreakers.[104] Bristol Icebreakers started operation in February 1974, running a phone-line two evenings a week. It was run by a collective of five, including two women. During the first four months, they handled 146 calls, 135 from men and 11 from women. Most of these came via the free advertisement which the *Bristol Evening Post* carried every day in its Service column. A group specifically called Bristol GLF was set up around 1974 by Eddie Cherrie, a trainee teacher originally from Scotland, who put up a notice in St. Nicholas Market giving his home address for contact. The group had a hard core of around 3–4 activists but a larger mailing list.[105] It was slightly more radical than CHE but there were no great ideological differences. Bristol GLF's main aim was to create a more visible gay presence by activities such as holding a picnic on the Downs and barracking the author D. J. West at a meeting in Bristol for making adverse comments about homosexuals. Bristol GLF published a single-page Newsheet in October 1974 and continued in existence at least until April 1975 but was defunct by the time Eddie Cherrie left Bristol in 1976. [106] A transsexual/transvestite group started in 1975, comprised largely of heterosexuals.

Women were active in the city's gay movement. The Gay Womens Group, based in the Bristol Womens Centre in Redland, was set up in summer 1974 and took part in a march through Bristol on International Women's Day in 1975. [107] At one point, over one hundred women were attending meetings.[108] The group began publishing the magazine *Move* in autumn 1974. This was a mimeographed monthly publication which started as a newsletter in September 1974 and then appeared regularly until September 1978, when it became intermittent before ceasing publication in 1980. *Move* contained a lively mixture of theoretical articles, personal experiences, letters, conference reports, news items and lists of useful contacts. It had a national scope and at the same time commented on the local scene. It was written from the perspective of women involved in the gay scene, who were not separatist but were quite prepared to point up the sexist aspects of gay men's behaviour. A few gay men helped with its production and it was sold in the pubs and clubs and by subscription.[109]

Lesbians in Bristol organised the Third National Lesbian Conference, which was held in the Central Methodist Hall between 27 and 29 February 1976.[110] A march was held from Queens Square to the Queen Victoria statue on College Green, where it was dispersed by the police. The conference consisted of plenary sessions and workshops on coming out, lesbian wives and mothers, abortion, bisexuality, lesbian publications, role-playing, aggression, CHE, theatre, orgasm, Wages for Housework and the Working Women's Charter. There was dissension between lesbian separatists and other women over the presence of a gay man who was helping with the creche and the intervention of the Wages for Housework and Wages Due Lesbians campaigns, which later caused serious divisions in the local women's movement.[111] The atmosphere was further disrupted when some women attending the conference were assaulted and injured by men at the Moulin Rouge Club, leading to the setting up of a Committee for Lesbian Action Now (CLAN) to protest at the incident.[112] After another similar incident six months later, protesters picketed the club and at the same time it lost its music licence.[113]

Despite their differences and occasional personal animosities, the groups were quite close together. Most of the activists knew each other and many were students or connected to colleges and universities and all of the same age group.[114] One later recalled that during the academic year 1976–77, there were openly gay student union officers in Bristol Polytechnic, Bath University and the Bath Academy of Art.[115] The Bristol Gay Alliance was formed in November 1974 by representatives of the Gay Liberation Front, CHE, Gay Soc, Equs and Gay Womens Group. It started holding open discussion meetings on Sunday afternoons in King's Club in March 1975 and in April that year was planning to hold a disco in the same club.[116] In 1976, Bristol Gay Activists' Alliance was formed and organised a picket outside a new branch of W H Smith in Broadmead, the city's main shopping precinct, on the day it opened as part of the nationwide protests against the newsagent's refusal to sell *Gay News*.[117] The Alliance was still in existence in 1979.[118]

Bristol Lesbian and Gay Switchboard

During the mid-1970s, activists came together to organise a series of initiatives in the city, including Bristol Gay Switchboard, the Bristol Gay Centre and a series of gay festivals and pride events. Bristol Gay Switchboard (later Bristol Lesbian and Gay Switchboard – BLAGS) started operation in February 1975 and was one of the earliest in the country outside London. The initiative grew out of the Gay Women's Group, because many of the calls they were receiving came from gay men. The driving force was Dale Wakefield, who was deeply involved in most of the initiatives in Bristol at this time. She set up the Switchboard with assistance from gay men in Gaysoc and GLF. The Gay Switchboard used the Women's Centre in Redland as their contact address but for around two years the telephone was located in a room in Dale Wakefield's house in Totterdown before moving to the Gay Centre (see below).[119] The service offering information and advice was open every day and by 1978 was receiving 3,000 calls a year, rising to 3,500 in 1979.[120] Over 70% of the calls came from men and the great majority came from Bristol and the surrounding area. The largest number of calls (846 in 1979) was for information about entertainment, while the next largest (471) wanted advice on legal, medical and sexual matters. 450 calls were silent, often indicating people too frightened even to talk about their sexuality. Initially, 30% of calls derived from advertisements in the *Bristol Evening Post* while another 18% cited *Gay News* as their source. By 1979, 43% of the calls were coming via *Gay News* and 21% via the local press.

Despite recurrent financial problems over the years, Bristol Lesbian and Gay Switchboard has continued to operate down to the present day. Many of the gay activists who worked in the various LGBT organisations which have existed in the intervening years have also been volunteers on Switchboard. In addition, there was a separate Lesbian Line, which operated from 1985 until around 2000.

Bristol Gay Centre

Dissatisfaction with the commercial scene and the need to find a more adequate location to house Switchboard led activists to consider setting up a Gay Centre along the line of the one in Edinburgh and they began to search for suitable premises.[121] In late 1976, the City Council offered to rent a building in Upper Maudlin Street and the group made plans to ask for a government urban aid grant. Before the arrangements could be finalised the premises were vandalised beyond repair (not apparently because of its intended use). After further searching, a lease on space on the top floor in McArthur's Building, a former maltings in Gas Ferry Road, was obtained and the Bristol Gay Centre opened in October 1978. The Centre started off with great enthusiasm, attracting a good crowd with Saturday and Sunday lunches, social evenings and monthly discos. It housed Gay Switchboard and was used by a number of groups, including CHE Bristol and Gay West, for some of their meetings. The Centre was funded entirely by voluntary donations, with no financial support from the Council. Many of the activists running the Centre were also involved in Switchboard and CHE Bristol.

Although this district is now being gentrified, at the time it was a derelict dockside area remote from the city centre. The building's isolated location and difficult access prevented the original concept of a drop-in centre developing and the Centre failed to attract people from the commercial scene. The committee struggled for some years to increase usage and raise more funds, issuing a newsletter to publicise its facilities, but the Centre was finally forced to close at the end of 1983, mainly because of the difficulty in getting volunteers to provide the services. The organisation continued in existence for another nine months in the hope of finding new premises but was dissolved in September 1984 and the remaining funds donated to Bristol Switchboard.[122] The idea resurfaced in October 1995, when a meeting was called to assess whether a lesbian and gay centre was feasible in Bristol. The meeting attracted 26 people who discussed what they wanted from a centre and a steering group was then set up to undertake a feasibility study. A potential user survey was circulated in May 1996 and the project announced that it would report back at an open meeting in April 1997 but nothing seems to have come of this proposal.[123]

Bristol Gay Festival/Avon Pride

The first Bristol Gay Festival was held in July 1977 and consisted of a fortnight of social events organised around the showings at the Arnolfini and Bristol Arts Centre of gay films drawn from the NFT's London lesbian and gay film festival.[124] The festival was put together in a little over a month to raise funds for the defence in the *Gay News* blasphemy trial.[125] This

McArthur's Warehouse, which housed the Bristol Gay Centre, 1978–83.
Photo: Chris Leigh.

festival was one of the first such ones outside London and was judged to be a great success, despite a small financial deficit.[126] Plans to hold another festival the following year went ahead in the face of sustained opposition from Conservative councillors, who objected to Bristol City Council letting the Corn Exchange.[127] There were also protests from some local vicars, while others offered support.[128] The Council confirmed its decision on a free vote, with Labour and Liberal councillors refusing to act as censors and pointing out that gays were ratepayers like anyone else. In the end, no event took place in the Corn Exchange because the proposed speakers were unable to make the specified date but the Festival programme expressed its "appreciation of the City Councillors who stood up to the anti-gay lobby in protecting our right to use a public building".[129] The rest of the Festival took place successfully and from then on the festivals were held fairly regularly under the names Gay Bristol Festival (1977–1982, 1985), Avon Pride (1987–1992), Pride West (1994–1996, 1999, 2001) and Pride Bristol (2010). The early festivals were organised by Gay Bristol, a group comprising the gay groups of Bristol and Bath, a number of commercial establishments and the Bristol Gay Centre. The later Pride West festivals and pride events continued to involve both voluntary organisations and businesses, with the Aled Richards Trust assuming an important role.[130] The festival programme usually consisted of a range of film showings together with cultural and social events. In 1988 and 1994–95, the festival included a march through the city centre. In 1990, the festival received financial support from Avon County Council and in 1995–96 from Bristol City Council but most of the funding had to be raised by the festival organisers and some years it ran at a loss.

Metropolitan Community Church

The Metropolitan Community Church originated in the United States. The Bristol branch was started in October 1975 by Angela Needham, who was also convenor of the Bath Gay Awareness Group for some months at this time.[131] She had been impressed by a service of the Church which she attended at a CHE conference. This was the fourth branch in the UK after London, Birmingham and Edinburgh. The Church originally started meeting in Bath but moved to Bristol, where most of the interested members lived. It soon ran into difficulties. It was asked to vacate the Bristol Council for Voluntary Services's building in Elmdale Road, which it was using for services, but was then offered a room in the University Settlement in Barton Hill.[132] The Church failed to attract enough members to be viable and had to be financed by Angela Needham, who was unemployed at the time. It closed after a short while but was revived in 1989 as the Living Springs Metropolitan Community Church, which continues to meet in Bath.[133]

CHE Bristol in the Later 1970s

By 1975–76, CHE Bristol appears to have become almost moribund. A newly-arrived member later recalled that some meetings were held with the curtains closed so that no-one could see in.[134] An influx of new activists, however, gave the group a renewed lease of life from 1976 onwards. Monthly Planning Meetings were instituted to organise the group's activities, the newsletter was revived and a programme of weekly Tuesday meetings started. In September 1977, the group launched a more substantial magazine entitled *Bridge*, containing articles on CHE, the gay movement in Bristol and elsewhere, topics relating to sexuality and lighter items such as fiction and crosswords. Five issues were published between September 1977 and September 1978.[135] In April 1977, the first Tea and Chat was held and the group's programme then settled down to a pattern of Tuesday evening meetings and Sunday afternoon tea and chats, which continued for the next five years. The Tuesday meetings comprised planning meetings, discussion groups and meetings with speakers. Some of these were held at the Folk House in Park Street and were publicised to people outside the group such as social and youth workers. Speakers included Rose Robertson of Parents Enquiry (a voluntary group aimed at helping young gays to come out and reassuring their parents), the headmaster of a local comprehensive school and the Governor of Bristol's Horfield Prison.[136] The group's greatest coup was to secure as speaker the Bishop of Gloucester, who had chaired the working party of the Church of England's Board for Social Responsibility, which produced a report on *Homosexual Relations: a Contribution to Discussion*. The talk which he gave at St. Paul's Church, Clifton, in December 1979 was his only public comment on the report and the group arranged for a press release to be sent to the local press and *Gay News*.[137] The Sunday tea and chats were for those just coming out or who preferred socialising. Apart from the speaker meetings at the Folk House, most meetings were held in members' homes or at the Gay Centre, where CHE Bristol celebrated its tenth anniversary with an evening's entertainment in April 1980.

CHE Bristol made regular donations to support Bristol Lesbian and Gay Switchboard, with which some activists were also involved, and affiliated to the NCCL and the National Abortion Campaign. It occasionally provided speakers for outside organisations and promoted the CHE tape/slide show on homosexuality. The group participated in the campaigns orchestrated by National CHE, writing to candidates in the general and local elections to ascertain their views on gay issues and lobbying local MPs on specific issues. Two campaigns to which it gave particular prominence in 1980 were the John Saunders case in defence of a handyman at a Scottish youth camp, who had been sacked simply for being gay, and the NIGRA campaign to legalise homosexual relations in Northern Ireland.[138] The group was proud to report that six out of ten local MPs voted for legalisation in Scotland and none voted against.[139]

CHE Bristol took part in the national campaigns in support of the *Gay News* appeal in 1978–79 and went on the Gay Pride marches in London, organising coaches to take people on some occasions. In 1980, the coach due to bring members back from the march broke down and the coach company arranged for another of its coaches which was in London that day to pick the marchers up. This coach was carrying members of the St. Teresa Ladies, a Catholic lay organisation, who were rather surprised at the company they were expected to keep on the return journey.[140]

Up until early 1981, the newsletter exuded a positive air of confidence. Four months later, however, the mood had changed and a period of introspection set in. At the AGM in April 1981, it was agreed that the newsletter would be produced by a collective and the format was changed from A5 to A4 to allow for cheaper printing and to give more space for members to express their views. In the following issues, members did indeed pour out their concerns about the future of the group, providing an insight into its difficulties, particularly the tension between political activity and social needs which was at the heart of CHE's malaise as an organisation. One correspondent asked why in a city the size of Bristol there was only a handful of activists.[141] Another drew attention to the threat of the burgeoning commercial scene to the voluntary movement: "We exist in a vicious circle. Because of the pubs and clubs we have insufficient membership to attract people away from these places and people will not desert these places in our favour while our membership is so low."[142] Yet another member made a more direct criticism of the group's Planning Meetings, urging that

> the articulate few curb their loquacity in the interest of ensuring that all views are thrown into the melting pot. [...] Those of us whom CHE Bristol has helped to come out [and] come to terms with our gayness are well aware of the sort of work – often informal, often on a one-to-one basis – which is inconspicuous and therefore goes largely unrecognised at Planning Meetings.[143]

In a piece of self-criticism intended to stimulate discussion, Chris Leigh, one of the most active members, suggested that CHE Bristol was dominated by a group of five or so individuals.

> This group can be summarised as follows: (1) Radical, anti-establishment, basically socialist in political orientation, supportive of other 'left-wing' issues (feminism, trade unionism). [...] (2) Highly politicised (with a small 'p') thus issues and lifestyles are perceived and interpreted in terms of ideologies, predominantly sexual politics. (3) Generally highly educated, very articulate with many years of experience in the gay movement. This Gang of Five can be readily identified by anyone who has spent 10 minutes at a Planning Meeting. They form a remarkably coherent and coercive power block. Without hesitation, I include myself within this caucus. The bulk of the Group's membership however is significantly different: (1) Politically middle-of-the-road or even apolitical. (2) Primary interest in the Group is social. Although supportive of the campaigning aspects of C.H.E., generally unwilling to become personally involved in non-social activities. (3) Comparatively new to the gay movement and pressure-group politics,

thus hesitant to express opinions – particularly to an audience of more than three. Possibly shy or unsure of their abilities and potential. This second group, which I will call the Silent Majority, is typified by the regular attenders of the tea & chats.

He noted an increasing divergence between the two groups: "Two virtually separate sub-groups have evolved, each with its own friendship networks. Each is suspicious or dismissive of the other." He did not believe the group's structure or politics were at fault – "I will argue that it is nearly always the 'left' which fires the challenges to established thinking" – but rather the lack of communication between the two divisions and urged members of the Silent Majority to speak up.[144]

One of the leading activists defended the importance of campaigning, referring to the ridicule and rejection suffered by "our gay brothers and sisters" and the emotional strength people got by working together: "That is why those of us who feel the injustice and hatefulness of our society will never stop campaigning."[145] On a more personal note, another correspondent discussed his feelings of guilt, because coming out was not an easy process for him.[146]

Following a successful disco held as part of the Gay Bristol Festival, CHE Bristol, together with the Gay Centre and Switchboard, organised a number of discos on the Lochiel floating pub, starting in September 1981.[147] In November 1981, CHE Bristol proposed greater cooperation with the Gay Centre and Switchboard in the areas of a joint newsletter, fund-raising and publicity, but this suggestion was turned down by the Gay Centre.[148] This was not enough to keep the group together and in January 1982, some of the more socially-minded members formed an independent gay social group called Avonscene.[149] One of the activists welcomed the new group and thought that it would be more attractive to those who wanted a social group or help in coming out.[150] Support for the Sunday afternoon tea and chats declined and the AGM in March 1982 decided to concentrate on the weekly Tuesday meetings.

The John Saunders campaign and other similar cases alerted activists across the country to the importance of employment legislation, since it showed that anyone could be dismissed simply for being gay. This was not a straightforward issue, however. When Bath CHE wrote to the seven Avon councillors for Bath suggesting the inclusion of a clause in employment contracts so that employees could not be sacked for being gay, only 3 replied and these, all Tories, were against the idea.[151] CHE Bristol activists also surveyed the attitudes of candidates in the 1981 Avon county elections and then turned their attention towards getting sexual orientation included in Avon County

Council's equal opportunities policy. On the advice of a sympathetic Labour councillor, the Bristol activists pushed for the anti-discrimination measure through the public sector unions NALGO and NUPE.[152] The suggestion was considered at length by various parts of the Council and in mid-1982, two members of the group were invited to a consultation meeting with the Leader of the Council and the Chairman of the Personnel Committee. It emerged that the Council had no objections to equal opportunities for homosexuals but felt that the term "sexual orientation" was too vague and could encompass paedophiles as well. The group noted that it had not been directly involved in the negotiations but that councillors had begun to realise the existence of a large minority who were homosexual "and recognise their duty to consult us".[153] In autumn 1982, the newsletter reported that the Council and unions were about to sign an equal opportunities agreement including the term "sexual orientation".[154] The Bristol Trades Union Council had also passed a resolution encouraging member unions to extend gay rights by negotiating the insertion of sexual orientation into equal opportunities agreements. "The passage of this resolution is a very encouraging step and CHE members should continue the work by now asking their unions what is to be done."[155] The newsletter also asked its members to support a campaign by Gay Rights at Work on behalf of a sacked lesbian care assistant.[156] In retrospect, this reflects the trend whereby effective campaigning on gay rights was passing to more specialised trade union and political lobby organisations from omnibus groups such as CHE. Nevertheless, CHE Bristol started work on a health education campaign, aimed at providing material to raise awareness about homosexuality among health and voluntary workers and agreed to produce a leaflet to distribute in order to alert gay men about a change in the police approach to cottaging.[157]

When in 1980 National CHE set up a Special Commission to consider its future (see Chapter 4), CHE Bristol made a submission, suggesting a radical change from the current centralised organisation to a less formal association of local gay organisations, with the activities at the national level restricted to matters of direct concern to gay people.[158] When the time came to implement the changes, CHE Bristol decided to register as a "Local Campaign Group", seeing no immediate prospects for a "Gay Community Organisation" in Bristol. "In practice, this will have no effect on the activities of CHE Bristol."[159]

The group regularly published its annual accounts: turnover never exceeded £800 and was usually much less. The maximum number of members was in the 80s.[160] In 1980 the group had 68 members, with about twenty regular attenders during 1981.[161] This rose to 71 at the time of the AGM in March 1981 but numbers fell to 51 in November 1981 and 42 in

February 1982.[162] By November 1982, after CHE implemented its structural reorganisation, CHE Bristol had only 19 local and 16 unexpired national members.[163] The remaining activists were keen to continue campaigning but recognised that the group was no longer viable. They decided to open negotiations with CHE Bath/Gay West with a view to amalgamation. At an Extraordinary General Meeting on 11 January 1983, the seven members present formally agreed to dissolve CHE Bristol on 31 January 1983 and to transfer its members and assets to Gay West.[164] One of the members present had also attended the very first meeting in 1970. In a brief retrospect, Charlie Beaton noted that "CHE Bristol appears like a parent and has now passed its time. The day of 'gay awareness for all' has passed and a new decade of confident socialising and sectional groups is upon us." With a touch of bitterness, he concluded with an epigraph for Bristol CHE: "Dissolved 1983, with clinical expertise, in favour of the new breed of hard-sell, value-for-money Gay West."[165]

Gay West agreed to hold more events in Bristol and its campaigning wing, Bath CHE, became Avon CHE in acknowledgement of its wider remit. Most of the Bristol CHE activists chose to concentrate their efforts on other activities, such as the Bristol Gay Centre, and did not join Gay West.[166] Some of those on the left became more involved in trade union activities and Labour politics. These developments will be discussed in Chapter 6.

The split with Avonscene and the dissolution of CHE Bristol illustrated the difficulties which faced CHE as an organisation. Its basic strategy depended on creating a mass movement which would lobby MPs in their constituencies in the hope of creating a majority in Parliament in favour of further law reform and other measures to advance LGBT rights. While it also encouraged its members to work at the local level, particularly in its education campaign aimed at securing a more understanding representation of homosexuality in schools, its main objective remained to create a large-scale national campaigning movement. However, many members joined primarily to meet other people and were not interested in campaigning, while others refused to join because they were put off by the campaigning image. CHE activists were aware that they needed to provide a good social environment to attract and retain members, particularly as the commercial scene began to develop, but in a voluntary movement, time and resources were limited and the more politically-aware activists wanted to devote their time to campaigning. Ultimately, CHE Bristol failed to resolve this dilemma but it left a legacy in the future development of the local LGBT movement. Activists in Bristol continued to look towards political involvement whilst Gay West concentrated on social activities. The following chapters will explore how these diverging strategies affected the history of the movement in the region.

3

Bath in the 1970s

Of all the gay places the world can afford,
By gentle and simple for pastime ador'd,
Fine balls, and fine concerts, fine buildings, and springs,
Fine walks, and fine views, and a thousand fine things,
Not to mention the sweet situation and air,
What place, my dear mother, with Bath can compare?

The word "gay" has acquired new meanings since Christopher Anstey first published his *New Bath Guide* in 1766 but his panegyric on Bath still applies. In contrast to Bristol ("for commerce and dirt ... renown'd"), Bath is the quintessential leisure city. It owes its existence to the hot springs, which formed the basis of its attraction as a resort both in Roman times and during the 18th century. The Georgian city was laid out to attract visitors with lodging houses and entertainment facilities like the Pump Room and the Assembly Rooms. The country's aristocracy and rising middle-class flocked to Bath during the season to take the waters as well as for shopping, gambling, dancing and finding advantageous marriage partners. In Jane Austen's *Northanger Abbey*, Mrs Allen looks out for the newest fashions as soon as she arrives in the city and she was not the only one. Bath and its shops were at the forefront of the consumer revolution of the 18th century.[167]

In the early 19th century, sea-bathing supplanted taking the mineral waters and the fashionable company removed to Brighton in pursuit of the Prince Regent and Mrs Fitzherbert. Bath reinvented itself as a retirement centre for the well-to-do upper and middle classes, who increasingly set the tone of the city through the 19th and first half of the 20th century. Besides the genteel squares and crescents, however, Bath also housed a significant amount of industry, principally printing and engineering (Stothert & Pitt's cranes were world-renowned) and an industrial working class. Most of this industry had disappeared by the end of the 1980s.

The opening of the University of Bath in the mid-1960s brought an influx of young people while improved transport links to London in the 1970s injected new life into its economy. The founders of the Bath Gay Awareness Group all came from elsewhere and recalled a state of "effervescence" in the city when they arrived, reflecting changing social attitudes. Bath was the scene of one of the main conservation battles of the 1970s, as campaigners fought to prevent demolition of large swathes of the old city in a battle which became known as the Sack of Bath.[168]

This situation changed completely in the 1980s. Increasing support for conservation and the cleaning of the buildings' facades led to a new popular appreciation of the city's architectural heritage and Georgian architecture became fashionable. Property prices rose rapidly as more and more young people wanted to live in the city centre. The city was designated a UNESCO World Heritage site in 1987. Bath was well placed to benefit from the emphasis on consumer culture during the economic boom of the 1980s. During these years the International Music Festival was a major event, starring world-famous opera singers. Bath regained much of its 18th century role as a leisure and retail centre. In recent decades, the city's total population has fluctuated around the 80–85,000 mark, a fifth of the size of Bristol. The city centre is quite compact because of its location in a valley and serves at the same time as a local market town, a regional shopping centre, a national cultural forum and an international tourist destination.

Bath politics have traditionally been dominated by its wealthy residents and the local business elite. In party terms, local politics have revolved around the split between Conservatives and Liberals, with Labour acting as the main opposition for the third quarter of the 20th century. During the first half of the 19th century, Bath was known as a hotbed of radical liberalism but this faded in the latter part of the century. The city's parliamentary representation was held almost continuously by the Conservatives and their allies from 1885 to 1992. From 1974, the Liberals replaced Labour as the runner-up and at the 1992 General Election, the Liberal Democrat Don Foster defeated the sitting MP, Chris Patten, the then Conservative Party chairman, in an election upset with national repercussions, continuing to hold the seat in the following General Elections. The Labour vote came a distant third, partly reflecting the decline of local industry and partly as a result of tactical voting.

Like Bristol, Bath was subsumed in Avon County Council from 1974 until 1996, when it was reconstituted as Bath & North East Somerset Council (B&NES), a unitary authority. Unlike Bristol, the Liberals retained a greater presence on the council up to the mid 1970s and, with the realignment of centrist politics during the 1980s, the number of Liberal Democrat councillors began to grow. Since B&NES was created, no party has had overall control of the council but the Liberal Democrats were the dominant party from 1995 to 2007, when the Conservatives took control until 2011.

Gay Subculture in Bath

Bath seems to have been designed for the homosexual flâneur. Where else can one stroll down Gay Street, turn into the architectural masterpiece of Queen Square and end up in Queen's Parade, overlooking what was formerly one of the city's busiest cottages? In Bath, as in Bristol and other provincial cities, the public toilets were one of the main sites where gay men met each other, both before and after 1967. There were several scattered around the city centre and various ones became notorious at different periods. The pattern of cottaging in the 1950s, and the risks involved, can be deduced from a court case which centred on the public convenience at the entrance to the Charlotte Street car park (still in existence but closed).[169] Nine local youths aged 16–18 were arrested in April 1953 and charged with conspiracy to demand money by menaces during the preceding months. At the magistrates hearing, four men who had been victims of the youths gave evidence as witnesses and were allowed to retain their anonymity, being referred to as W, X, Y and Z. They described how they had been approached and threatened by the defendants. One had been beaten up and had to go to hospital with a broken nose. The encounters took place at the Charlotte Street convenience but one man stated that he had seen one of the defendants "at a number of conveniences which he visited". One man had offered to give a boy a lift and while he was starting his car, the other youths jumped in and threatened him. Another man invited a youth back to his flat, where the youth threatened him with a hammer and demanded money. Despite this, the man saw the youth again in his flat a few days later and this time a watch was stolen. The original complainant knew one of his assailants and asked him by name not to hit him. One defendant told the police that "The idea was to get talking to a man and after reaching a nice quiet spot, the man would commit an improper act." Then the rest of the gang would come up and give two alternatives: the police or money. The defendants were remanded in custody and all nine pleaded guilty at the Somerset Assizes, where three were jailed for a year, with the rest receiving lesser sentences.

The press reports throw some interesting light on patterns of cottaging before 1967. The case came to light because the man who had been beaten up complained to the police. The police chose to prosecute the assailants

The founders of Bath Gay Awareness Group in July 1972. Photo: Courtesy of the Bath Chronicle and Bob Illingworth.

rather than the victims because the case involved blackmail and gave the witnesses immunity from identification (and presumably prosecution), even though the original complainant testified in court that "an act of impropriety took place" in the car park. Some men used to visit several conveniences and would use them to meet partners with whom they would then go off to have sex elsewhere. Local youths were aware of the way gay men used cottages and would turn to queer-bashing either to extort money or, as one told the police, to give them "a good hiding to satisfy my feelings."

Another convenience which figures in accounts stood in a secluded location in the Royal Victoria Park until it was demolished and replaced by the Pavilion Cafe (where Gay West now holds its Christmas dinners). In the 1970s and 1980s, the most notorious cottage was located in Marlborough Lane, a few hundred yards down the hill from the Royal Crescent, one of the city's major architectural monuments. This toilet was closed and demolished in the mid-1980s to make way for an access road to a car park.

A toilet in the Saw Close, opposite the Theatre Royal and close to the Garrick's Head gay pub, also had its adepts. This has been demolished too. In the 1990s, the sites most frequently mentioned were Sydney Gardens and Rainbow Woods, where public conveniences were located adjacent to wooded areas, allowing men to combine cottaging with open-air cruising. These sites frequently figured in the discussions of the Policing Initiative (see Chapter 9).

The longest-running gay pub in Bath was the Garrick's Head, next to the Theatre Royal. According to my mother, the Garrick's Head had a reputation as a gay pub before the Second World War and it may well have gone back much further, benefitting like the Salisbury in London from the tolerance extended to the eccentricities of theatre people. A long-time gay resident of the city confirms that the Garrick's Head was gay before the war and that people used to come over from Bristol to go there.[170] In 1976, a local guide to Bath pubs noted "...the Garricks Head is now the watering hole for the actors and stage staff of the Theatre Royal next door. [...] Both [bars] have velvet curtains, plenty of tables and a thriving limp-wristed bar stool community..." In fact, lesbians and gay men mainly used the Green Room on the left-hand side of the entrance. In its later days, this was something of a misnomer as the room was furnished in red plush, with signed photographs of actors and actresses who had appeared at the theatre adorning the walls. The Garrick's was first listed in *Gay News* in January 1974.[171] The Garrick's Head was quite notorious locally and one long-serving Gay West committee member recounted that his mother discovered he was gay when his uncle saw him coming out of the pub.[172] It ceased to be a gay pub at the end of 1997, amidst protests from its LGBT customers.[173]

In the early 1970s, the Regency Ballroom, situated in the Saw Close not far from the Garrick's Head, tried to turn itself into a gay pub. The Bath Gay Awareness Group newsletter referred to it as a new gay pub in November 1972, it was listed in *Gay News* from March 1973 and the group held its first disco there in September 1973.[174] The Bath pub guide described the Regency as "Very smooth chic pub. [...] They certainly relish their image as a gay bar, though it's more a pose than a reality..."[175] By December 1973, however, the newsletter was noting that "it looks as though the Garrick's Head has settled back into being the gay meeting place for most Group members. The Regency has become so popular that the hets have nearly crowded us out."[176] However, the newsletter still mentioned it as a gay pub.

Over the years, a number of other pubs have also been patronised by gay people for periods of time. In late 1988 the Volunteer Rifleman's Arms advertised in the Gay West newsletter and the landlady told the group that she would welcome gay customers.[177] With the growth of the pink economy during the 1990s, two pubs assumed the modern form of gay pub, with an openly gay ethos explicitly seeking to attract LGBT customers, with rainbow flags prominently displayed outside to proclaim their identity. The Bath Tap (formerly the Devonshire Arms) at 19 St. James's Parade, was converted into a gay pub in October 1996 and opened a dance area in the basement in 1997.[178] For several years it was popular with younger lesbians and gays but in February 2010 it was sold and the new owner said that it would no longer be regarded or listed as a gay venue.[179] Mandalyns (which had once been the Lansdown Arms) at the bottom of Lansdown Road, was taken over and renovated by a landlady in 2002. A pub guide published the next year noted that Mandalyns billed itself as "a pub for all sexualities"and was a splendid example of how an old boozer could be transformed into a popular twenty-first century hangout without losing sight of what pubs were all about.[180] The Smith Bros pub in Westgate Buildings had originally been a wine vaults. In 2004, against the opposition of the two existing gay pubs, the Eldridge Pope brewery turned it into a gay bar called DYMK [Does Your Mother Know] but this venture was short-lived and the bar later reverted to a straight pub, complete with sports television (a sure way of driving out gay customers).[181] At the time of writing in 2010, only Mandalyns, under new ownership, remains as a lesbian and gay pub.[182]

Gay clubs in Bath have had a mostly ephemeral existence. Georgy's Club, located in a cellar at 14 George St., was once Bath's only striptease nightclub but in 1972 it was taken over by the former manager of the Moulin Rouge in Bristol, Reginald Valentine.[183] He turned it into a gay club and as such it became known as Valentine's. In 1975, it was described as a mixed straight/gay club but by April 1976 it was reported to have gone totally straight.[184] The Adam Room in Nero's, also in George St., on the other hand, was described at this time as "all gay friendly atmosphere. Not too big in luxury surroundings. Drinks reasonable food available after 11 pm. Run by Gay Committee – never any trouble".[185] In September 1976, a new gay womens group called "Wings" launched a disco night at the Adam Room.[186] Henry's, located under Pulteney Bridge and functioning on Sunday evenings, opened in early 1980 but closed around the end of the year following prosecution for a licensing law infringement.[187] The Underground club was run by a well-known gay owner, Bill Ayres, but was not a gay club as such. The Bath Tap ran a club in its basement from 1997 onwards.

Publicans in country areas who wanted to attract gay customers faced a much more difficult task. In October 1986, the Gay West newsletter carried an advertisement for the White Hart in Crewkerne near Yeovil, which was planning to operate one of its rooms as an exclusively gay bar on

Thursday and Friday nights.[188] When local opponents of homosexuality got wind of the idea, they started a campaign in the local press, which deterred the pub's other customers and forced the landlady to drop the plan, amidst considerable financial loss.[189] When Jaspers tried to start a gay night in Glastonbury in 1995, the fuss in the local press stopped it opening and the landlord lost his job.[190]

Bath Gay Awareness Group/Bath Gay Group/Bath CHE

In keeping with the *genius loci*, the gay movement opened in Bath with a performance. The first recorded activity was carried out by the Gay Liberation Front in 1971. Under the heading "Street theatre at Bath", the GLF's magazine *Come Together* reported,

> Over the weekend of the 4th, 5th and 6th of June, GLF Street Theatre participated in the Bath Civic Festival. Two actions were performed; a heavily symbolic liberation involving the ultimate rejection of conditioning and oppression by the liberated homosexual, and a rip-off of the Trial Scene from Alice in Wonderland, relative to us. Both were extremely effective; visually as entertainment, and propaganda. Our audience was stereo-typed bourgeoisie, so it was to our surprise that the majority of reaction was warm and positive. A Bath GLF Group is getting it together right now![191]

This very public inauguration set a marker for the Bath gay group, whose main achievements were to be in the public sphere.

The origins of the Bath group were very different from that of CHE Bristol, being associated with students at the University of Bath.[192] One of the group's founders, Bob Illingworth, a post-graduate, was seeing a psychiatrist, who eventually told him to accept that he was homosexual and put him in touch with another of his gay patients and a friend. Another early member, Norman Lapper, wrote a letter to the student newspaper following a lecture on homosexuality given by a visiting speaker. The letter, which was published anonymously in March 1971, asked whether a sympathetic student or member of staff would be willing to make contact with homosexuals and give them an opportunity to discuss their problems either individually or in groups.[193] The University Chaplain wrote in the next issue, suggesting that a study group on current social problems which the chaplaincy was hoping to sponsor in the following term might offer a situation for discussion and participation.[194] As a result of these various contacts, a group began meeting in the autumn, when the students returned from the summer vacation.

The Bath Gay Awareness Group celebrated its 10th anniversary in November 1981, which indicates that it was actually founded in November 1971. It made a conscious decision to meet in the town rather than the university and included both University of Bath students and other students and non-students. The name Bath Gay Awareness Group was chosen to distance it from the "stuffy" image of CHE and the "outlandishness" associated with GLF. The aim of the group was to help people to come out and accept their homosexuality, rather than to provide a social programme. In the early days, each person attending a meeting had to give their name and say "I am gay and proud of it". Two of the founders were interviewed on the University's internal television service but did not encounter any reaction. Students were either radical or not interested.

One early meeting appears to have been quite eventful. In March 1972, the convenor of CHE Bristol went over to Bath to attend a meeting.[195] He found that the group consisted of about eight people, mostly students at Bath University, and that at least one was a CHE member. He went on:

> The meeting took place in a bed-sitter and had been advertised on posters. The most interesting part of the evening was when the landlord burst in unannounced and ordered us out. He, the landlord, alluded to an unwritten rule that guests had to be out by 11 p.m. and that it was past that time. The tenant refused whereupon the landlord returned with a policeman. No definate [sic] conclusion to the dispute was reached.

The Bristol convenor asked CHE to ascertain whether this constituted harassment of homosexuals or whether the landlord was within his legal right to ban public meetings on his property. In the early days, however, the Bath group did not generally have much contact with CHE Bristol.

By July 1972 the group was sufficiently well-organised and confident to give an interview to the local paper, which was accompanied by a photograph of five people gathered round a coffee table.[196] This interview came about because one member had a woman friend who knew the paper's liberal-minded editor. Describing it as a newly-formed group, the *Bath Chronicle* reported:

> They call themselves gay. And in their world, as in Gay Lib, the word means homosexual. But they are breaking away from Gay Lib because the movement has become mixed up with political revolutionaries. Hence Bath Gay Awareness Group. It was started by David Barton, a 23–year-old law student who stood unsuccessfully as an anti-tunnel

candidate in the city council elections. [...] It is a social group in which homosexuals can become aware of themselves. They help each other by talking freely about their attitudes over cider and cups of coffee to the sound of a record-player. And they want to make other people aware of the fact that homosexuals don't necessarily regard themselves as being a problem and should be accepted as members of society who have simply opted for an alternative way of life. They do not plan to parade about the streets with placards. Says Mr Illingworth, 'In Bath you can't go about with banners. But we want to break down the conspiracy of silence by being open.' Richard Watkins, a horticulture student at Bath University is recruiting volunteers to sell copies of Gay News in Abbey Churchyard.

The article said the group had about twenty members, including students, a surveyor, an education researcher, a few women and two men who were married with children, and met weekly in a flat overlooking the Royal Victoria Park. It also gave the group's phone number. The photograph was taken a few days later and because no women members were present, a heterosexual feminist who was not a member agreed to appear for the sake of gender balance. Later, in October 1972, members of the group appeared with CHE Bristol and some GLF Rad Fems on the Harlech TV programme *Now It's Your Say* on Gay Liberation (see also Chapter 2).[197]

Despite their reservations about GLF (some of whose members had become associated with the Angry Brigade), the Bath Gay Awareness Group is listed in the first *Gay News* listing in May 1972 under National Gay Liberation Front groups.[198] In its December 1973 newsletter, however, there is a reference to one person looking after the CHE side of things and another the GLF side.[199] After the disintegration of GLF in 1972–73, the group became increasingly involved with CHE, but as an associate rather than a full member and it continued to have a more free-spirited aura derived from GLF.[200]

The Bath Gay Awareness Group soon began to organise itself more formally, starting a typescript newsletter in October 1972, which, in various formats, has continued almost uninterrupted down to the present day.[201] It held its first AGM in February 1973, at which officers were elected and a membership subscription instituted.[202] In October 1974, the group held a meeting to discuss a new constitution. "It is hoped to settle once and for all time the arguments that have been raging over the groups [sic] future."[203] The Constitution which was adopted by the E.G.M.s on 17th and 24th October [or November] 1974 listed the aims of the group as "a) to provide an enlightened environment where gay people can meet together.

b) to promote an awareness of all forms of human sexuality within both the group and society. c) to support all other groups which promote the aims of sexual liberation. d) to work in close association with other local CHE groups to establish CHE groups down the South West peninsular [sic]." The Constitution also stated that "The group will be a full member of the Campaign for Homosexual Equality". Membership would be open to all who supported the aims of Bath Gay Awareness Group but "a group member does not have to be a national CHE member".[204] The mixture of broad liberationist aims and specific provisions regarding CHE suggests that the constitution represented a compromise between the two strands of opinion. There was also a pressing practical reason as a constitution was needed to allow the group to open a bank account.

Initially meetings were held on different days of the week but from January 1975, they settled down to a pattern of weekly meetings held on Thursdays. During 1973 and 1974, the group held its meetings in the upper floor of the Liberal Association headquarters at 1 St. Michael's Place. As if in anticipation, this building had once been occupied by a beerhouse called the Queen.[205] From 1993 onwards, Gay West has used the ground floor for its Saturday morning Rainbow Cafe, completely unaware of its previous association with the group. Members of the Bath Gay Awareness Group used to meet informally in the Grapes pub in nearby Westgate Street until the landlord objected to two women with their arms around each other and asked them to leave.[206] From 1975 onwards, it met in committee members' homes, initially in Fairfield Road and later in Rivers Street. Outside meetings, members regularly met informally in the Garrick's Head.

The early 1970s saw Bath Gay Awareness Group embroiled in a series of campaigns, which had important implications for freedom of the press and access to information. Two were on the surface purely local issues – campaigns to get the local newspaper to publish advertisements for the group and the local library to stock *Gay News*, while the third – the trial of *Gay News* on obscenity charges, had national repercussions. But in reality, all three had major implications, involving the right of homosexuals to participate in their own name in the public sphere. That this was no formality is indicated by the opening of all mail addressed to the group's post box by the Post Office during 1973.[207]

In 1972, the group started two local campaigns, which were only to achieve success nearly ten years later. Encouraged by the sympathetic article which the *Bath Chronicle* had published in July 1972, the group tried to insert a paid contact advertisement, only to be refused. When Bob Illingworth went to see the Managing Director and pointed out that the group had already been featured in the editorial section, he was told that the

St. Michael's Place, Bath, where Bath Gay Awareness Group held its first public meetings in 1973 and, later, the venue for Gay West's Rainbow Cafe from 1993 onwards, seen in July 2008. Photo: Robert Howes.

newspaper reserved the right to refuse advertisements as it saw fit. Pressed further, the Director eventually explained that he thought that homosexuality was a gross abnormality and not suitable to appear in the advertisement section, which represented the newspaper itself.[208] This reflected a pattern of inconsistency across the provincial press at this time, with some papers, such as the *Bristol Evening Post*, accepting advertisements from gay groups without question, while others rejected them.[209]

At the same time, the group wrote to Bath Municipal Libraries asking them to stock *Gay News*. The Director replied saying they were unable to make a decision owing to the imminent reorganisation of local government. He also declined to display the CHE poster on the noticeboard, which was reserved for official announcements, but sent a registration form for the Directory of Local Societies, maintained by the Reference Library. This appears to be the first time that a public institution took cognisance of the group's existence.[210]

The third campaign was part of the ongoing struggle at the national level over the visibility of homosexuality. As described in Chapter 1, powerful elements in the legal establishment fought a long rearguard action to restrict access by homosexuals to the public sphere, from the trial of the alternative magazine *IT* for publishing contact ads for gay men in 1971–72 to the prosecution of the London bookshop Gay's the Word for importing books about homosexuality in 1984–85. On 31 October 1973, the Bath police raided a wholesale warehouse owned by Johnsons Central News Agency and seized over 10,000 magazines and newspapers. These included titles such as the *Times Literary Supplement*, the *Spectator*, *Railway Modeller* and *The Lady*, which were later returned to the company. Also seized was *Gay News* issue no. 34, and this was not returned but included among the publications to be prosecuted for obscenity. *Gay News* only heard of the case through the managing director of Johnsons, as the wholesaler rather than the newspaper was to be prosecuted. As it pointed out, it could have been condemned as obscene without even knowing about it. *Gay News* engaged a barrister and when the trial started at Bath magistrates court on 17 April 1974, it emerged that no-one, from the police to the public prosecutor, had actually read the paper – the case was based on its name alone. It took the police a quarter of an hour to find the relevant copy and as soon as the magistrates had read it, they ruled that the issue was not obscene.[211]

CHE was affiliated to the National Co-ordinating Committee against Censorship and members of Bath Gay Awareness Group attended the convening meeting of the committee at the local level. "We went with a mandate from the group to commit it to helping in Bath; it will be good for us to get involved in local activities which are separate from the group. Many of the issues involved in fighting censorship are directly relevant to our campaign activities."[212] A silent demonstration was staged outside the Guildhall on the day the trial began and four members of the Bath Co-ordinating Committee of the Campaign Against Censorship handed out leaflets and copies of *Gay News*.[213] Members of BGAG took part in this demonstration.[214]

Gay News were awarded costs of just £250 for their legal bills of £1715. They launched an appeal and within three weeks had raised enough to cover the costs. The Gay News Bath Fund raised over £1500, showing the high regard in which the paper was held by its readers.[215] A similar prosecution of *Gay News* and the lesbian magazine *Sappho* was mounted in Bournemouth in February 1975 and again dismissed, relieving *Gay News* of legal pressure until the notorious prosecution for blasphemy brought by Mary Whitehouse in 1976.[216] The Bath case helped establish the principle that a publication by gays addressed to a gay audience and talking about concerns to gays was not per se obscene.

The group was active in other forms of campaigning. It sent 50 questionnaires to candidates in the 1973 Avon County Council elections but only 13 candidates replied. All replies except from the National Front were favourable. It then sent out 70 questionnaires to candidates in the Bath District elections.[217] The group also took part in the national campaigns to canvas the views of parliamentary candidates preceding the General Election in October 1974, sending questionnaires to candidates in 9 local constituencies.[218] In June 1974, the group's convenor, Angela Needham, was elected onto CHE's national executive.[219] Committee members were active in CHE national politics, attending and reporting back on the CHE conferences in Morecambe, Malvern and Southampton, as well as the NUS Gay Rights Conference in Sheffield and the first international gay conference in Edinburgh.[220] Malvern was widely seen as CHE's most successful conference and the exhilaration was shared by the Bath representatives. One wrote: "Malvern was more than just another conference, ot [i.e. it] was an experience in release and gay emancipation."[221] At the local level, the group was in contact with schools and it organised a meeting with local clergy in November 1974.[222]

In 1975, however, the group went into decline and during the later 1970s, its activities largely comprised weekly social and discussion meetings in committee members' homes and occasional pub evenings and outings. It organised a meeting of the CHE National Council in Bath in March 1976 and continued to send questionnaires to candidates in local elections.[223] The tension between socialising and campaigning which characterised Bristol

CHE was also evident in the Bath group. In February 1975, the convenor wrote: "As I see it campaigning is an essential part of the groups [sic] activities [...] It is necessary to campaign on two levels; personally by living a life which is openly gay, and also collectively by trying to change society so that no one is hung up about sex or sexuality, be it there [sic] own or someone else's." At the same time, the newsletter editor remarked: "Some of us want to campaign, and some want to socialise, and if there is not patience or understanding, one or the other sub-groups will dominate and thus destroy all that has gone before."[224] Only a small number wanted to campaign and the amount of work involved inevitably led to frustration. Nigel Collins, the group's longest-serving activist, commented after drafting questions for candidates in the May 1976 local elections: "the questionnaire does mean that at last we have done something constructive [...] of course when I say 'we' have done something constructive, I mean the same old tiny handful of people as always. I for one am getting extremely pissed off with slogging my guts out over B.G.A.G. and getting absolutely no feedback whatsoever, good or bad."[225] Fewer than a third of the candidates replied to the survey, although of these 65% were in favour of an end to discrimination.[226]

In February 1977, the *Bath Chronicle* again rejected the group's application to publish an advertisement.[227] The newsletter regularly lamented the low attendance and appealed for ideas to make the group more attractive. In April 1977, the convenor complained: "Attendance at meetings will have to improve drastically if B.G.A.G. is going to continue as a viable group. In March attendance was very sporadic [...] A very valid comment was made concerning the lack of discipline at meetings which means that discussions tend to turn into friendly chats and vice versa. Social evenings also tended not to be sufficiently different from usual meetings to persuade people to attend."[228] In his last newsletter contribution in June 1977 before departing, he wrote: "it would be nice to report that my successor will be taking over a thriving, well attended group. This is not the case" while Donald Branch, a former convenor, who was moving to Bristol, wrote: "We have allowed the excuse of lack of support to prevent us doing many things of which we have been capable. We have not followed up contacts with people in education, the clergy, the press and local government, which we could have done. We are small but committment [sic] is what really counts."[229]

For much of 1978 the newsletter was reduced to a single sheet. In November 1978, however, the group was able to announce that the *Bath Chronicle* had reversed its policy on advertising and agreed to accept an advertisement from the group. Initially it still refused to carry a telephone number, although this restriction was later dropped. As a result of the first advertisement, the group received five letters of enquiry.[230] With an influx of new people, the group was energised. On 5 January 1979, it held a disco in the basement of the Labour Party headquarters, Century House, which was judged "amazingly successful", with 108 people turning up. Profits from further discos in Century House provided funds for the group. A questionnaire prepared by the National Gay Lobby was sent to all the local MPs and prospective parliamentary candidates in the forthcoming 1979 General Election and the answers summarised in the newsletter.[231] Two members of the group followed up the reply by going to a meeting with Chris Patten, the Tory candidate (who became the MP for Bath following the election), which they admitted was "rather nerve-racking". "If he is elected then he said he would welcome further information from us on the matter and I got the impression that his general attitudes would be good if an attempt was made in Parliament to improve the present laws."[232] At the same time, it was decided to drop "Awareness" from the name of the group as it sounded rather dated and from April 1979, it became the Bath Gay Group.[233]

Nevertheless, when David England became convenor in autumn 1979 he painted a dismal picture of dropping attendances, especially of women, weekly meetings devoid of anything to interest anyone and a group which had all but ceased to exist as a campaigning organisation.[234] He continued to warn about the dangers of complacency, which reflected the feeling of the time. "The anger and indignation at the repression of gays seems to have subsided, and many gays seem to think that there is nothing left to fight for – they are quite content with life as long as no one actually bothers them personally."[235] The group continued to flat-line through 1980, with a small number of members continuing the traditional letter-writing to MPs on gay issues and the weekly meetings in members' homes. One MP wrote back that "we knew his views and that persistant [sic] enquiries could only lead to alienation!"[236]

During 1981, however, things began to change and a new mood of optimism and confidence began to percolate through the group. The newsletter expanded and was produced by photocopying instead of stencils, giving it an improved appearance. From May 1982 onwards, it included the names and phone numbers of the committee, a practice which has continued almost unbroken since. Thanks to an approach from the Mayor of Bath's Charity, early in 1981 the group started using the Bath Centre for Voluntary Service (BCVS) building in Abbey Green for meetings.[237] This gave it a prominent venue in the centre of the city and links which were to be important for the later development of Gay West. The successful discos improved the financial situation and the group began to see that other activities besides the traditional lobbying could be effective forms of campaigning. It also became more adroit in its relations with the media. The convenor wrote: "More money, more members, more campaigning .. hopefully it will have not escaped anyone that the group has been doing rather well."[238]

A meeting with the local clergy in January 1981 was reported in the *Bath Chronicle*, the first time it had given the group press space for a long time.[239] The group took up the campaign to get *Gay News* into the public libraries again in earnest in 1980, by which time the libraries were run by Avon County Council. Initially the request was turned down by the Conservative-controlled council but when Labour took control in 1981 following council elections, the group tried again, with support from CHE Bristol.[240] The new leisure committee reconsidered the matter and eventually agreed to make copies available in the three main libraries in Bristol, Bath and Weston-super-Mare. The subscription would be paid for jointly by the Bath Gay Group and CHE Bristol. This break-through was carried as a news item on local radio, with an interview by the group secretary Roland Attwell, and in the local press, where it generated correspondence between opponents and members of the group. The BGG newsletter editorialised: "Gays in the area have made one small step to-wards being allowed to be a full part of society, we must carry on our work despite the setbacks, our gains are more important to us as they help to bolster our confidence. [...] The media in all its forms gives the gay movement a chance to air its views, we must sieze [sic] every opportunity we can to do this."[241] In the short term, this proved to be something of a Pyrrhic victory, since *Gay News* collapsed in April 1983, but the group had established an important point of principle in this and its campaign to publish advertisements in the *Bath Chronicle*, namely, that homosexuals had the right to make their voice heard in the local public sphere.[242]

The group canvassed the views of parliamentary candidates preceding the General Election in May 1979, wrote to local M.P.s about Northern Ireland and the John Saunders case in 1980 and started preparing in 1982 for the next General Election.[243] At other times it surveyed the opinions of candidates in local elections and planned a survey of all 54 Bath city councillors in 1982.[244] The group initially had high hopes of the new Alliance of the Liberals and SDP but were disappointed when the sexual orientation clause was deleted from the SDP Constitution.[245] In summer 1982, Bath CHE put on a theatrical performance entitled *Peers, Queers and Commons*, as its contribution to the Bath Festival and the Bristol Gay Festival. The write-up described it as an "amusing, infuriating and sometimes moving look at how Parliament has responded to attempts to obtain equality for gay men and women." Its author, Stephen Jeffery-Poulter, subsequently turned it into a detailed history of the parliamentary struggle for law reform between 1950 and 1990, which was published under the same title in 1991.[246]

The group gained a higher profile when one local paper, the free weekly *Bath Herald*, published a number of articles about it, including its survey of candidates in the council elections, its attempts to talk to schools and a two-page spread on David England and Roland Attwell.[247] Roland Attwell welcomed the publicity for the group, commenting humorously that "the Herald is fast becoming the mouthpiece for Bath CHE".[248] This interest was carefully cultivated by the group. "Over the past month the Bath Herald has carried articles about the group on various aspects of our work. We hope that this will bring the subject of homosexuality out into the open. The back ground work has carried on, this is lots of information sent to the Chronicle and the Herald, this appears to have worked."[249] This publicity came at considerable cost since Roland Attwell's high profile meant that he faced prejudice and even assault at the factory where he worked.[250]

Building on its success, the group became quite adept at working with the media. On Remembrance Sunday, 8 November 1982, it laid a wreath in the shape of a pink triangle at the Cenotaph in Victoria Park in memory of the homosexuals killed in the concentration camps or who gave their lives during the wars. This was vandalised later that evening and had to be replaced.

> On behalf of the group a press release was issued to the Bath Evening Chronicle about the incident and the action they had taken. Next day the paper carried a report headed "Pink Triangle Vandals" next to a photograph of the main Wreath laying ceremony. Perhaps a few more people will be aware that so many gay women and men gave their lives for the cause of freedom.[251]

The group also found that other means could be used to spread the message. After successfully raising some money through that traditional stand-by of voluntary organisations, the jumble sale, it decided to organise a spring sale, appealing to city shops for items to sell. "We will be quite open about what CHE stands for, but in addition we will also inform the shop that half of the net profit will be going to a local Charity [...] We will be helping the group, and perhaps get some Press coverage too, but most important (in my opinion. Ed.) we will be helping those who cannot help themselves."[252] Members of the group visited over 300 city centre businesses and with the items donated were able to take a total of £145, donating £75 to a local special needs school. The newsletter thanked the shops which had made donations and also named and shamed "5 shops that were openly hostile towards CHE, ranging from disgust to open abuse.

[…] These shops however, represented only 1.7% of all the premises visited and, as a whole the exercise has been an overwhelming success in the field of public relations."[253]

The group undertook outreach work where it could. In 1975, members of the group spoke to a meeting of Chippenham Young Conservatives.[254] It was particularly keen to talk to schools and colleges as part of CHE's education campaign. In 1974, three members of BGAG addressed a meeting of Chippenham College of Education at Rudloe Park Hotel on some of the problems faced by homosexuals in society. Two committee members also spoke to 16 year olds at a comprehensive school in Bristol. "They had to answer some tough and at times very intimate questions but the kids responded well and seem to be very aware both of problems faced by homosexual couples as well as heterosexual couples in society."[255] When Angela Needham went to talk to a group of Bath youth leaders, on the other hand, she was shaken by the hostility and lack of support she encountered.[256]

Later attempts to contact headteachers and arrange visits to schools in Bath in the early 1980s were, however, ignored, perhaps as a fallout from the heightened concern about paedophilia resulting from the PIE trials.[257] The group had more success with mothers and future mothers, addressing housewives' groups in Chippenham, Melksham, Frome, Warminster and Derry Hill. When three members of the group addressed the Derry Hill Young Homemakers, they used a tape-slide kit on homosexuality produced by Tyneside CHE and were asked afterwards if the tape-slide show could be shown to the local youth group.[258]

The same tape-slide show figured in a more difficult assignment, when "a handful of group members" met with an inspector and a sergeant who dealt with community relations in the Bath police district. "The Inspector acknowledged that gays were an invisible minority in the police field of work." The meeting discussed indecency offences and police surveillance of public toilets. On the subject of police training,

> the Officers said they would welcome any help the group could give towards a better understanding of the gay situation by the recruits and it was agreed that an official approach by the group to the Police authorities be made, with a view to providing speakers and possibly showing of the CHE Tape-Slide kit to recruits. This could be another bold step forward for BATH CHE's Campaigning work.[259]

This initial contact with the police was slow to bear fruit but a member of Gay West was later directly involved in the setting up of the

Avon and Somerset Constabulary's police liaison group.

During 1981, divisions started to appear in the group. The more politically minded, notably David England and Roland Attwell, wanted to strengthen its links with CHE while others preferred to maintain the status quo.[260] In September 1981 a ballot of members was held on whether to change the name of the group to Bath CHE, with proponents arguing that it would help the group's growing political influence, while opponents who wanted to retain the name Bath Gay Group pointed out that it emphasised the individual nature and identity of the local group, clearly stated its role and was more likely to attract women, young people and those who were put off by the image of CHE. The ballot resulted in a split vote, with 18 for becoming Bath CHE and 13 for remaining Bath Gay Group. An EGM was held on 24 September 1981 to decide whether to make the group a full and integral part of National CHE and those attending the meeting voted 7 to 3, with 1 abstention, for a new Constitution to implement the majority decision.[261] This stated that "Bath CHE shall be a constituent group of National CHE and its National Council" and declared that "Membership shall be open to all who agree with the aims of CHE, and pay an annual subscription"; those who could not totally agree with the aims of CHE could take out a separate subscription in order to receive the newsletter but they could not vote on items which directly affected CHE.[262] Welcoming the decision, England wrote: "CHE is the only national gay organisation committed to fighting for the rights of gay women and men and despite it's [sic] faults your support even if it's only financial by paying your subscription is vital."[263] This resulted in a split, with a number of members who objected to the bureaucracy associated with CHE leaving to form a short-lived group with more social aims, including Nigel Collins who had kept the newsletter going through the difficult years of the later 1970s.[264]

The only other group recorded in Bath at this time was "Wings", a gay womens group, which launched a disco night at the Adam Room in September 1976. "Wings" said that "Ours is a purely social thing" and gave the Bath Gay Awareness Group as its contact address. It listed its aims as to become the only all-female gay group for Bath and the surrounding district, provide a base for meetings and all social activities, establish an affinity with other women's groups at both local and national level, give backing and support to those who wish to fight in legal and political battles, and publish the occasional newsletter for local gay women.[265] Despite its name, this group never really took off and does not seem to have lasted very long.

4

Gay West in the 1980s

The Creation of Gay West

During the late 1970s, CHE nationally comprised around 100 local groups in England and Wales, with an elected national Executive Committee (EC) which coordinated campaigning and political lobbying, although much of this was carried out by the groups at the local level. Falling membership, increasing financial problems, widespread criticism of the organisation's bureaucratic methods and a series of resignations from the EC led to the holding of an Extraordinary Conference on 1 March 1980 and the creation of a Special Commission to inquire into the role and future development of CHE. This produced a Majority and a Minority Report. The Majority report recommended a major restructuring of the existing organisation, while the Minority report argued that CHE had become irrelevant to most gay people's needs and advocated that it should evolve into two interlinked organisations, one exclusively devoted to campaigning and the other to the social and caring needs of the community. CHE's Annual Conference in August 1980 adopted the principles of the Minority Report, involving a split between CHE's social and campaigning activities, together with some of the proposals of the Majority Report. A working party was set up to examine how to implement the recommendations and after its findings were debated at the CHE Conference in 1981, the final decisions were taken at the National Council meeting in June 1982. The reorganisation of CHE included the creation of a new national Gay Community Organisation (GCO), which formally came into being on 1 September 1982. [266]

The GCO started off with high ambitions, including the creation of a chain of commercial enterprises, which would be owned and operated by gay people for the benefit of the gay community as a whole, with profits being reinvested to give GCO a secure financial basis. Enterprises envisaged included bars, discos, cinemas, saunas, coffee shops and gay centres. These were to provide a varied programme of social activities, ranging from athletic and sporting events to literary and music clubs or cookery classes. The local gay community was to be a caring organisation, helping members who lived alone or were sick, visiting those who had been sent to prison and supporting any who lost their job because of discrimination. It was also to encourage the provision of gay housing and temporary accommodation. Local CHE groups were advised on how to reconstitute themselves as gay community organisations, together with streamlined CHE groups consisting of campaigners only. The new GCOs were to be autonomous organisations, although affiliated to national CHE and the national GCO. It was envisaged that the GCOs would become registered co-operative societies, with the members as shareholders, allowing them to hold buildings and other assets.

The initial high hopes foundered owing to a lack of financial and technical expertise and by mid-1983, only eight local GCOs had been set up (in Bath, Bexley, Hastings, Hampstead, Southampton, Coventry, Luton and Swindon). More local groups were set up but the national organisation got bogged down in discussions over structure and finance, and was forced drastically to scale back its plans. CHE itself continued in existence as an organisation for activists but gradually lost influence during the 1980s.

Bath CHE implemented the recommended changes at an EGM on 16 September 1982 when it reconstituted itself as Bath Gay Community Organisation (or Bath GCO) and took the name Gay West, retaining Bath CHE as a campaigning committee.[267] The names Bath Gay Community and Gaylink were considered by the Committee but rejected in favour of Gay West.[268] CHE Bristol had already lost most of its members who preferred social activities when Avonscene was set up at the beginning of 1982 and the group saw no prospects for setting up a GCO in Bristol. The remaining activists were more interested in campaigning and decided to register CHE Bristol as a local campaigning group. Meanwhile, however, Gay West began to recruit members in Bristol as well as Bath and, with falling numbers undermining its viability, the CHE Bristol committee decided in December 1982 to merge with Gay West.[269] On 31 January 1983, CHE Bristol was formally dissolved and its members and assets transferred to Gay West, while Bath CHE became Avon CHE in recognition of its wider remit. One lasting result of this process of merger was that, while Gay West always had many members in Bristol, it was generally identified with the smaller city of Bath.

The history of Gay West can be divided into three phases. The first from its foundation in 1982 until the early 1990s was a period of growth and optimism, with buoyant membership, a very active social programme and an outward-looking concept of the group's potential role in local civil society. From the early 1990s to the mid-2000s, the group turned in on itself, as it faced competition from an increasing array of other local LGBT organisations, falling membership and uncertainty over its role. From the mid-2000s, the group appears to have stabilised, concentrating on its weekly Saturday morning coffee shop in Bath, which attracts a regular clientele and continues to provide an open door for new members, and also offering a small number of additional social activities.

In most respects, the 1980s were Gay West's golden age. Membership increased from 39 when Bath CHE held its AGM in June 1982 to 250 by the end of 1989. Despite the increasingly sombre climate in which it operated, with the spread of HIV/AIDS and AIDS hysteria, the group's outlook was generally optimistic. As the newsletter put it in February 1985 under the heading, "Off to a Good Start", "If the first two weeks of January are anything to go by then it looks as if 1985 is going to be a good one for Gay West." The following chapters will concentrate on analysing the group's structure and activities during this period, although also covering some earlier and later developments. These chapters will look at individual aspects of Gay West, including its internal organisation, its search for identity, its relationship with other LGBT people and groups, as well as with politics, civil society and the public sphere, before going on to discuss how Gay West reacted to changing circumstances in the 1990s and 2000s.

The idea of a group of gay men and women organising themselves openly was still something of a novelty in 1982 but the structures and methods the group adopted were traditional and well-tested. Bristol and Bath, like the rest of Britain, have a rich history of local voluntary associations reaching back to the 18th century, with well-understood methods and structures for self-organisation.[270] Some of the social movement organisations which sprang up from the 1950s onwards adopted these formal structures, including CHE. Gay West, like its predecessor groups, followed in this tradition and adopted the full panoply of a classic voluntary society, with a constitution, Annual General Meeting, elected committee, minuted committee meetings, formal membership through subscriptions, written accounts, a monthly newsletter and a library. This contrasted with the much looser organisational structure of GLF and the lack of formal organisation adopted by other social groups in the area, such as Chris's Coffee Club (3Cs) and Men Meeting Men (3Ms), which depended on the initiative of a small number of individuals who took on leadership roles.

Gay West was formally constituted at an Extraordinary General Meeting (EGM) held at Bath Centre for Voluntary Service in Abbey Green on 16 September 1982. A notice was circulated to members of Bath CHE informing them that the Committee had tabled motions to dissolve Bath Campaign for Homosexual Equality and replace it with a Gay Community Organisation, to transfer all the assets of Bath CHE to this Gay Community Organisation and to adopt a provisional constitution which was included in the notice.[271]

After considerable discussion and voting on amendments at the EGM, the proposed Constitution was adopted by the group, with a couple of procedural changes.[272] This Constitution replaced the Constitution of Bath CHE adopted on 24 September 1981, which in turn replaced an earlier BGAG Constitution dating from 1974. CHE Bristol also had its own constitution. A comparison of these constitutions reveals the changing aims and concerns of the group, as well as an increasing formality in organisation.

Constitution

Both CHE Bristol and the Bath Gay Awareness Group had formal written constitutions. I have not been able to trace the original Bristol CHE Constitution but in the CHE archives at the LSE, there is a heavily amended typescript document dated 7 March 1972 and headed Campaign for Homosexual Equality – Bristol Constitution. It is not clear whether this is an actual constitution or a draft for discussion but in its preamble it refers to the Revised Constitution of Bristol CHE Group-1 (November 1971) and a Vote of Co-operation of Bristol CHE Group-2 (February 1972). At all events, during the period of conflict over direction of the group, some constitutional changes were made at a general meeting in September 1973, which, according to the convenor, shifted power from him to the committee, and a more formal draft constitution was circulated to members and accepted with a few procedural amendments at another general meeting in December 1973. This defined CHE Bristol's status as "a constituent group of the organisation, The Campaign for Homosexual Equality (CHE) and its National Council" and laid down that its aims would be the same as the National Campaign with special reference to the Bristol Area, namely:

> a. promote the principle that the homosexual has an equal right to self-fulfilment and can make an equally positive contribution in our common quest for the betterment of society and the happiness of all; b. fight for absolute equality at law between homosexuals and heterosexuals and to campaign against all forms of legal or social discrimination against homosexuals; c. campaign for improved sex education in schools in order to stop the process by which existing attitudes towards homosexuality are maintained; d. provide a counselling service for the alleviation of the problems encountered by homosexuals; e. support

the inauguration of local groups and social centres where homosexuals and others can meet in congenial surroundings.

Membership was open to all who supported the aims of the National CHE, who paid the required subscription and who were admitted to membership by the Committee (preferably joining nationally as well). The remaining clauses covered general meetings, the committee, officers, elections, finance and amendments to the constitution.[273]

A number of amendments were made by the new wave of activists who took over the group in the mid-1970s and the Constitution was re-drafted in 1980–81.[274] At the first Planning Meeting in August 1977 it was reported that no copy of the group's Constitution could be found but this seems to have been rectified because in January 1978 an amendment was passed to ensure that only fully-paid up National members could be members of the group. In March 1980, the AGM agreed to draw up amendments to bring the Constitution into line with current practice and in September 1980 a member was asked to prepare a first draft of a new Constitution, which was presented at the Planning Meeting in November 1980. This was circulated to members and approved at the AGM in March 1981. The aims of the group were now:

> a) to foster the development of greater gay awareness amongst homosexual people; b) to undertake public education about homosexuality; c) to work to protect existing gay rights; d) to campaign to extend gay rights; e) to provide a congenial social atmosphere for gay people; f) to undertake the befriending of isolated and lonely gay people; and g) to provide access to counselling and information for gay people with problems that may or may not relate to their homosexuality.

Membership was open to all who supported the aims of the group and paid the annual subscription. There was also a procedure set out in case the group was dissolved.[275]

The earliest extant constitution of the Bath group is entitled "The Constitution of Bath Gay Awareness Group as adopted by the E.G.M.'s on 17th and 24th October [or November] 1974".[276] The aims of the group were both very general and quite specific: "a) to provide an enlightened environment where gay people can meet together. b) to promote an awareness of all forms of human sexuality within both the group and society. c) to support all other groups which promote the aims of sexual liberation. d) to work in close association with other local CHE groups to establish CHE groups down the South West peninsular [sic]." The Constitution stated that "The group will be a full member of the Campaign for Homosexual Equality". The provision that membership would be open to all who supported the aims of Bath Gay Awareness Group but that "a group member does not have to be a national CHE member" reflected the hybrid origins of the group, taking in both liberationist and reformist views. The Constitution also set out some basic rules for subscriptions, meetings, group officers, working parties and Annual and Extraordinary General Meetings.

The Constitution adopted at the EGM on 24 September 1981 defined the group's name as "Bath Campaign for Homosexual Equality (CHE)" and its status as "a constituent group of National CHE and its National Council, and a member of the CHE South Wales and South West of England Region". Membership was to be "open to all who agree with the aims of CHE, and pay an annual subscription". In addition, a separate subscription scheme would operate for those who could not totally agree with the aims of CHE. This would allow them to receive the newsletter but they would not be members of Bath CHE and would not receive any benefits which CHE members received. Only full CHE members would be able to vote on items which directly affected Bath CHE. The aims of the group were virtually the same as those of CHE Bristol and based on National CHE.[277]

The Constitution adopted on the creation of Gay West on 16 September 1982 was headed "Bath Gay Community Organisation" but stated that the group's name would be "Gay West". The group was to work towards the establishment of a national Gay Community Organisation and was to be affiliated to the national Campaign for Homosexual Equality. Membership would be open to those people who agreed with the aims of the group and who paid the annual subscription. The aims were defined as:

> (a) To provide Social, Educational and Material Facilities for gay men and women. (b) To provide help and support for gay people with problems. (c) To work with other local gay groups towards an integrated gay community as an alternative to the commercial scene. (d) To take up local issues which affect gay people, and to work towards obtaining equal treatment of gay people by the local community. (e) To promote, at a local level, the principle of absolute equality before the law for homosexuals and heterosexuals.

The Constitution set out detailed rules for the composition and election of the Management Committee, which was to consist of a

Chairperson, a Membership Secretary, a Treasurer, a Campaign Secretary and a Social Secretary. Other clauses set out rules for committee meetings, the management of the group's finances and other procedural matters. Three clauses set up a Campaign Committee, which was to be called Bath CHE (changed to Avon CHE when CHE Bristol was dissolved and its assets passed to Gay West in January 1983) and would have the automatic right to request up to twenty percent of the group's annual funds and other safeguards.[278]

The Constitution was amended at the September AGMs in 1984, 1986, 1988, 1992 and 1993. The title was changed to "Gay West Constitution" but most of the amendments comprised procedural alterations or related to the size of the committee. The aims remained unchanged. The 1988 amendments revised the provisions for the Campaign Committee in response to the complaints over Gay West's perceived lack of action over Section 28. The Campaign Committee was to comprise a maximum of 10 members and would be nominated at the AGM, with provision to co-opt members to fill any vacant places. A proposal by the committee to limit membership to those aged 18 and above was defeated at the AGM in September 1992.

Between 1997 and 1999, however, the Constitution was radically re-written. In September 1997, a Definition was added which stated that "The Group shall be a social and support group for gay and bisexual men and women." The aims were amended so that aim (a) now became "To provide social activities, information and support services for gay and bisexual men and women", the provisions about helping and supporting gay people with problems and providing an alternative to the commercial scene were dropped and the last two aims rephrased as follows: "c. To promote the principle of absolute equality before the law for homosexuals and heterosexuals d. To take up local issues that affect gay people." Other changes introduced a minimum age of sixteen for membership, gave the committee the right to refuse membership to any individual and to terminate the membership of any members who brought the group into disrepute or acted in a disruptive or counter-productive way. Short job descriptions were included for the Chair, Secretary, Treasurer, Membership Secretary and Social Secretary and the detailed arrangements for the Campaign Committee were replaced by a provision allowing the setting up of sub committees to handle special projects "for example campaigning and events." A clause on financial gain was introduced which said "No member of the Group shall make any financial gain from their involvement, except through specific trade advertising", although claims for reasonable expenses were permitted.

Further amendments were made at the September 1999 AGM

77

when the definition of the group was changed to "The Group shall be a social and support group for gay men, lesbians, bisexuals and all other persons of a gender minority. Heterosexual persons who wish to support the Group, its aims and equal opportunities policy, are welcome to join as associate members." This distinction was carried over into the clause on membership, which for the first time restricted membership to "gay men, lesbians, bisexuals and all other persons of a gender minority". In theory, this was a major step away from the original stipulation that membership was open to all who agreed with the aims of the group but it seems to have been motivated by a desire to modernise the wording rather than any specific issue and had no practical effect. An equal opportunities clause was introduced at the same time and a provision introduced for the dismissal of a committee member should a majority of the committee deem their behaviour to be disruptive or inappropriate, or they were not fulfilling the responsibilities as detailed in their job description. A few minor changes were made in September 2006.

Committee/Officers

The Management Committee of Gay West is elected at the AGM in September each year. The outgoing chair usually gives a report and has sometimes published an Annual Report, although not consistently. The Management Committee has always had a Chair, Treasurer, Membership Secretary and Newsletter Secretary/Editor. At times there have also been other posts such as General Secretary, Social Secretary/Events Coordinator, Campaign Secretary/Coordinator and Coffee Shop Host, as well as a varying number of committee members without formal responsibilities. Individuals have sometimes been co-opted onto the Committee. The Committee normally meets once a month and produces minutes which can be made available to members on request. In the 28 years between 1982 and 2010, just over one hundred people have served as committee members.[279]

As with any group of people working closely together, there have been occasional clashes on the committee, particularly where strong-willed individuals have come into conflict with the rest of the committee, leading to resignations and some bitter recriminations. The most important such event was the resignation of the Chair, John Bescoby, in December 1988, after the Committee criticised him for asking a fellow committee member to resign without prior reference to the rest of the Committee.

Membership

Membership is open to all who agree with the aims of the group and who pay the annual subscription. For a long time there was no stipulation over the sex, gender or sexual orientation of members but in 1999, a constitutional amendment restricted membership to gay men, lesbians, bisexuals and all other persons of a gender minority, with heterosexuals able to join as associate members. In practice, this change had no effect. The group's membership has always consisted of both men and women but always with a predominance of the former.

Statistics for membership are patchy and have been drawn from committee minutes and newsletters.[280] Only a few figures have been found for the Bath and Bristol groups which preceded Gay West but it is unlikely that membership at any one time of either group ever exceeded 100 and attendance at meetings was usually much less. CHE Bristol had 73 members in 1972.[281] A survey carried out by CHE Bristol in late 1973 revealed that 70% of the group's members were paid-up members of the National organisation, their average age was 41 and 15% were women.[282] In 1980 the group had 68 members, of which about twenty were said the following year to be regular attenders.[283] This rose to 71 at the time of the AGM in March 1981 but then fell to 51 in November 1981 and 42 in February 1982. According to a retrospective note written at the time of dissolution, CHE Bristol's maximum membership was between 80 and 90.[284] No figures are available for the early days of Bath Gay Awareness Group. The group's membership was 26 in May 1980, 34 in April 1981 (26 full CHE members plus 8 BGG only) and 39 at the time of Bath CHE's last AGM in June 1982.[285]

The group's membership continued rising after Gay West's formation in September 1982, standing at 57 in November and 62 in December. There was an increase in membership following the merger with CHE Bristol but many of these transferred members failed to renew. Nevertheless, by the time of Gay West's first AGM in September 1983, membership had risen to 106.[286] When Avonscene folded at the beginning of 1984, some of its members joined Gay West, boosting numbers.[287] By September 1984, membership had risen to 150 and remained about this figure until September 1985. It then began to grow steadily, reaching 204 in May 1986 and 244 in November 1987. It then hovered between 240 and 250 until December 1989, after which it again began to grow, reaching 305 in January 1991, 355 in June 1991 and a peak of 404 in January 1992. The figures remained around 380 for the first third of 1992 but then began a period of decline, with the number dropping to 317 in January 1993 and 271 in May 1993. From then until January 1996 it fluctuated between a low of 241 and 297. By February 1996 it had grown to 310 again and fluctuated between 295 and 348 until September 1998 when it was 299. From then on, although the figures are not complete, there seems to have been a steady downward

BCVS building in Abbey Green, Bath, where Gay West held its Saturday morning Coffee Shop, 1983–1993. Photo: Robert Howes.

trend reaching 214 in September 1999, 160 in September 2000, 149 in May 2001, 119 in November 2001 and 95 in April 2002 before recovering slightly to 102 in May 2003. During most of 2004, membership was fairly stable in the 90s and from 2005 onwards it remained in the 80s, standing at 83 in November 2010.

The majority of members have always been men and the proportion of women members has fluctuated greatly. The number of women members was initially small. The earliest available figures for September 1985 show 18 out of a total membership of 155 (11.6%). During 1986 and 1987, the number hovered around 20, representing about 10%. One of the effects of Section 28 was for the first time to criminalise female as well as male homosexuals, leading to an upsurge in lesbian activism and an influx of women members into Gay West. The numbers grew steadily from 24 in December 1987 to 40 in December 1988, 62 in December 1989, 83 in December 1990 and 146 in December 1991. The number of women peaked in January 1992, with 153 out of 404, representing 37.8% of the total membership. The number fell during the course of this year but continued to hold around 80–100 from January 1993 to mid-1998, after which there was a steep decline, with women's membership down to 42 in September 1999, 23 in September 2000 and single figures by April 2001.

With the growing number of women members, the committee decided in February 1991 to create the post of Assistant Membership Secretary to deal with women's membership. The two posts were re-designated Men's Membership and Women's Membership in September 1992 and this was incorporated into the Constitution at the AGM in September 1993. This arrangement lasted until September 1999.

Gay West and its predecessors did not gather or publish data on the socio-economic background of its members, so the following is largely subjective and based on observation or report. What is immediately striking is the wide range of backgrounds and occcupations of the group's members. Many of the leading activists in the 1970s were students, mostly post-graduates, in their twenties, sometimes younger. Two of the most energetic chairpersons in the 1980s came from an older generation born before the Second World War. John Bescoby had a business and academic background.[288] He had previously been chair of Tyneside CHE and moved to Bath on retirement. Being newly-retired and full of energy, he threw himself into organising Gay West. John Pritchett worked as an office manager in the private sector, while a few members had their own small businesses. Other occupations represented in the group's membership included lawyer, academic, teacher, student, architectural technician, social worker, librarian, civil servant, police officer, office worker, manager, salesman, chef, car dealer, bus driver, gardener, carpenter, male nurse, factory worker, shop assistant, electrical technician, IT worker and antique dealer, as well as the unemployed and the retired – in short a cross-section of middle- and working-class occupations.[289] One feature that characterised many of the leading activists was that they had moved to the area from elsewhere, either to study or to work. Others, however, were born locally and spent most of their lives in the area, while at least two committee members came from local farming families. In direct contrast to the general pattern of LGBT migration, one long-serving activist moved from London to Bath when he took early retirement, specifically because of Gay West's existence.[290]

Gay West has always had a reputation as a Bath-oriented group but a survey of the men's membership in December 1994 found that 15½% came from Bath itself, 26% from the Bath postal district and 53% from the Bristol area.[291] In September 1998, of a male membership of 225, 105 (46%) were living in the Bristol area and 64 (28%) in the Bath area.[292] The situation was largely unchanged in September 2010: of 88 members, 19 (21.6%) came from Bath and 42 (47.7%) from Bristol; if the 8 members living in South Gloucestershire (now virtually a suburban extension of Bristol) are added to the city's figure, then 56.8% of the membership live in the Bristol area.[293] In June 1996, a survey of half the male membership (100 out of around 200) gave the following breakdown by age: under 21: 2%; 21–25: 12%; 26–30: 7%; [21–30: 19%]; 31–40: 31%; 41–49: 24%; 50+: 24%.[294]

A recurrent cause of concern for the committee was that many members rarely attended the group's events. In early 1985 a questionnaire was sent out to try to establish why this was so. Reasons given were lack of transport, clashes with other interests or work and an impression that the group consisted of cliques who were not friendly to new members.[295]

Recruitment

Potential members found out about Gay West by means of occasional advertisements in the local press (newspapers, Venue magazine), listings in LGBT publications, referral from befriending and counselling services such as London and Bristol Lesbian and Gay Switchboards and word of mouth. Advertisements were brief and ran along the lines of "Homosexual? Bath Gay Group Meets Weekly"; "Gay? C.H.E. The Group for Homosexual Men & Women in the Area, our Friendly Events Include : Meetings : Outings : Socials : Discos"; "Homosexual Men and Women For Friendship and Support Join Gay West" and "Homosexual Women and Men Meet Weekly in Bath", together with contact details.[296]

Traditionally the main means of approaching the group were by writing to the postal box (P.O. Box 586, Bath BA1 2YQ) or phoning a contact number. These contact numbers were the home phone numbers of certain members of the committee, who provided advice and counselling to callers thinking of coming out, gave emergency help to people who had been arrested and also had to endure occasional abusive phone calls. Where possible, both a male and female contact and numbers in Bath and Bristol were given. Since 2000, the group's website (www.gaywest.org.uk) has become an increasingly important way of advertising the group's existence and means of approach for new members.

Finances

The group offers membership in exchange for a subscription. This has generally been expected to cover the cost of producing and mailing the monthly newsletter, with its diary of forthcoming events. Other sources of income have included profits from discos, jumble sales, auctions, raffles and special events, plus collections at social events and donations. In 1990, the group applied to Avon County Council for a grant but was unable to proceed with the application because it could not get its accounts audited in time. Thus, until 2005 the group received no external funding, from public or charitable sources. In that year, it obtained a grant of £900 from the Quartet Foundation to help towards the cost of running the Rainbow Cafe and in 2007 it received £1,100 from the Allen Lane Foundation. In 2002, Gay West considered registering as a charity but decided against on the grounds that it would be of no benefit to it and would add complications. With occasional alarms and calls for restraint from Treasurers, the group has always managed to maintain a positive financial balance. Annual turnover has grown over the years, partly because of inflation, but has never exceeded £5,000.

The income raised has been spent on producing and mailing the newsletter, room hire, publicity, office and coffee shop equipment, subscriptions to other organisations and expenses. During the 1980s and 1990s, when membership was buoyant and discos profitable, the group accumulated significant funds and was able to make donations to other organisations and causes. In July 1997 it had a bank balance of £4,800 and made donations of £1,000 to Bristol Lesbian and Gay Switchboard and £500 to the Stonewall Equality 2000 initiative. Over the years it made many donations, usually of much smaller amounts, to a number of LGBT organisations such as the London and Bristol Switchboards, Legislation for Lesbian and Gay Rights, Gay Sweatshop, the Terrence Higgins and Aled Richards Trusts, and various LGBT disabled groups. It also made a point of making donations to national organisations like the NCCL and

John Bescoby, Chair, 1983–84 and 1986–88, in July 2007. Photo: Robert Howes.

local charities such as the Bath Centre for Voluntary Service (1984), Bath Samaritans, St. Marks Community Centre (1985), Dorothy House hospice (which had agreed to take AIDS patients), as well as towards a minibus for a special needs school in Bath (1986). In this way, it achieved quite a high profile amongst the local LGBT and mainstream communities.

Newsletter and Diary of Events

The Gay West committee has always attributed great importance to the newsletter, which they have seen as the main justification for the membership subscription and a means of keeping in touch with members, even those who do not come to events. Whether or not members read it from cover to cover, its regular appearance through the post is a reminder of the group's continued existence.

Both the Bath and Bristol groups produced newsletters for a good part of their existence. These were sometimes rather irregular and a few issues have disappeared. The early newsletters were produced by typing and stencils or photocopying in foolscap or A4 format, and present a fairly amateurish appearance. They generally consisted of a list of forthcoming events, news items about the group, National CHE, conferences and local events, and occasional articles on issues relating to sexuality. CHE Bristol began producing a newsletter entitled *Chewssheet* in the autumn of 1972. The first issue (which I have not been able to locate) was called *Chews* and had a parish magazine format but this was so complicated to duplicate that subsequent issues were produced in straightforward foolscap.[297] The first page was printed on yellow paper with a crude masthead, with the other pages in a variety of colours held together by a single staple in the top left hand corner. As well as the usual list of events and news items, the early issues contained some longer articles on various aspects of homosexuality. The name *Chewssheet* was dropped after the April-June 1974 issue and simple duplicated sheets with the title Newsletter or Newsletter and Diary of Events were issued monthly during the mid- 1970s. In September 1977, the group launched a more substantial magazine entitled *Bridge*, containing articles on CHE, the gay movement in Bristol and elsewhere, topics relating to sexuality and lighter items such as fiction and crosswords. Five issues were published between September 1977 and September 1978.[298] A new series numbering for the newsletter was started in 1979.[299] This was called simply Bristol CHE Group and appeared fairly regularly at approximately monthly intervals until late 1982.[300] Initially it was printed as four A5 pages on a single folded A4 sheet, with a letraset masthead comprising the name of the group and a sailing-ship logo. In April 1981, it adopted an A4 format in order to allow more pages for the debate which was then going on in the group.

The Bath group's publication was called Bath Gay Awareness Group newsletter and appeared roughly monthly throughout the 1970s, with a possible gap in 1975. It had a simple typescript appearance and was duplicated or photocopied in A4 or folded A5 format. As the group began to flourish in 1981, the newsletter became larger and was given a separate cover with a variety of different patterns but appeared less frequently. After criticisms about the cost of the newsletter, the committee decided in June 1982 to try a new format based on an A4 sheet folded to A5 containing events for the coming month, committee contacts, a short convenor's comment slot and forthcoming events.[301] In addition to the monthly diary of events, there would be a more substantial supplement, issued on a quarterly basis (which appeared later in the year as *Gay Link*). The A5 format had already been used for the May 1982 Diary of Events and became the standard for the newsletter from July 1982 onwards, giving a much neater and more professional appearance. With the change in format, the newsletter began regularly to publish the names of the committee and their telephone numbers.

From July 1982 onwards, the newsletter has appeared regularly each month, except for a double Christmas issue for December/January. Over the years the title has changed: Gay West Diary of Events, 1982–May 1988; Gay West the Diary, June 1988–June 1995; GW Frendz Diary, July 1995; GW Frendz the Diary, August 1995; Gay West Diary, September 1995–December 1996/January 1997; The Gay West Magazine, February 1997–December 1997/January 1998; Gay West Magazine & Diary, February 1998–December 1998/January 1999; The Gay West News, Magazine and Diary, February 1999–March 2000; Gay West Magazine, April 2000– . For most of that time it has retained the A5 format, with a single-colour cover and white inner pages. The number of pages has varied over the years, as has the layout, which improved with the advent of computer technology in the 1980s. Between February 1998 and October 2003, the newsletter adopted an A4 format, printed on glossy paper with a two-colour masthead and photographs. This format was eventually dropped because of the increased expense and the magazine reverted to the A5 format, nowadays usually consisting of 8 folded pages.

The Gay West newsletter has always carried the Diary of Events or programme for the forthcoming month or so, the names of the Gay West committee and their telephone numbers, and listings of local and national LGBT community organisations. In addition, at different times it has carried messages from the Chairperson, editorials from the newsletter editor, profiles of committee members, reports on Gay West activities, news items of local, national and international interest, newspaper clippings, notices from other LGBT organisations, humorous pieces, correspondence from members and advertisements for commercial venues and services.

Though editors have frequently complained of a lack of response, the letters from members have from time to time provoked controversy or reflected divisions within the group. Editors have occasionally resorted to some of the journalist's tricks of the trade. In 1996, correspondents called Francis and J wrote a number of provocative letters, which caused a flurry of correspondence. Later, the editors quietly let readers know that Francis and J were a deliberate creation to stimulate debate in the newsletter.

During the 1980s and 1990s, the newsletter carried announcements from LGBT organisations and advertisements for gay and gay-friendly businesses, notably hotels. From August 1992 onwards it carried a few personal adverts. For three months in 1997, the newsletter even carried an advertisement on its back page for the private health insurance scheme BUPA.

In February 1998 new editors took over and changed the format of the magazine to A4 printed on glossy paper and with a single colour masthead. By the summer the treasurer became alarmed at the extra cost. When the editors heard of this they reacted by producing a "no-frills" version with fewer pages printed on ordinary paper for the September 1998 issue. The differing views of the treasurer and editors were aired in the next issue and the more spartan version continued until March 1999, when a new editor reinstated the glossy format.

During 2000 and 2001, the magazine began to include some more explicit cartoons, short stories and photographs of men. A former chairperson wrote twice to complain about the sexual content, which he thought gave a poor impression of the group to outsiders, and eventually resigned from the group over the issue.[302] The chairperson at the time reluctantly accepted the resignation rather than risk losing the editor.[303]

Beginning in August 1982, the group produced a quarterly magazine known as *Gaylink*, similar in its content and A5 format to CHE Bristol's earlier *Bridge*. This was intended as a supplement to the monthly Diary of Events and was to contain "a balance of serious and light-hearted articles including a regular series of articles by members of particular professions, a review of the events of the preceding quarter [...], reviews of films and plays, cartoons, and in future editions: a crossword and poetry".[304] *Gaylink* ran to four issues.[305] From then on the Diary of Events was expanded to include some of this content.

Library

The committee decided to set up a library of books and videos in June 1982. A library of books which members could borrow for a small sum was gradually built up and housed in a cupboard at the venues for the weekly Bath coffee shops. From 2000, the library also comprised (non-sexual) videos and later DVDs but shortage of space meant that many of the books and later some of the videos had to be disposed of. The group also subscribed to magazines such as *Gay Times* and made this and some of the free newspapers and magazines such as *Capital Gay*, *The Pink Paper*, *Boyz*, *Fyne Times* and *one80* available to members at the Coffee Shop.

Social Activities

Social events have been one of the main attractions of the group and the reason why many joined. During the 1970s, both the Bristol and Bath groups settled down to a pattern of weekly meetings, which had a large social element. As Gay West became more popular in the mid-1980s and membership increased, the number of social activities also grew, so that by August 1985, for instance, there was at least one event on 27 out of 31 days. These included regular weekly activities such as the Saturday-morning Coffee Shop in the Bath Centre for Voluntary Service building and the Monday-evening aerobics class in St. Marks Community Centre, both in Bath. Other events included theatre visits, parties, walks, pub visits, video evenings, opera and musical evenings, Sunday teas, swimming sessions, consciousness-raising groups, picnics and discos. Some of these events were held in members' homes while others were outings to public venues. For several years during the 1980s an annual highlight was a party held in a member's flat in the Royal Crescent on the opening night of the Bath Festival, culminating in a grandstand view of the firework display. This member also regularly organised group visits to the Theatre Royal where a phalanx of members sat in seats booked under the name "Gay West". The group also organised seasonal events such as an annual Christmas dinner and short holidays in Torquay (February 1984, 1985), Amsterdam (1985), Portugal (1985), Paris (ca. 1995) and other resorts.

Speaker Evenings/Celebrities

A staple of CHE groups in the 1970s was the speaker meeting, when an outside speaker, from within or without the gay movement, was invited to come and address the group. In the early days when information on LGBT topics was still difficult to come by in the mainstream media, this was a good method of disseminating new viewpoints, stimulating discussion and giving meetings more than just a social dimension. CHE Bristol achieved something of a coup in December 1979 when it got the Bishop of Gloucester to speak on his recently-published report on homosexuality (see Chapter 2). Eventually

*Gay West newsletter –
small format.*
Photo: Robert Howes.

*Gay West newsletter –
large format.*
Photo: Robert Howes.

this type of meeting fell out of favour as the pool of speakers was exhausted but occasionally Gay West continued to arrange talks by prominent LGBT speakers or local people working in areas relating to LGBT interests such as doctors or the police. The most high-profile speaker was Peter Tatchell, the chief organiser of the Outrage! group, who gave a talk to Gay West in December 1990.

In 1992, two members of the group proposed reviving the more traditional type of speaker evening and arranged a series of events at the Crown & Anchor pub in Weston, Bath. The first was held in January 1993, with a speaker from Bristol Outrage!. Further meetings were held in the following months, including an out-gay policeman from the Lesbian and Gay Police Association (LAGPA) and the Conservative MP for Kingswood, Rob Hayward (who later came out as gay), but the evenings ran into a number of practical problems, failed to attract many people and were abandoned after July 1993.

With the growth of celebrity culture, the group was able to make use of its connections to invite famous actors or prominent LGBT activists to attend its events. The actress Fenella Fielding, who was appearing at the Theatre Royal, visited the Coffee Shop on 9 March 1985. Michael Cashman, who played the gay character Colin in the TV soap *Eastenders* and was a leading member of Stonewall, was the star of a Desert Island Discs meeting on 4 March 1990 and also visited the Coffee Shop on 15 May 1993. Forty people came to Peter Tatchell's talk on 5 December 1990. Simon Callow, another leading actor and gay activist, visited the Rainbow Cafe on 4 April 2009.

Coffee Shop/Rainbow Cafe

The single most important activity of Gay West is undoubtedly the Coffee Shop, now called the Rainbow Cafe, which runs every Saturday morning in the centre of Bath. This regular event is now the group's main focus and it seems likely that without it the group would have folded long ago, like so many others. The Coffee Shop was initially suggested as an experiment in late 1981 because the committee wanted to get away from the Thursday evening meetings in members' homes and establish something regular where people could just drop in and to which new people could come.[306] A Bath CHE Saturday Meeting Centre for coffee, chat and snacks was scheduled at the Bath Centre for Voluntary Service (BCVS) building on 4 February 1982 but because of bad weather only a few people turned up and the idea was dropped for the time being.[307] It was revived at the end of the year and the first regular coffee meeting was held on 8 January 1983. The entry in the Diary of Events read: "Sat 8th GAY WEST COFFEE SHOP: good quality coffee and home-made cakes will be served between 10 am–12 noon in the upstairs room of the BCVS, 3 Abbey Green, Bath".[308] Thus, without fanfare, began a regular event which has now been running for over twenty-five years. The Coffee Shop continued to meet on the first floor of the historic BCVS building in the heart of the city for the next ten years. A large table had to be moved each week to make room for those attending and at times the number of people was so great that they spilled out onto the staircase. Originally, coffee was to be served at tables by waiters but this was soon dropped in favour of self-service. By January 1984 the group's Diary of events was noting that "'The 'Coffee Shop' is one year old this month and though perhaps not quite in the form originally intended, seems to have settled as a very successful regular Saturday morning event."[309]

In May 1991, the first Coffee Shop in each month was moved to St. Michael's Day Centre for a six-month trial because of improved disabled access, while on the remaining Saturdays it continued to meet in Abbey Green. During April and May 1992, it met most Saturdays in St. Michael's because of building work in the BCVS building but reverted to the previous split arrangement in June 1992. In February 1993 the BCVS asked the group to use a downstairs room in Abbey Green, which proved to be too small and inconvenient. Changes in personnel on both sides had also led to a weakening of the links with the BCVS and so the decision was taken to move the Coffee Shop completely to the St. Michael's Community Centre in August 1993, where it has continued to meet ever since. St. Michael's was originally owned by MOBAC and now by Age Concern. Unbeknown to those involved, this was the same building where the Bath Gay Awareness Group had held its first public meetings in the Liberal Association rooms on an upper floor in 1973.

In June 1995, the group's publicity material was given a make-over to give it a more modern image and the Coffee Shop was relaunched as the Rainbow Cafe, with improved facilities and tableware, a wider choice of refreshments and rainbow flags prominently displayed in the window. A proposal on cost grounds to move the Rainbow Cafe to St. Marks Community Centre in Widcombe, some way out of the city centre, was rejected by a ballot of members in early 1998. Four years later, falling membership, a lack of volunteers to serve coffee and increasing costs for room hire and public liability insurance led the committee to consider moving to the Bath Tap (a local gay pub) but it eventually decided to remain at St. Michael's. For a while during the early 2000s the Rainbow Cafe ran at a loss and the committee worried about the drain on group funds. Since the mid-2000s, however, numbers have stabilised and around 20–30 people now attend the cafe, consisting of both regulars and occasional visitors.

Some are members but others are not; forms for joining are available but visitors are not obliged or pressed to become members.

Volunteers serve the refreshments on a rota basis. In May 1986 the committee asked for volunteers to act as a host at Coffee Shop to welcome newcomers and introduce them to existing members. Concern to avoid a cliquish and unfriendly atmosphere led the committee in 1989 to introduce a host, who is responsible for ensuring that new people are welcomed and introduced into the group.

The Bath coffee shop is a public space and is now the main channel through which people first encounter Gay West. It has had its ups and downs and the committee minutes are peppered with worries about the fall in numbers attending and difficulties in getting volunteers to serve refreshments, yet it is widely recognised as the group's most successful activity. Several attempts have been made to copy it elsewhere. Coffee shops in Bristol and Weston-super-Mare have enjoyed some initial popularity but none has lasted in the long-term. These are detailed below. Similarly, attempts to provide coffee or tea shops to attract women have been successful to begin with but then fizzled out. These are discussed in the section dealing with the role of women (see Chapter 5). Other groups have also tried to copy the formula but again without lasting success. It seems that the Coffee Shop/Rainbow Cafe's presence in the centre of Bath and the city's function as a regional shopping and leisure centre have allowed it to continue attracting people, who come not only from Bath but from Bristol and the surrounding areas as well.

A Bristol coffee shop which met on the last Tuesday evening of the month in the Service 9 social centre started in February 1987 and continued until the end of 1989, when Service 9 closed down. For a trial six week experiment starting in December 1989, a member organised The Pink Rock Cafe as a weekday coffee shop meeting on Thursday evenings in his home to play rock music but this was not continued. Coffee evenings continued to be held on the last Tuesday of the month in members' homes in the Bristol area until May 1997, when they moved to the more public venue of the Arnolfini and Watershed arts centres. In May 1998, they reverted to being held in people's homes. When in May 2001 Berkeley, the former Campaign Co-ordinator who was by then working for the Terrence Higgins Trust West (THT West), suggested starting a coffee shop in Bristol, the committee was very concerned about the potential competition with the Bath Rainbow Cafe coffee shop and repeatedly warned him not to hold it on a Saturday morning.

In 2000, the THT West proposed to Gay West setting up a joint Rainbow Cafe in Weston-super-Mare as part of its HIV/AIDS prevention outreach work. This venture began on a trial basis in October 2000, meeting once a month at the Crossroads Centre, Graham Road, Weston-super-Mare, and was initially quite successful, with up to 20 people attending. Attendance began to fall off in April 2001 but the committee persevered for another eighteen months until October 2002, when they decided it was not viable. Some people continued to meet informally in the Foresters pub in Alexandra Parade, Weston until the summer of 2005.

Locations

In contrast to Bristol, where a Gay Centre was established and might have succeeded in a more accessible location, Gay West had no realistic prospect of acquiring its own premises. It was therefore obliged to use other premises, both private and public, for its events. It carried on the tradition established by the predecessor groups of holding many of its social functions in members' homes. These included Sunday teas, parties, video and record evenings and so on. It also organised social events in public areas, such as walks and picnics in the countryside or pub evenings in gay and straight pubs. For its regular weekly events, however, it used the premises of other voluntary organisations. The Saturday morning coffee shop was held in the Bath Centre for Voluntary Service building at 3 Abbey Green and later in the MOBAC/Age Concern building in St. Michael's Place, while the Monday evening aerobics classes, which ran during the second half of the 1980s, took place in St. Marks Community Centre in the suburb of Widcombe. These were premises used at other times by other organisations and so Gay West's events became routinised and part of the everyday round. This stands in marked contrast with the Bristol Gay Centre, and indeed the modern commercial scene, where LGBT events are held in dedicated spaces, often away from mainstream locations. In this way, the practical requirements of Gay West's social activities helped to integrate it with local civil society. This process was not always uncontentious, as will be seen later in the section on discos (Chapter 9), but occurring week in, week out over the years, was undoubtedly one of the group's major contributions to greater acceptance of LGBT people.

5

Questions of Identity

The total population of Bristol is around half a million and that of the area covering Bristol, Bath and the surrounding region about one million. If we exclude children and the very old, this leaves about 300,000 in the city or 600,000 in the region in the socially-active age range. Taking a conservative estimate of 2% of the population, this means that there must be at the very least 6,000 men and women with an exclusive or predominantly homosexual orientation in Bristol and 12,000 in the region. Using a more realistic estimate of 5% would give 15,000 and 30,000 respectively. In contrast, nationally, CHE's highest membership figure was about 5,000. Even at its peak, Gay West's membership was only 400 and during the 28 years between 1982 and 2010, just over one hundred people served as Gay West committee members. One Bristol activist estimates that there were around 30–40 core people who were active in organising things in the city over the years, which means they could all fit into a singe-decker bus. Clearly, only a small proportion of the total LGBT population joins voluntary groups and an even smaller number have taken an active role in organising them. The following comments therefore only apply to a small proportion of the LGBT population in the area.

   This chapter deals with questions of identity, which are a major issue for new social movements and have been the subject of much academic debate. These concerns can be summarised as the way people come to recognise themselves as homosexuals, the image which gay men or lesbians form of themselves and project to others, their relationship to other gay people and to non-gays as individuals and their attitude to broader society, both gay and mainstream in general. The concept of identity in the early days of the gay movement held a fairly straightforward binary distinction between gay and straight. Under the pressures of day-to-day activism and new intellectual concepts developed during the 1980s and 1990s by postmodernist writers and philosophers such as Michel Foucault, the conception of self adopted by different parts of the LGBT movement changed and became increasingly fluid and complex. Historians such as Jeffrey Weeks and David Halperin criticised the essentialist view that homosexuals have always existed as a distinct category and have argued for a social constructionist interpretation which sees the identity created by LGBT people as a work in progress.

These influences were reflected in academic discourse and in the developing terminology adopted by LGBT activists, as the gay movement changed to lesbian and gay, then lesbian, gay, bisexual and transgender (LGBT), or more radically, to queer. Amongst lesbians, there was a ferment of controversies and ideas in the 1980s, leading to the creation of new identities such as radical feminism, lesbian separatism and others, often in bitter conflict with each other over issues such as pornography and lesbian S/M, which were later dubbed the "sex wars". In the United States, postmodernism and feminism contributed towards the development of queer theory in academic circles, while the impact of AIDS led queer activists to reject the gay and lesbian label as too bound up with mainstream American identity politics.[310] Groups like ACT-UP and Queer Nation took a much more militant stance than the reformist groups.

Similar developments on a smaller scale also occurred in the UK during the 1980s, particularly in London, with conflicts among revolutionary, radical and libertarian lesbians over access to the London Lesbian and Gay Centre and the Lesbian Summer School, until lesbian separatism began to fall out of favour in the late 1980s.[311] Outrage! was set up by queer activists in London in May 1990 to undertake direct action non-violent politics.[312] These debates rippled out and found an echo in the provinces. In Bristol, a separate Lesbian Line was set up in 1985 and ran alongside the pre-existing Bristol Lesbian and Gay Switchboard until around 2000.[313] A womens group published *The Bristol Radical Lesbian Feminist Magazine*, which produced at least two issues in 1986.[314] Bristol Outrage! was founded by two activists who had worked with Peter Tatchell in London and held its first meeting at the Watershed in March 1992.[315]

Gay West was not involved in the academic debates but was not immune to some of the practical implications of the arguments among activists. At the same time, it has worked at establishing its own identity in response to the pressures and opportunities which have presented themselves in the course of its activities. This chapter looks at how the group has sought to help new members establish a gay or lesbian identity during their coming out process, how it has sustained its members' identity through its social activities and how it has moulded the group's own identity through its relations with the rest of the LGBT movement and with other local LGBT people.

Helping People to Come Out

One of the aims set out in Gay West's constitution was "To provide help and support for gay people with problems." In practice, this has mainly meant helping people to come out. Members of the committee, particularly the telephone contacts, devoted large amounts of time to helping people who contacted the group to talk through their problems and overcome their doubts about their sexual orientation. Callers included gay men and women, concerned parents, the wives of gay men and frightened young lads.[316] These people usually got in touch after seeing an advertisement in the local newspaper or being referred by the Bristol Switchboard. Sometimes committee members met them in neutral venues such as pubs to put them at their ease before introducing them to the group. Some never got as far as attending a group meeting, many came once or twice to find their feet and then moved on to the commercial scene, while others became active members of the group.

The importance of groups like Gay West and its predecessors in acting as a stepping stone can be summed up in this quotation from a member of Bath Gay Awareness Group in 1974:

> I need hardly state this as I'm sure that most, if not all, of you have gone through the same experience at some stage in your lives – 'coming out' is not an easy process. One needs to make contact with other gay people, preferably in an empathetic and enlightened environment (which was what the group gave to me) and one needs to absorb a sense of group identity – to let it sink into one's consciousness that one is no longer 'the only one in the world' and that, at long last, one belongs. Through my involvement in the group, I've found my gay identity and together with it, self-acceptance; and with self-acceptance has come a greater piece [sic] of mind and a kind of quiet contentment with life – hence the happier ans [sic] less hung-up person I am today.[317]

The motivation of activists, many of whom have spent many hours and in some cases much of their lives in unpaid work for the movement, often stemmed from this initial contact. Some activists first contacted the group as part of their coming-out process and having come to terms with their gayness, wanted to help others in a similar situation – to give something back to the group. This is particularly the case of young people and those who were previously married. Others have been involved in the LGBT movement elsewhere and joined Gay West when they moved to the area in order to meet other people. A number of people who joined for these reasons then went on to develop a political consciousness and become activists.

Developing Members' Identity

Until 1999, the group did not feel it necessary to police the boundary with the straight world. On one level, this was redundant, since anyone who joined a group with "gay" or "homosexual" in its title has already taken a major step in adopting an LGBT identity. The group's main concern has been to publicise its existence and help people who are already thinking of coming out. Since prejudice against homosexuality remained strong for many years, the group's membership was largely self-selecting. However, sexuality was not formally a qualification for membership. Both the two precursor groups and Gay West adopted the formula that membership was open to all who supported the aims of the group and who paid the required subscription. The aims essentially were to support LGBT rights. Only in 1999 was membership formally restricted to "gay men, lesbians, bisexuals and all other persons of a gender minority", with heterosexuals being offered associate membership. In practice, this has not been an issue: although a few straight friends and relatives of group members have attended meetings, the group's activities have generally not attracted heterosexuals and as a mainly social group, it has not proved a target for political entryism.

One issue rarely discussed in the early days was bisexuality, which posed some difficult questions for the straightforward binary divide between straight and gay. Nevertheless, at least two of the chairs and a number of other members have been previously married and had children. In September 1997, in line with the increasing emphasis generally on diversity, Gay West included "bisexuals" amongst the people it was aiming to serve as stated in its constitution. In 1999, Sid Roberts, a former chair and previously married, wrote about the difficulties of deciding on a sexual role and the common occurrence of same-sex behaviour among men who would not categorise themselves as gay.[318] A number of other articles published at this time also mentioned bisexuality.

In the 1970s, there was a great deal of debate in CHE groups about the nature of homosexuality. Guest speakers, drawn either from within the movement or from outside, were invited to address meetings, in the case of CHE Bristol in the Folk House, while articles and correspondence in newsletters described personal experiences and set out theoretical arguments. By the early 1980s, speaker meetings largely fell out of favour, although the group continued to hold discussions on topical themes and occasionally hosted big name speakers – for example, Peter Tatchell spoke to a meeting in December 1990. The group made an unsuccessful attempt to revive speaker meetings in 1993. The newsletter regularly contained news and information on LGBT issues and polemics erupted on the letters pages from time to time. The group also on a few occasions put on awareness-raising groups along the lines pioneered by GLF.[319]

Such conscious efforts to build identity within the group were rare, however. The group's energies were largely devoted to social activities and, paradoxically, this in itself was a powerful reinforcement of identity. In an environment where the media and public opinion routinely cast gays as abnormal and the only role models widely available were the camp stereotypes portrayed by media personalities like Larry Grayson and John Inman, to engage in ordinary social activities under the banner "Gay West" was a powerful lesson in the normality of LGBT people. While to some participants social activities were a form of escapism, to others they were a means of bolstering their self-confidence. In practice, this could be a complex process. As one student wrote:

> Although I had read about homosexuality I still had to overcome some of the myths and misconceptions that are perpetrated about the gay world. [...] I have learnt that gay people, apart from the fact of being gay, are like any other group of people. There exists within the gay community a great diversity of taste, political persuasion, characteristic [sic] and career choice shown by the people within that group. [...] I have learnt that 'coming out' is an ongoing process, not a sudden revelation. That gay is good. [...] I also realise that gayness can be an uneasy mantle to wear. Social groups like Gay West are only the tip of an iceberg that I have encountered but I have gained much comfort from that source. I realise that being gay doesn't stop the problems of everyday life; that being gay is not a problem in itself; that it is no help to be introverted about being gay. Gay West has helped me to begin to come to terms with these things and I would like to thank you all for being so friendly and <u>normal</u>![320]

Relations with the LGBT Movement

An important element in the activities of Gay West was its relations with other LGBT organisations. These had practical effects – the exchange of information, support for political campaigns, etc. – but they were also a means for the group to affirm and strengthen its gay identity. Links with other related organisations helped integrate Gay West into the broader LGBT movement.

The mechanisms of these links were affiliations and subscriptions, financial donations, attendance at meetings and conferences, exchange of newsletters, participation in campaigns, and practical assistance with events and projects. The highlight of these activities was a trip to London to take part in the annual Pride Marches in the capital. As well as the formal links, it is important not to underestimate the informal links: some Gay West members were also active in other organisations, particularly the Bristol Lesbian and Gay Switchboard.

Both Gay West's predecessor organisations had been affiliated to National CHE and CHE Bristol, in particular, had given especial importance to this connection. Gay West itself was born out of a restructuring of CHE at the national level. During the 1980s, these links weakened. The National Gay Community Organisation failed to establish itself on a solid basis and Gay West decided at the AGM in September 1984 not to re-affiliate to the National GCO, which in any case closed down shortly after.[321]

During the early years of Gay West, the CHE legacy remained quite strong, with regular news items and articles about CHE in the newsletter.[322] During 1986, the committee regularly discussed the group's affiliation to CHE, questioning the organisation's involvement in non-gay political causes, such as a donation to the Irish Prisoners Appeal, and its failure to communicate with Gay West. It suspended its affiliation between August 1986 and January 1987 and continued to maintain a watchful eye on CHE activities, being particularly hostile to attempts by paedophile activists to influence CHE policy. The group allowed its CHE membership to lapse in September 1989 but renewed it in March 1991. Membership lapsed again in March 1992 and the group does not appear to have renewed it after that. New national organisations were established by political activists in the late 1980s. After some debate, Gay West affiliated to the short-lived Organisation for Lesbian and Gay Action (OLGA) in 1987 and distributed information about Stonewall campaigns during the 1990s. Its only international link came in the form of an invitation from a Dutch group in Alkmaar to attend its Pride celebrations in 1991 but this was not followed up.[323]

Gay West maintained both formal and informal links with other local LGBT organisations. It held some of its events at the Bristol Gay Centre until this closed down in 1983 and made donations to the Bristol Lesbian and Gay Switchboard. Several of its members were actively involved as volunteers with Switchboard, which also referred some of its callers to the group. Gay West participated to a varying extent in the organisation of the successive gay festivals and pride events in Bristol and organised some events as part of the festival programmes. The group also sent representatives to the early meetings of the Aled Richards Trust and made regular donations to it. Gay West's most lasting and consistent involvement with other local LGBT organisations was to list them in its newsletter and to publish news items and announcements about them. As well as free publicity for the organisations concerned, this indicated to Gay West members that the group was part of a wider regional LGBT culture and network.

Besides the more political groups, there were also a number of other

Picnic in Dyrham Park, early 1990s.
Photo: Vince Baughan, Julian Vagg.

social groups, which were potential competitors to Gay West. Avonscene was started by breakaway members of CHE Bristol as an independent social group in January 1982.[324] Despite some occasional friction, Gay West publicised a number of Avonscene events.[325] When Avonscene folded at the beginning of 1984, many of its members joined Gay West.[326] Another group, Amicus, started around 1985 and a number of joint social meetings were held over the following years until around 1990.[327] Many members of Gay West have also been members of the national Gay Outdoor Club, which holds walks and other leisure activities in the area.

The most fraught relationships have been with two other social groups, 3Ms and 3Cs, which initially were seen as possible competitors for members. 3Ms (Men Meeting Men) was an American-style supper club set up by John Bescoby in 1990, a year after he resigned as chairman of Gay West. Events were held on Saturday evenings in members homes and everyone attending was expected to bring some food and drink. Chris's Coffee Club, often referred to as 3Cs, was set up by Chris Brown quite independently of Gay West in June 1990.[328] He was relatively new to the area and organised weekly coffee evenings in his home in Bristol as a way of widening his social circle. He began with a single advertisement in the local paper and received a dozen phone calls, as a result of which six people, complete strangers, turned up. They set about getting to know each other but after a few weeks only one of the original people was still coming. The group expanded by word of mouth, however, and was soon thriving, at its largest attracting 70 people a night. Chris had a hundred mugs in his kitchen. On discovering that Bristol Lesbian and Gay Switchboard was in debt, Chris Brown started giving money collected at the coffee evenings to Switchboard and eventually joined as a fundraiser, raising some £5,000 for the organisation. Meanwhile, other members expanded the group's activities to include theatre visits, Sunday lunches, outings and short holidays away. After 13 years, the numbers coming to the coffee evening dwindled to around 20 and Chris Brown withdrew, passing the group on to another Chris – Chris Watkins, who continued to develop the group's social programme. In contrast to Gay West, neither 3Ms nor 3Cs initially had any formal structure, membership or chairperson. They issued occasional circulars publicising forthcoming events but depended very much on the energy and interest of individuals who did the organising.

In the early years there was a certain amount of mistrust between Gay West and the two groups. Gay West objected to 3M's attempts to recruit members at its meetings and declined to include 3Ms events in the Diary of Events.[329] In October 1990, the Diary editor sharply reminded John Bescoby of the "unfortunate circumstances" surrounding his departure "evidently calculated to cause the maximum possible damage".[330] In early 1995, members of the Gay West committee and the organisers of 3Cs held a meeting to discuss problems which had arisen between the two groups and agreed to allow a certain amount of mutual promotion of activities through leaflets and the distribution of information. This occurred intermittently over the following years, despite occasional prickly relations. In reality, there was a considerable overlap of membership between the three groups and relations mellowed over the years. In April 1998 the newsletter printed an article by John Bescoby about 3Ms and during 2001–2003 it published a series of articles and reminiscences by him.[331] In the later 2000s Gay West held a number of joint events with 3Cs, including an occasional ten-pin bowling competition for a trophy. In 2010, 3Ms and 3Cs merged to form a new social organisation, Gays Meeting Gays South West (GMG), which had more of a formal structure.[332]

In the early days of both the Bristol and Bath groups, there was quite a close relationship with the local universities. In Bristol, the University of Bristol Students Union Gaysoc also functioned as CHE Bristol's Youth Group in the early 1970s and Trevor Locke was active in both areas. Several of the founding members of the Bath Gay Awareness Group were either students or staff at the University of Bath, although they wanted the BGAG to be a local rather than a student group. These links soon weakened. Students spent only part of the year in the area and were more involved in their own LGBT societies. There were nevertheless still occasional contacts and exchange of information, and Gay West used Bath University's facilities a few times to hold its discos.

London Pride Marches

In the 1980s, Gay West was the main representative of the organised LGBT movement in Bath and its surrounding area, while outside this immediate catchment area, it co-existed with other organisations in Bristol and with the national LGBT movement. The most important affirmation of Gay West as part of a wider movement was its participation in the London Pride Marches, held each year in June or July and, along with the Switchboards, perhaps the most tangible continuing legacy of the GLF. Members of the group regularly went on these marches in London during the 1980s and 1990s. In 1987 a group of Gay West members took the group's banner on the march and a picture of members relaxing in Hyde Park before the march appeared in the *Observer* in 1989.[333] In most years between 1986 and 1997, the group regularly hired coaches and sold tickets to anyone in the Bath and Bristol areas who wanted to go on the London Pride march. In 1993 and 1994, Gay West hired a total of three coaches. Although there were occasional disputes with other organisations over the arrangements, notably with Lesbian Line over the group's refusal to run a women-only coach in 1989, this was one of the ways in which Gay West raised its profile amongst non-members.[334]

The marches produced different effects on those who went on them. One member who had "always taken a rather sceptical view of demonstrations and marches" went on his first march in 1986 and concluded: "I am not sure what the March actually achieves but it generates a friendly atmosphere and feeling of solidarity simply through being a large gathering of gay people." To others, they were liminal occasions when the normal routines of the heterosexual world were overturned. A long-time CHE activist wrote of the same march: "It's always heartening to see masses of other people who are like you – your brothers and sisters stretching back as far as the eye can see. The banners tell you that there are people from just about everywhere and representing all kinds of interests. [...] this is a day which always gives a lift to those taking part."[335] In 1988, the first march after the passing of Section 28, a member noticed that:

> ...passers by, shopkeepers and theatre workers, gave cheers, waves and applause. And to the delight of us marchers, a troop of crimsoned bandsmen managed a corporate grin and some sheepish waves. [...] On the Tube back to Earls Court, the highest camp of the day – on one side of the platform, two lesbians; on the opposite one, roughly 100 gays. And the repartee flew, little arrows of wit and battering rams of camp inuendo. Like the whole day, it was brilliant and unforgettable![336]

Gay West's Reputation in the Local LGBT Community

The group's identity was also partly formed in reaction to the way it was perceived by other local LGBT people. The number of people who have either been members or attended Gay West events over the years must run into several thousands but this is only a small proportion of the local LGBT population. While many of these may not have acted on their homosexual impulses at all or restricted their activities to anonymous cruising and cottaging, many others are active on the commercial gay scene without becoming involved with the organised LGBT movement. Probably most of these would never consider joining a voluntary group but others may have been put off by the way Gay West was viewed externally.

Despite bearing all the hallmarks of a middle-class voluntary organisation, class does not seem to have loomed large in perceptions of the group (indeed, several of its most active members have had working-class origins or occupations). Rather, the main perception was of a group of older men and it is sometimes referred to as "Grey West".[337] In a culture which prizes youth and good looks above all else, this proved a major disincentive to many people. As one member frankly recognised "Locally, the primary criticism of GayWest has always been its reputatio:n as a group for older gays, (and among lesbians, older gay men)."[338] A student activist put it more brutally when he referred to the group's "reputation as a bunch of 'ageing Tupperware Queens'"[339] Gay West promptly organised a Tupperware party in order to live up to its reputation but this ironic response failed to alter this aspect of the group, which became increasingly pronounced over the years as the gay scene expanded and became more specialised.

Another contentious area was the question of respectability and acceptable behaviour. While many have celebrated camp as an essential part of gay culture, others have regarded it as an embarrassing hangover from the days of the clandestine subculture. An echo of this conflict can be found in an anecdote recounted by one interviewee, which illustrates the way the group was viewed by some on the scene. A flamboyant young man, well known on the Bath scene, came to a group meeting and was told to shut up by a member of the committee. Later at a party in the Theatre Royal, he launched into an attack on Gay West, telling its members to "p*** off" because "this ain't no f***ing tea party!" and was cheered by the audience.[340]

The impression of conformism might have been confirmed by an editorial on the Europride march in London in June 1992, in which the editor criticised "the public behaviour of many gay people which I find sometimes to be both 'outrageous' and sometimes beyond the bounds of decency for public acceptability."[341] This did not go unchallenged by other Gay West members, however. A former committee member wrote that he had seldom felt so angry about an editorial in any gay publication: "If the injustices levied against us are to be overcome then we must demonstrate and act, publicly, very loudly, and by any means necessary. Public acceptability can kiss my arse."[342]

Incidents such as the one in the Theatre Royal reveal some of the tensions between Gay West and those who preferred to socialise on the commercial scene. Nevertheless, most of the time, the two groups managed to co-exist amicably and members of Gay West regularly used the commercial scene. As we shall see in a later chapter, the group's discos provided an opportunity to reach out to those who preferred the commercial scene and were one of its most popular events.

Responses to Increasing Diversity

The debates about identity which divided the LGBT movement in the 1980s reflected the increasing diversity of LGBT people and inevitably had an impact on Gay West. The committee deliberately tried to keep party politics out of the group, which in the context of the time meant left-wing politics. Perhaps mindful of the demise of CHE Bristol, it argued that they did not belong in a group mainly devoted to social activities (see Chapter 6 for more discussion of politics). There was little discussion of race or ethnicity and no awareness of disability issues until a disabled group raised the question of accessibility. The debate amongst radicals and academics about "queer" found no echo in the group. Other issues, such as ageism, which was important given Gay West's image as a group for older men, and the parochial but nevertheless important issue of the balance between Bath and Bristol, were discussed occasionally. The issue which proved most contentious, however, particularly during the late 1980s and

On the way to the London Pride March, mid 1980s. Photo: Vince Baughan, Julian Vagg.

1990s, was the role of women. During this period, many gay organisations added the word "lesbian" to their names to recognise their commitment to the representation of women. A change in name to "Lesbian and Gay West" was discussed several times in 1990–91 but not in fact adopted. Nevertheless, there was a long running debate over how the group should respond to its women members and to the changes in lesbian identity in the 1980s.

Gender Trouble

The primary aim of both CHE and Gay West was homosexual equality and gender equality was an integral part of this vision. The precursor groups and Gay West promoted themselves as mixed groups open to women members and, indeed, both Bath Gay Awareness Group and Gay West had women convenors, as well as a considerable number of women committee members. Nevertheless, women were always in a minority. The proportion of women members has fluctuated greatly, from around 10% in the mid-1980s to a high point of nearly 40% in early 1992 (see section on membership). The absolute number of women members has also fluctuated, from 18 in September 1985, rising to a maximum of 153 in January 1992, then declining to around 80–100 from mid 1992 to mid-1998, after which there was a steep decline, with women's membership down to single figures in the 2000s.

Individual men and women formed many enduring personal friendships and many women had no problems socialising with men and working with male committee members. Nevertheless, the role of women in Gay West was often conflictual and was regularly discussed by the committee. Some of the women involved in the early days were strong personalities well able to hold their own against the men but even at this time there were tensions. At the discos inaugurated by Bath CHE in 1979 (which attracted many non-members as well), men and women gathered together on separate sides of the room and rarely interacted, foreshadowing one of the problems later faced by Gay West. Between gay men and lesbians there is little of the sexual attraction which often tacitly animates mixed groups. While political groups can focus on their shared ideological or practical aims, social groups experience greater difficulty in finding a glue to bind people together.

The role of women in Gay West was discussed by the committee in November 1982 and discussions became more frequent in 1987, as the number of women joining the group began to rise. This coincided with two developments amongst lesbians at the national level. The bitter disputes between the various tendencies, centred around the London Lesbian and Gay Centre, led many women to reject the notion of rigid lesbian separatism which had been influential in the early 1980s. At the same time, the campaign against Section 28, which applied to lesbians as much as gay men and particularly incensed those already in what the clause dubbed "pretended family relationships", provided a pratical incentive for lesbians to work with gay men. Lesbian activists were at the forefront of the campaign, most famously invading the BBC Six O'clock News studio and abseiling into the House of Lords. The outcome of these events was a new generation of lesbians who had a strong sense of their identity and needs but were more willing to interact with men.

Gay West welcomed the influx of new women members, based on its long-standing commitment to gender equality, but conflict soon developed over the question of "women-only" spaces. The idea of safe spaces for women to meet, free from the unwanted attentions of men, was one of the major gains of the women's and lesbian movements, which many lesbians wished to retain. This ran directly counter, however, to Gay West's view of itself as a mixed group dedicated to practising equality. This posed a dilemma which was frequently wrestled with by the committee but never adequately resolved, with the result that while many women became

Gay West banner on the London Pride March, mid 1980s.
Photo: Vince Baughan, Julian Vagg.

members, few regularly attended events.

The problem is summed up in the following exchange in the October 1990 newsletter. A lesbian wrote:

> I joined GayWest to meet other lesbians. [...] I've given up going to coffeeshop because I always come away depressed and despairing. At least 3 times I've been 50% of the female population in the room. As a young lesbian, I feel more isolated at Coffeeshop than I do in most 'heterosexual' settings. [...] The fight against homophobia means nothing to me if we can't acknowledge that the lesbian and gay community is a diverse community, made up of many different people with differing needs. Those who wish to live and socialise in single sex groups should be left to do so in peace.

In a belligerent reply, the (male) editor defended the group against the letter-writer's accusation of sexism and asked "Is the fact that Coffeeshop is male dominated the fault of the men who turn up, or the women who could turn up but don't bother?" He continued:

> Gay West supports and provides women-only, and men-only events, precisely because of the reasons you have stated above (creating a comfortable environment etc). We do not, however, believe that dogmatic, totalitarian separatism, is conducive to good relations and understanding between lesbians and gay men. We oppose gender-based apartheid. Dogmatic separatists, like those at Lesbian Line, are as irrelevant in the fight against sexism and homophobia, as they are intolerant.[343]

In June 1987, woman members organised a meeting to find out why there were so few women members and came up with a number of suggestions. The event was listed in the newsletter as a "Women-only evening" but with a note explaining: "This is not the start of segregation within the group but a one-off get-together of our women members to get to know each other better and to try to find out what Gay West can do to appeal to them more."[344] Six out of Gay West's 24 women members attended this meeting, plus five others, and discussed why so few women joined the group, what events they attended or would like to attend and ways of attracting other women to Gay West activities. Most of the women present said their main concern was whether there would be other women at events; they liked the discos because they were confident other women would be there. It was therefore suggested that women should contact one another to check whether they would be attending events and that women committee members could be focal points of contact.[345] Transport and childcare were also problems. One suggestion floated around this time was to put on a number of single-sex events and this was accepted in principle by the committee in May 1988. From May 1989 onwards, a number of social events were listed in the newsletter as "Women's" or "Women-only".

The number of women members doubled from 1987 to 1989 and this produced some mutterings among the men. In August 1989, the editor of the Diary responded to comments about "the women taking over", pointing out that there were now 50 women members or roughly 20% of the membership; more women than ever before on the committee, including the chairperson; women's phone contacts in both Bath and Bristol and an increasing number of women-only events. "This means that lots of men are prevented from going to events that they won't have gone to anyway!" He pointed out that many gay groups were exclusively male, or the women formed a tiny minority, whereas Gay West was almost unique in having men and women members working side by side. "The group is changing all the time as new members join and get involved. If the number of women is growing surely it is a measure of success rather than cause for alarm."[346]

During 1990–91, members engaged in a sometimes sharp debate about the role of women in the group. In September 1990, women held another meeting to discuss their problems and a survey was sent out with the October diary. This produced a number of ideas, notably over transport problems, facilities for children and the disabled, and ideas for hosting events. Meanwhile the committee decided to appoint a Women's Events Coordinator, with the aim of getting at least one women-only event each month, and a number of successful women-only events were organised during the winter of 1990–1991, attracting between 15 and 25 women.

In March 1990 and again in June 1991, the idea was raised by both men and women members of renaming the group "Lesbian and Gay West". This provoked replies from two women, one of whom wrote: "A large number of gay women hate the word 'lesbian' and frankly shy away from those organisations that blazen the word!! [...] PLEASE, do not alter the name of our group, GAY WEST says it all for me and a large number of it's [sic] female members."[347] An older woman member added: "Had I even thought I would be called a Lesbian – a lady undesirable in the past – I would have gone back to the closet and shut the door fast!"[348]

The increasing number of events labelled 'Women-only' during late 1990 caused some resentment amongst male members. In March 1991 the committee decided to list events hosted by women as "Event for women" and that "Everybody welcome" should also be added where appropriate. From May 1991, events listed in the newsletter were coded either W for "Event for women" and E for "Everybody welcome". There were suggestions that some events should be listed as "Men only". The committee initially rejected this, preferring to restrict the labelling of events, but queried the number of events hosted by women which were women-only. In December 1991, however, the newsletter announced that there would also be some men-only events, although they still wanted to see mixed events to balance things out. In March 1992, one long-standing male member wrote to the newsletter arguing that by and large the women in the group had no wish to socialise with the men and suggesting that it would be better to have two distinct groups under the Gay West banner. This, together with the editor's accompanying note using the term "girls", provoked a number of letters from women trying to explain why they found it difficult socialising with men. Subsequent letters from both a woman and from men urged more tolerance and the advantages of working together.

In early January 1991, women hosted the coffee shop, attracting a large contingent of other women, and it was decided to continue this arrangement in the following months. Increasingly, the committee's efforts concentrated on finding a coffee shop-style formula which would satisfy both the specific needs of the women and the wishes of the group as a whole. November 1992 marked the beginning of the Women's Tea Shop, held initially on the first Saturday afternoon of the month and then twice a month in the Women's Centre in the basement of the Greenleaf Bookshop, at 82 Colston Street, Bristol. At first it attracted about 20 women a month but numbers dropped during 1993. Many of the women attending were referrals from Lesbian and Gay Switchboard or the bookshop rather than Gay West members, and with only a few stalwarts coming regularly, the Tea Shop closed in October 1993.

By February 1995 very few women were attending the Bath Coffee Shop. In August 1995, an article entitled "Women's visibility" traced the rise and fall of women's participation in Gay West, which reached its peak between 1988 and 1992. "The Bath Coffee Shop buzzed with an excited air with a good mix of men and women, giving the event a very welcoming atmosphere, especially for first-timers. Gaywest had 'come of age' and was truly a social group for all comers." Membership then began to fall and although it had recently recovered, with almost a third being women, events were no longer mixed nor were there many women-only events. The article went on to consider possible reasons for women's reluctance to get involved, suggesting that the women might have formed a large circle of friends through the women-only events and continued to meet socially. They no longer felt the need to advertise events, thus creating a closed shop situation and denying all those who followed, in need of a friend. It asked for members' views on why so few gay men and women now got together for social events.[349]

Shortly after the coffee shop in St. Michael's was transformed into the Rainbow Cafe, a separate Womens Space in an adjacent room was started in July 1995, meeting on the last Saturday of the month. This was hosted by women and initially attracted 25–30 women, so that at times the room was overcrowded. The main Rainbow Cafe continued for men and those women who preferred mixed company. The Women's Space ran monthly until November 1996, when it went fortnightly. The committee wanted the main Rainbow Cafe to remain mixed and worried about a split developing but the women committee members argued that many women came to a women-only cafe who would not wish to enter a room dominated by men. At the beginning of 1997, the Women's Space moved to the Bath Tap and began to run every Saturday morning under the name Rainbow Cafe for Women. It was renamed Diva's in May 1997 and in the summer was attracting an average of over 30 women but closed at the end of 1997 following disagreements among the organisers. A non-Gay West group called Diva's in the Afternoon continued to meet at the Bath Tap on Saturday afternoons. A table was reserved for women in the Rainbow Cafe but most stopped coming. Over the summer of 1998, the group tried a monthly women-only cafe at St. Michael's from 1–3 p.m. after the main Rainbow Cafe but this only lasted about four months.

In March 2000 the magazine published a news item about the Bristol gay pub Roosters turning into a straight table-dancing club and suggested that "a few of the lesbian brigade may salivate at the thought of dishy dollies thrusting intimate parts in their faces".[350] The front page of the next issue, under the title "Sisters are doing it for themselves. Is Gay West really just 'a gentleman's club'?" carried a serious article in which two women ex-members gave their reasons for no longer belonging to the group. Inside, two letters, both from men, pointed to the Roosters article as a reason for the lack of women members. "The complete lack of understanding of women is staggering".[351] The following issue contained a letter from one of the women who had run Diva's, in which she reported that she had brought up the subject of Gay West at the last 35+ Group [a breakaway from Diva's]:

> Of those who had heard of GayWest, no-one was interested in joining or rejoining. One ex-member said women didn't need GayWest because they could network well enough without it. She also said that it was not possible for busy people to plan events weeks in advance. Another woman said she had found KENRIC much more valuable because it's run by women for women. No-one was prepared to consider what GayWest should do to attract more women. [...] Sorry there's nothing positive to report.[352]

This debate continued in the subsequent issues and women continued to be members of Gay West but the numbers dwindled away to only three in February 2004 and there were no more women committee members until July 2008 when a Women's Officer joined the committee for just over a year.

As well as the social events put on for women by Gay West, there were also women-only discos which were organised by other people but publicised in the newsletter, such as Hint of Pink in Bristol and Desert Hearts in Bath in the early 1990s. The number of local groups catering for lesbians increased during the 1990s and the fall in Gay West's women's membership in part was the result of the growth of an increasingly diverse and fragmented scene in Bristol during this period (see Chapter 8).

Relations with Other Minorities

In contrast to the regular agonising over the number of women members, there has been little discussion of the relevance of the group to the ethnic minorities, despite the fact that Bristol has long had a substantial black population. Members of ethnic minorities have come to the coffee shop and taken part in group activities but the membership remains predominantly white. There has been no suggestion of overt racism but rather a feeling that the issue does not concern the group. In March 1973, CHE Bristol reported that "Various imigrant [sic] communities have been informed of our existence and facilities" but this was one of the very few occasions on which a conscious attempt was made to contact ethnic minorities.[353] In 1986, a correspondent in the newsletter raised the question of racism and apartheid. In reply, the chairperson accepted "that Gay West is almost, but not exclusively, white, and I agree that it is a shame. There is no reason why it should always stay that way since our membership is open to anybody regardless of colour, but we cannot go out and recruit non-white people. We have to wait for people to come to us – if they want to."[354] The question was only rarely discussed by the committee. In one of the few instances, in 1991, a woman committee member suggested that more should be done to encourage black people to join the group, including running an anti-racist workshop. She was asked to contact existing black groups, but nothing seems to have resulted from this.[355]

Disability was also largely ignored until September 1989 when GEMMA, a group for disabled lesbians, pointed out the problems disabled people faced in trying to find out whether they would be able to get to the events advertised. The group then made a concerted effort to include accessibility information in the newsletter. One of the main reasons given for moving from Abbey Green to the St. Michael's Community Centre and staying there was the improved disabled access, which has enabled people in wheelchairs to come to the Rainbow Cafe on occasion. The group also made some donations to organisations for disabled LGBT people. However, when the newsletter reprinted an article which had originally been published in the free *Bath & Keynsham Advertiser*, stating that "People who belong to GayWest never feel isolated", a member wrote in to say that he took great exception, pointing out the difficulties for housebound and physically restricted people in getting to the coffee morning in Bath. He was supported by another member who complained about the lack of public transport. The editor offered to arrange lifts for isolated members and asked for other suggestions.[356] The episode pointed to the difficulty in deciding what support it was feasible for a voluntary group to provide.

Age Concern

In many ways, the elephant in the room for Gay West has been the question of age. In common with the rest of Western society, there are an increasing number of older LGBT people and, as a recent work points out, with the passage of time, there are now three generations of gay men who have lived through the years of gay liberation, each with different experiences of coming out and with different current needs and perceptions.[357] One striking feature of the early days was the age of the activists. Although it is not possible to establish the membership's average age over time, it is noticeable that many of the most active members in the 1970s were in their twenties. Indeed, two committee members celebrated their 21st birthdays while in office. People who were 20 in 1970 are now (2010) approaching retirement age. Over the years Gay West has attracted members from all age groups (though very few teenagers) but even in the 1980s, the group had a reputation for attracting older men and the profile of the members has visibly aged since then. At the same time, the group has had to confront the question of how to deal with young people who approach it, taking into account on the one hand the needs of those just coming out and on the other the legal ramifications of the age of consent.

Between 1967 and 1994, when the age of consent was reduced to 18, it was illegal for young men under 21 to engage in homosexual acts. In December 1987, the committee noted that it had no policy on age limits but generally did not encourage people under 18 to come to events and must make the law clear to them. Later, it stated that they would normally refer people under 18 to one of the local youth groups. During 1992, the committee discussed a proposal from the diary editor to introduce personal contact adverts and in this context it also decided to propose setting a minimum age of 18 for membership. In September 1992, a constitutional amendment was presented to the AGM but rejected by a narrow majority. The editor suspended publication of personal ads pending clarification of the situation and the committee decided it needed legal advice, although noting that "overall it was preferable to be able to offer support to under 18's than to carry personal ads."[358] In October 1993, the committee discussed the question of enquiries from persons under 21 and agreed that anyone enquiring would be made welcome and support offered. The matter came to a head in November 1994, some months after the age of consent was reduced to 18 by Parliament, when the group received a request for information from a 15-year-old boy. Fearing that the letter could be from an anti-gay group to see the group's reaction, a carefully-worded reply was sent pointing out that the legal age of consent was 18. Following advice from one solicitor, the committee decided to include the phrase "I'm over the age of consent" on the membership application form, noting: "Although the Committee felt it was a shame that we had to abide by this Law that we had campaigned against we also had to protect the general membership."[359] At the next committee meeting, it was decided to take further legal advice and the consensus of the letters from four solicitors was that there would be no legal case to answer if the group should have any members below the age of consent as long as it was not encouraging sexual activity between members.[360] However, when the Constitution was extensively re-written in 1997, a minimum age of sixteen for membership was introduced.[361]

Problems occasionally arose when older members made unwelcome sexual approaches to new younger members. In 1988 a young member of the group alerted the committee that another young member had recently been subject to this sort of behaviour. The committee published a warning in the newsletter and later wrote to the older person concerned, with the result that he left the group.

At the other end of the scale, Gay West had a reputation as a group for older men. Although in the early years there were members in all ranges from twenties upwards, as time has gone on, the age profile of the group has risen. This issue was rarely addressed directly but in June 1991, one of the younger members wrote an article criticising ageism in the gay community and those who rejected Gay West because it attracted older people. A couple of years later, Vince Baughan, another of the younger members, remarked: "One criticism I have heard regularly levelled at Coffee Shop, and ultimately Gay West, is that it is over populated by old men. I have even heard the extremist view that perhaps someone should suggest to the oldies that they are not welcome." He thought that that was no way to solve a perceived problem. "The senior members' needs are as equally important as any other group members' needs, so you youth-ist, abolitionists should have a care. You should not ban the oldies." Instead, they should get their young friends to attend Gay West events.[362]

Since then, the attendance at the weekly Rainbow Cafe has come to be dominated, albeit not exclusively, by those over 50. This appears to reflect both the overall ageing of the UK population and the changing needs of the generation of (mainly) gay men who have lived their adult lives in the post-1967 age of legalised homosexuality. While so much of gay culture and the commercial scene remain geared to the youth market, the voluntary sector provides a space for older LGBT people to socialise freely.

Bath vs. Bristol

One issue which was discussed surprisingly rarely was the relationship between the Bath and Bristol activities of the group. During the 1970s, CHE Bristol was a much larger and more active organisation than Bath Gay Awareness Group but the split caused by the creation of Avonscene meant that when the group merged with the newly-formed Gay West in 1983, it was the Bath group which dominated. This led to the anomalous situation in which a group based in the smaller city also covered its larger neighbour and, as a result, Gay West has always had a more precarious position in Bristol than Bath. This issue was addressed in an editorial headed "Us and them" published in the October 1989 newsletter, which noted that although more of the members lived in Bristol than Bath, Gay West continued to have an image as a Bath-based group. The P.O. box address was Bath, the bank account allowed cheques to be made payable to Bath GCO, the regular events such as Coffee Shop and discos were held in Bath and the majority of the committee members lived in Bath. There were historical reasons for this but "Although Gay West is made up of former groups from both cities, somehow it is the Bath end which has retained its identity more strongly than Bristol." The 1989 AGM was held in Bristol, there was a monthly Bristol coffee shop, a double entry in *Gay Times* giving Bristol phone numbers as well as Bath and both the chairperson and membership secretary lived in Bristol. "None of this will stop some remaining convinced that Gay West is a Bath group."[363]

The impression that Gay West is primarily a Bath-based group has undoubtedly made it difficult for the group to make inroads in the Bristol scene. On the other hand, the group continues to draw on Bristol for a substantial part of its membership and committee members, and many Bristolians continue to travel over to Bath on Saturday mornings to go to the Rainbow Cafe. Bath's leisure and retail facilities provide a major additional attraction, so that a visit to the Rainbow Cafe becomes part of an enjoyable day-out, meeting friends for lunch or going shopping. At the same time, it seems likely that the existence nearby of a major city like Bristol, with a large LGBT population to draw on, has made Gay West viable in a way that a group in a city the size of Bath would not be if it stood in isolation.

6

Politics, the Market and Civil Society

This chapter discusses developments during the 1980s. It looks at the relationship between LGBT activism and mainstream politics, showing how events at the local level affected national developments while not always conforming to the national agenda. It contrasts the different paths taken by Gay West and the activists who chose not to join it and compares the opportunities offered by political activism with those which stemmed from the market and civil society.

In his comparative study of the relationship between the LGBT movements and the political systems in Britain, the United States and Canada published in 1998, David Rayside shows how in a highly centralised system like Britain's before devolution, there were relatively few points of access for social movement activists, allowing the party in government effectively to block change if it was not positively disposed. More decentralised federal systems, on the other hand, offer multiple points of access, allowing activists to work at one level when they find themselves blocked at another.[364] Paradoxically, the UK structure, which remained relatively centralised despite devolution, worked in favour of LGBT interests when a governing party showed the political will to implement equality policies in the 2000s.[365] In Britain in the 1980s, however, the scope for political initiatives at the national level was effectively blocked and LGBT activists found themselves increasingly on the defensive against encroachments on civil rights, most famously with the Section 28 campaign of 1987–88.

In 1980 Parliament voted to extend the provisions of the 1967 Act to Scotland. In 1984, the Criminal Law Revision Committee, which had been asked by Roy Jenkins, Home Secretary in the preceding Labour government, to review the law on sexual offences, presented its final report, the last of a series of four produced by itself and the Policy Advisory Committee on Sexual Offences. These recommended a reduction in the age of consent for homosexual relations to 18, which was still short of equality at 16 as advocated by LGBT activists.[366] Even these modest proposals were shelved and the recommendation to reduce the age of consent to 18 was not implemented until 1994. The British political system showed that it was no longer capable of generating reform from its own resources. The legalisation of sex between men over 21 in Northern Ireland in 1982 was the result of a decision by the European Court of Human Rights, and for the next two decades the most effective pressure for reform came from activism at the European level, which increasingly recast gay rights as human rights. In the longer term, this enabled the British political system to begin to overcome the log jam caused by the perceived hostility of public opinion to LGBT issues, starting with the lowering of the age of consent to 18 in 1994, but in the short term the prospects were bleak.

During the 1980s, CHE continued to survive but was much reduced in influence. Most activists concentrated on the AIDS crisis but in 1987, the Organisation of Lesbian and Gay Action (OLGA) was born out of a fractious conference held in London as a more left-wing alternative to CHE. Both OLGA and CHE were immediately pitched into the battle over Section 28. Although a defeat in the short term, the wave of activism which this campaign unleashed was to have major repercussions in the following two decades.

By 1982, it was clear that the Conservative government was at best indifferent to LGBT rights and that further law reform was unlikely to be achieved by the classic technique of lobbying MPs to try to secure a favourable majority for a free vote in Parliament. When CHE restructured itself in 1982, the LGBT movement in Bristol and Bath developed in opposite directions, reflecting the different inclinations of the activists involved and the differing opportunities offered by the political cultures of the two cities. Activists in Bristol concentrated on developing autonomous lesbian and gay institutions or deepened their involvement in trade union activities and local Labour Party politics, continuing trends which were already visible in the last days of CHE Bristol (see Chapter 2). In this they were able to tap into the city's tradition of reformist Labour politics. Bath, on the other hand, had no such tradition and its political culture was still conservative in the 1980s, albeit with a growing liberal trend. It also had a smaller population base, not large enough to support a gay centre. The two precursor groups (like CHE in general) had maintained an uneasy mix of social and campaigning activities in the 1970s. The Bristol activists broke this tension by increasing their involvement in mainstream politics, while Gay West opted to distance itself from party politics and concentrate on social activities.

Gay West's activism was therefore limited to the traditional non-partisan campaigning activities of its predecessors. In 1982 Bath CHE had started lobbying the prospective parliamentary candidates but this had to be cut short when the General Election was called at short notice in 1983; instead Gay West representatives went to talk to some of them, including Chris Patten, who was re-elected as MP for Bath.[367] Gay West's survey of Bath City councillors produced a poor response. The group's campaigning activities were generally low-key but its second chair, Gareth Wynn-Jones, was flamboyantly out and in March 1983, led a protest outside two newsagents in Keynsham which had refused to display the group's postcard, resulting in some local press publicity.[368] In June 1987, the Campaign Secretary reported that he had circulated a CHE questionnaire to all parliamentary candidates in Bath and Bristol: three completed them and five offered to meet representatives of the group. Prior to the 1997 General Election, the Campaign Committee prepared letters to send to the candidates, inviting them to speak at the Rainbow Cafe.

Developments in Bristol: LGBT Activism and the Labour Party

After the demise of CHE Bristol, some activists concentrated their energies on developing the Bristol Gay Centre but its financial difficulties (it never received any public funding, unlike the London Lesbian and Gay Centre) and its isolated location meant that it never became a popular meeting place and it was forced to close at the end of 1983. For the next two years, the LGBT voluntary movement in Bristol remained at a low ebb, effectively limited to the Bristol Lesbian and Gay Switchboard, the university Gaysoc and social groups such as Gay West, Avonscene and Amicus. Only in 1985 did the movement pick up again, with the foundation of Lesbian Line, the Gay Men's Health Network in Avon and the Gay Bristol Festival in June that year.[369] There was also a radical lesbian feminist group which produced a magazine in late 1986.[370]

CHE campaigning was based on the assumption that any future improvements in LGBT rights would be the result of a free vote in Parliament on a matter of conscience, as had happened with the 1967 Act. It therefore concentrated on lobbying MPs and prospective parliamentary candidates in an effort to build up support across all the main parties. In the changed political climate of the 1980s, the Bristol activists, in conjunction with left-wing activists elsewhere, adopted a new strategy of trying to get the Labour Party to include a commitment to LGBT rights as part of its official party policy, in the belief that it would be more likely to be implemented as government policy if and when Labour returned to power. This eventually proved to be a very effective strategy, although in the short-term, it propelled gay rights into the middle of the party political battle, giving right-wingers a convenient whipping-horse and alienating some gays who were not Labour Party supporters.

The activists who formed the core of CHE Bristol set about deepening their involvement in the political process beyond the intermittent lobbying of election candidates. Chris Leigh carried out a detailed statistical analysis of the results of a questionnaire sent to candidates standing in the Avon County Council elections on 7 May 1981. An edited version was sent to all 76 Avon councillors with a view to seeking support for a proposal to change employment contracts in order to prevent discrimination on the grounds of sexual orientation.[371] After the demise of CHE Bristol, Chris Leigh helped run the Gay Centre. Donald Branch had been a member of Lancaster GLF while a student and convenor of the Bath Gay Awareness Group during 1975–76, before moving to Bristol and becoming involved in CHE Bristol. He joined the Labour Party in May 1979 at the time of Margaret Thatcher's election victory.[372] Donald Branch was living with Charlie Beaton at this time and they moved to Southville in 1980. Charlie Beaton had learnt about political organisation and formed his ideas about homosexuality in CHE Bristol but saw that the future lay in working through the trade union movement. A social worker, he joined the local government officers's union NALGO (later Unison after NALGO merged with NUPE and COHSE) and, as the first person to come out at a stewards meeting, found that he was pushing at an open door.[373] Both he and Donald Branch became active in Labour Party politics, joining the local constituency party in Bristol South. This produced a change in the geographical focus of gay activism. Traditionally, the middle-class suburb of Clifton, located north-west of the city centre and including the University, had been the home of progressive political movements, such as the suffragettes and gay liberation. This was a district of large Georgian and Victorian houses which by the 1970s had been mostly subdivided into flats, bedsitters and student accommodation, and had a large gay population. The move of LGBT activists into the Bristol South constituency transferred the centre of political activity to the southern part of the city, comprising the middle class Edwardian suburb of Knowle and the council estates further south.

The first politician of national stature to come out unequivocally for gay rights was Tony Benn, who was MP for Bristol South-East until 1983, when the constituency was abolished. In 1981, he wrote a foreword for the NCCL book *Gay Workers: Trade Unions and the Law*, in which he said there should be absolute equality in law between heterosexual and homosexual men and women.[374] He does not seem to have had links with the local movement, however. Local LGBT activists were more closely involved with Dawn Primarolo, who, starting as a county councillor, became vice-chair of Avon County Council's Equal Opportunities Council in 1985 and prospective parliamentary candidate for Bristol South following the controversial deselection of the sitting MP, Michael Cocks. In 1987, she was elected to Parliament, the first woman MP for Bristol since 1945, and she subsequently held a number of government posts after 1997. As a prospective parliamentary candidate, she spoke in favour of gay rights at a meeting of the Labour Campaign for Lesbian and Gay Rights in Bristol in 1986 and she remained a strong supporter of LGBT equality after election to Parliament.[375] Donald Branch was chairman of the constituency party at the time Dawn Primarolo was first elected to Parliament and so gay men had a profile in the local Labour Party.[376] Avon County Council proved a good launch pad for political careers and other councillors who subsequently became MPs were Valerie Davey (Bristol West) and Roger Berry (Kingswood), both of whom supported LGBT equality legislation in Parliament. Consequently, as a result of these contacts, local gay activists knew half-a-dozen Labour MPs by first name after 1997.[377]

Charlie Beaton and other Bristol activists joined the national Labour Campaign for Lesbian and Gay Rights (LCLGR). This had replaced the Gay Labour Group in 1978 and took a more active stance from 1981 onwards.[378] At its second attempt, it succeeded in getting a motion on lesbian and gay rights put on the agenda for the Labour Party annual conference in 1985. To do this, activists had to follow the complicated party rules and get motions passed by local ward and constituency meetings. In 1985, the Bristol South Constituency Labour Party seconded a motion to the Labour Party conference from the Hornsey and Wood Green CLP opposing all discrimination against lesbians and gay men and calling on the NEC and Labour local authorities to take a series of practical measures to implement a lesbian and gay rights policy.[379] Charlie Beaton addressed the conference as Bristol South delegate in support of the motion, admitting to feeling terrified while he was doing so. The motion was passed by a 55% majority, followed by larger majorities in 1986, 1988 and 1994.[380]

The Party leadership was not keen to take the issue on board, given its associations with the "loony left" but eventually an explicit commitment to LGBT rights was included in the Labour Party manifestos for 1987 and 1992. The 1997 manifesto was much vaguer on the subject but once in power, the New Labour government made a serious effort to reduce the age of consent and do away with Section 28. Despite a bitter rearguard action by opponents in the House of Lords, the government of Tony Blair succeeded in the 2000s in passing a whole raft of measures securing equality and protection for LGBT people. Consequently, of all the events described in this work, LGBT activism in the Bristol South Labour Party was the activity which had the most far-reaching effects at the national level.

Steve Atack and the Liberal Party in Bath

Bath's political culture was characterised by a complex and volatile mix of conservatism and liberalism, which led to the unexpected ejection of its sitting Conservative MP, Chris Patten, in 1992. During the 1970s, the national party considered most sympathetic to gay rights was the Liberal Party and many CHE activists had a background in Liberal politics. After the trial of its former leader, Jeremy Thorpe, in 1979 for attempting to murder a former male lover, a case characterised by rumour and evasion, Liberals became rather sensitive about homosexuality and although official Liberal policy remained favourable, politicians on the ground preferred to downplay the subject. This was forcefully brought home in Bath with the controversy over the choice of its prospective parliamentary candidate.

In 1980, Steve Atack was selected to contest the Bath seat for the Liberal Party at the next general election. As national chairman of the Young Liberals, Atack had been an out gay activist. In March 1980, shortly after his selection, a campaign was started by dissident members of the local party to reverse the decision. This was led by the former constituency agent, Ray Wardle, who had also applied to be a candidate. Despite the opposition, Atack initially held on but some nine months later he was forced to resign.[381]

Bath CHE was not directly involved but it had some dealings with the local Liberals. During 1973 and 1974, Bath Gay Awareness Group used the local Liberal Party headquarters in St. Michael's Place for meetings.[382] Bath CHE's convenor, David England, stood unsuccessfully as a Liberal candidate in the Bath City Council elections in 1980.[383] Referring to the news of Atack's resignation, the newsletter remarked that "we within the group have lost a good friend" and went on: "It would be foolish to assume that all gay people are welcome within every political organisation even the Liberals. [...] Steve was willing to possibly be the first openly gay MP if elected, but sadly this chance has passed by for the Bath constituency."[384] When Wardle, by now a Social Democrat, wrote to the *Bath Herald* the following year to attack a report on Bath CHE's survey of candidates, David England and Roland Attwell, writing on behalf of the group, and another correspondent were able to reply with a polite but scathing demolition of his views.[385] Twenty-five years later, the Liberal Democrat Stephen Williams became the region's first out MP when he won Bristol West in 2005 but, at the time, the affair signalled that Bath Liberals were unlikely to be very receptive to any attempt to raise the profile of gay issues through that party.[386]

Bob Osborne and the Bath Conservatives

As described in Chapter 3, the Conservative Party had held the Bath parliamentary seat continuously since the 1920s. It is difficult now to recall that Margaret Thatcher was one of the relatively few Conservative MPs who voted for homosexual law reform in the 1960s. During the 1980s, however, her government became increasingly hostile towards gay rights, which became inextricably mixed up in the battle between the Conservative government and the urban left in local government. This bitter struggle resulted in the introduction of Section 28 in 1987–88 (see Chapter 7). Nevertheless, beneath the homophobic rhetoric, the Conservative party was not monolithic nor was it uniformly anti-gay. TORCHE (Tory Campaign for Homosexual Equality, 1977–93) urged the party to adopt a more pro-gay policy. Rob Hayward, MP for the Kingswood constituency on the outskirts of Bristol (1983–92) expressed interest in the aims of Gay West and talked to members at a discussion evening in February 1992. Later he came out as gay, but only after he had left Parliament.[387]

Some of these different currents within the Conservative Party were reflected at the local level. In October 1981, the Conservative agent in Bath became involved in controversy at the University when he helped the University Conservative Association produce a booklet for freshers which poked fun at homosexuals and women. The Student Union called an emergency meeting to demand withdrawal of the booklet and a written apology under threat of withholding funds to the student association. The agent claimed that he had printed the booklet but not read it. "'If it is offensive I wouldn't support it,' he said. [...] Told that the jokes were about homosexuals, bi-sexuals and women, Mr Statham commented: 'In the Rag magazines I have bought they always seem to make a whipping post of these things.'"[388] In the event, after an inconclusive union general meeting, a ballot of students resulted in a large majority against withdrawing the booklet.[389]

Five years later, however, there was a new agent in the post. In November 1986, the *Bath Chronicle* reported that "The Conservative agent for Bath, Mr Bob Osborne, has been elected secretary of Gay West."[390] Bob Osborne had come to Bath the previous year from the West Midlands where he had also been a Conservative agent. Soon after arriving in Bath, he joined Gay West and as he had been on the committee of a gay group in the Midlands he was soon invited onto the Gay West committee. He made no secret of his involvement in the group and his name appeared with the rest of the committee on the newsletter. As the group was not party political and at the time was little involved in public campaigning, he did not see any problem. When the newspaper informed him that it was publishing the story, he contacted the chairman of the Constituency Association and Chris Patten, the M.P., who both assured him of their support. The chairman told the *Bristol Evening Post* that he couldn't care less about his private life. It was not relevant and, as far as they were concerned, there was no conflict and no comment.[391]

As Patten was a junior minister and a rising political figure, the story was picked up by the national press and short reports appeared in the *Daily Telegraph*, *Daily Express* and the *Sun*, which headlined the story "Top Tory runs club for gays".[392] While Tory leaders in the city voiced their support for Bob Osborne, some members of the Constituency Association led by a retired Brigadier started moves to force him to resign. At a tense meeting of the executive committee, these moves were defeated by a large majority and, instead, his critics resigned from the Association.[393] Osborne's supporters in the local party hierarchy advised him to sit it out. The Gay West committee decided that any request for information about Gay West from the press should be referred to the committee and asked members not to respond to provocative letters in the paper and let the issue die.[394] This is what in fact happened.

Bob Osborne noted that several of his critics resumed friendly relations during the General Election campaign six months later and he continued to serve on the Gay West committee, although he eventually decided to change career away from politics. Looking back after twenty years, he thought that Chris Patten had no problem personally about homosexuality and did not wish to appear anti-gay in liberal Bath. Patten had voted for the decriminalisation of homosexuality in Scotland in 1980. Patten made no comment in public but assured Osborne that he would support him publicly if necessary. Bob Osborne surmised that Patten spoke to people behind the scenes but wanted to avoid upsetting those whose political support he needed.[395]

The episode showed that the Conservative Party was not as wholeheartedly anti-gay as some on its right-wing might have wished. The outing of Bob Osborne by the local paper also demonstrated that, in this period, it was impossible to detach homosexuality from politics. Nevertheless, the group tried as far as possible to stay clear of direct involvement in party politics, concentrating on its relationship with the commercial scene and local civil society.

Relations with the Market : the Commercial Scene

While campaigning occupied only a small part of Gay West's activities, its members were in daily contact with the market. Many of the pubs which had catered for a gay clientele before 1967, such as the Radnor and the Garrick's Head, made the transition to legality. The traditional gay pub, however notorious, did not advertise itself as such and sometimes catered for straight customers as well as gays, often using separate bars. Gay pubs were joined by gay dance clubs and discos, which gradually metamorphosed into the increasingly sophisticated and visible commercial gay scene of today. Few of the traditional gay pubs survived in the long run, however. By the mid-2000s, none of the pubs and clubs which comprised the gay scene in Bristol and Bath in the 1970s was still catering for a LGBT clientele: the scene had completely changed. The general improvement in facilities and the development of a gay village around Bristol's Old Market in the 2000s reflect what many critics see as the commodification of gay culture.[396] The market increasingly caters to the pink pound by providing the elements of a commodified gay life-style (clubs, restaurants, pubs, city-centre flats, etc.) but in doing so erects barriers to those who do not enjoy a high disposable income (entry fees, cost of drinks, late-night taxis, designer clothes, high rentals, etc.), let alone those who do not come up to the required standards of physical appearance because of age or body characteristics. For most of the 1980s, however, the commercial scene remained much as it had been in the 1970s: the Elephant and Oasis dominated the Bristol scene and the Garrick's Head remained the main gay pub in Bath.

The division between the market and the voluntary movement was not rigid. The owners of commercial establishments, some of whom were themselves lesbian or gay, also participated in movement activities, mainly through fundraising or providing a venue. The Oasis club in Bristol put on an annual garden party to raise funds for Bristol Lesbian and Gay Switchboard, Michael's Restaurant regularly provided prizes and sponsorship for special events and most of the commercial venues participated in the annual Avon Pride festivals. As well as altruism, this reflected a common practice of many businesses in proving their community credentials but it also provided a personal link between the voluntary and commercial sectors. Other entrepreneurs became directly involved in some non-profit activities, for example the owner of Just club was a regular participant in the Policing Initiative (see Chapter 9).

Researchers have pointed to the role of other organisations in sustaining social movements, such as churches in the case of the American black civil rights movement, local branches of trade unions for the British peace movement and neighbourhood solidarity organisations in the British urban movements.[397] A similar, albeit complex, role was played by gay pubs for the LGBT movement in the UK, at least in the provinces. Lesbian and gay activists had an ambivalent attitude towards gay pubs, which were often seen as unfriendly and exploitative. One of the aims expressly set out in Gay West's 1982 Constitution was to work towards an integrated gay community as an alternative to the commercial scene. Nevertheless, activists regularly used gay pubs for socialising and they were one of the main points of contact with lesbians and gays who were not members of the group. As the Bath Gay Awareness Group newsletter remarked in 1973: "For anybody who is at a loose end on Friday or Saturday nights – you can usually find someone from the Group in the Green Room of the Garrick's".[398]

The uneasy nature of the relationship with gay pubs can be seen in the case of the Garrick's Head in Bath. The Garrick's Head had been a gay pub long before 1967 and the pub made the transition into the new commercial scene, being listed in the Gay News Gay Guide from its inception. The Garrick's was in fact a mixed pub, with gays mainly frequenting one of the bars (the Green Room), while the other bar was usually straight. Straight customers sometimes came into the Green Room, usually unwittingly.[399] The Garrick's Head was the main gay pub in Bath and was treated as their local by many gays who had nothing to do with Gay West. It was also frequented informally by members of the group, who met there before other events or went for lunch after the Saturday Coffee Shop. For years the pub was run by a landlord who was happy to have gay customers and many lesbians and gays regarded the Garrick's Head as "their" pub. When the pub re-opened after a refurbishment in the early 1980s, however, its friendliness towards gay customers began to vary, depending on the attitude of a series of new landlords. The pub had a noticeboard which served as a barometer of the current mood. At times the landlord allowed the noticeboard to advertise Gay West and other gay events, at other times, all such notices were removed. In friendly periods, the pub sold Gay News and tickets for the group's discos, while at other times, the attitude was distinctly frosty. The committee kept an eye open for changes and regularly tried to make sure that the pub remained friendly towards gays.

In March 1987, the committee noted that the noticeboard had been removed and there were rumours about the landlord's attitude; they agreed to write to him to enquire about the situation. The landlord did not reply, so the group's chairman, John Bescoby, approached him with a request to put up the Coffee Shop notice.

> This had been refused as the landlord said other customers did not like
> gay notices, but he did not mind the pub being listed in the gay press.
> John thought it was impractical to suggest a boycott as there were many

non-members of Gay West who had always gone to the Garrick's and were likely to continue doing so. William thought we should search our consciences before using a pub which was no longer friendly but quite prepared to take our money. The consensus of opinion was to encourage members to go somewhere else after coffee on Saturdays and consider an alternative meeting place for theatre visits.[400]

A year later there was a reference to getting a Coffee Shop notice put up and the Switchboard numbers advertised again. In November 1989 it was again noted that the Bristol Lesbian and Gay Switchboard benefit poster and all specifically gay things had been removed. In January 1990, however, the committee recorded that the Garrick's had a noticeboard on which Gay West and other gay and lesbian organisations could advertise and that the pub would distribute copies of the *Pink Paper*.

In December 1990, there were more problems when the landlord refused to display a notice for the Metropolitan Community Church service. After discussion by the Campaign Committee, the committee decided to send a letter to the Administrator at the Theatre Royal, which owned the pub, drawing attention to the advert for the Garrick's Head in *Gay Times* and expressing the group's concern. This had some effect, as the group received a letter from the Garrick's managers which refuted all comments made and the committee agreed to follow up the offer of a meeting involving the Theatre management. By July 1995, the Theatre was making its 1805 Rooms available for group discos and the Garrick's was keen to be involved as most people met there for a drink before the discos. The group held discos in the 1805 Rooms between summer 1995 and March 1998 and the Garrick's Head placed advertisements in the group's newsletter in 1995–96.[401] In November 1997, however, the committee, alerted by a number of members' experiences, minuted that "the current anti-gay vibrations from the Garrick's Head is cause for concern. Perhaps the group can play a part in making sure Bath does not loose a long, established gay venue."[402] A month later, it noted that the "'Garricks Head' has definitely become a straight pub."[403] This was confirmed by an article in the *Bath Chronicle*.[404] In April 1998 the committee complained that the Garrick's management had ripped up and thrown away ten tickets to the group's disco which it had been given to sell. It considered sending an invoice but in the end decided not to. The newsletter reported that the Garrick's Head had refused to sell tickets or display a poster for the disco: "Inconceivable under the old ownership."[405] In July 1998 the committee heard that some gays who had not heard about the pub's change of policy were still using it but effectively this period marks the definitive end of a long history when the

Garrick's Head was Bath's main gay pub.

The demise of the Garrick's Head as a gay pub was partly due to competition from a newcomer. In October 1996, the Devonshire Arms in St. James's Parade was renamed the Bath Tap and re-opened with the clear aim of catering primarily for the LGBT market. Gay West's first formal contact with the Bath Tap was in late 1996 when the women, who were dissatisfied with the Women's Space at the Rainbow Cafe, decided to try meeting there for three months. From then on references to the Tap regularly crop up in the minutes. At the end of 1997 the Bath Tap opened its cellar as a club and in February 1998 agreed to liaise with Gay West to avoid clashes of dates over discos. When the St. Michael's Centre closed for refurbishment in August and September 2002, the Saturday morning Rainbow Cafe moved temporarily to the Tap. The committee, already worried about the financial viability of the Rainbow Cafe due to increased room hire costs, public liability insurance and falling attendances, considered moving permanently to the Tap and were assured of a very warm welcome from the landlord. They thought that if they did so, they would have to "consider an introduction system similar to BLAGS when people can meet others in a safe meeting place"[406] In the event, the Cafe returned to St. Michael's but the Tap option was considered again a year later. However, after hearing that when the group returned from the Tap following the refurbishment of St. Michael's, no-one had said they would prefer the Rainbow Cafe to be at the Tap, they decided to stay at St. Michael's. This reflects a lingering unease with the commercial scene and the feeling that people just coming out would be intimidated by having to enter a gay pub alone.

Two other gay pubs in Bath opened after 2000, Mandalyns and DYMK (Does Your Mother Know). The group does not seem to have had any formal dealings with DYMK, which in any case only lasted a short time, or initially with Mandalyns. However, in April 2010, it held a coffee morning there when its usual meeting place was temporarily unavailable, which helped establish relations with the pub's new owners.

Gay West's links with the pubs in Bristol were not so close but it made a point of holding its Christmas dinner at the Griffin in 1987 soon after it opened as a gay pub and continued to use this pub occasionally for meetings and social events, such as Sunday lunches. Since September 2006 the group has held a monthly pub evening in Bristol as a successor to the Bristol coffee evenings, first in the Old Market Tavern and then in other pubs in the area. In the mid-2000s, as part of the group's drive to attract more members, the Chair negotiated some discounts for members in the Bristol Clone Zone shop (since closed) and the two saunas in Bristol and Bath.

The Garrick's Head pub, Bath, in June 2009. Photo: Robert Howes.

Civil Society

The following quotation appeared under the heading "Pause for Thought" in the January 1985 newsletter:

> We are part of society, part of the world, w[h]ether we or society like it or not and we have to learn to live in the world and the world has to live with us and make use of us. Not as scapegoats, part of the world's collective unconscious it would rather not come to terms with, but as who we are. Just as in the long run it will have to do with all the other bits and pieces of humanity that go to make up the whole human picture. Society isn't a simple organism with one nucleus and a fringe of little feet, it is an infinitely complex living structure and if you try to suppress any part of it by that much, and perhaps more, you diminish, you mutilate the whole.[407]

When John Pritchett became Chairperson for the second time in October 1991, he quoted this passage again, noting that:

> as probably the largest gay social group in the country we now enjoy considerable recognition, not only in the gay community but with other organisations as well. We need not only to expand our contacts with other groups but also to build on our existing relationship with such people as the BCVS, St Marks, Citizens Advice Bureau, St Michaels, the local Health Authorities and others who support us and recognise us as part of society.[408]

Although in interview, John Pritchett disclaimed any knowledge of the concept of civil society, the strategy endorsed by these quotations was implicitly one of integrating Gay West into local civil society.

During the early 1980s, Gay West found that there were other ways of campaigning beyond the traditional letter-writing and demonstrations. In January 1985, as Chairperson, John Pritchett drew the following conclusion from his experiences while collecting jumble for the group's jumble sale: "On a personal note I was asked four times what the initials Bath G.C.O. stand for, and an honest answer proved that it was no deterrent to people either giving or buying jumble. Just another opportunity to be a little more visible in the community."[409] Later in the same year, John Pritchett wrote in the newsletter: "We are still fortunate in the support that we receive from the BCVS which enables us to continue the Saturday morning Coffee Shop, and now through the Aerobics we have been able to form a closer relationship with the people at the St. Marks Community Centre." The group had a stall at the Centre's recent Summer Fair "and this received the total support of other stall holders. Whilst we maintain our contact with other gay groups this contact with the BCVS and St. Marks helps our position in the community, and we should strive in the future to improve our relationship with non gay organisations."[410]

The group's relationship with the Bath Centre for Voluntary Service (BCVS) was one of the major factors in Gay West's success in the 1980s. The group made regular use of the BCVS building for meetings and events and this allowed it to maintain a stable public presence in the centre of Bath, in contrast with its predecessor, which only occasionally met in public buildings. The BCVS building in Abbey Green was an attractive old building in the very heart of the city, close to the major tourist attractions and the main shopping street, where the group held its weekly Saturday morning Coffee Shop and a number of other events. Although there were some physical constraints (a steep staircase to the first floor where the Coffee Shop was held and a large round table which had to be moved to one side and replaced each week), this building, belonging to the voluntary sector, had the major advantage of being free of any connections with the market (e.g. pubs), the state (council premises) or organised religion (church halls). The Saturday coffee shops were therefore able to create a temporarily free LGBT space. The building was easy to find and had no negative connotations to put off first-time visitors. The present location in St. Michael's Place also shares some of these advantages, although the obvious associations with the owners, Age Concern, may deter some younger LGBT people.

The connection with the BCVS came about by chance, when the group was still the Bath Gay Group. The group was written to by the Mayor of Bath's Charity through its P.O. Box number, offering its resources. This approach was probably the result of the higher profile which the group had achieved through the questionnaire it sent to all Bath candidates in the local elections in 1980 and 1981 and the articles about it in the *Bath Herald*. Roland Gonzalez Attwell thinks that the Charity was trying to be inclusive. The group was looking for somewhere to meet and so Roland took the letter into the BCVS and asked if they could hire a room.[411] The first event scheduled to use the BCVS building was the meeting with the Bath clergy on 28 January 1981.[412] The next use was the CHE South Wales and South West Groups Regional Meeting on 28 February 1981. The group used the BCVS building for occasional events and meetings but it was the weekly Saturday-morning Coffee Shop, which started in January 1983, that cemented the relationship.

Gay West used its connection with the BCVS to raise its profile in the local voluntary community and beyond. The group consciously set out to foster relations with the BCVS, as can be seen from this extract from the November 1984 newsletter:

> The Committee have decided that part of this year's profit from the Jumble Sale should be given to a local 'good cause', and we think that the best way to make use of the money will be to make a donation to the Bath Centre for Voluntary Services. These Centres throughout the country have passed a vote to support local Gay groups, and the Bath centre is a tremendous asset to this group. We use it not only for some of our Thursday meetings, but every Saturday of the year for the Coffee Shop which is now such an established and popular feature of Gay West. We are extremely lucky to have this facility in such a central spot, and due in no small part to the charm of our ex Chairperson [John Bescoby] we enjoy a very good working relationship with the people at Abbey Green.[413]

The group made a number of donations to the BCVS and got involved with the running of the organisation.[414] John Bescoby, who was again Gay West's chairman, was appointed to the BCVS executive committee in June 1987 and other members of the committee were elected or co-opted onto the BCVS's management and equal opportunities committees in subsequent years. In July 1988, Gay West had its own stall at the BCVS fair in Abbey Green and ran the coffee and refreshments in the building. John Bescoby "felt that it had been a good public relations exercise in making Bath more aware of our existence", adding waspishly that he "was disappointed that many of those who were most critical about G.W. failing to have any impact on public opinion had not turned up to help on the stall."[415]

The relationship with the BCVS was extremely important for Gay West but was not free of tensions. In summer 1988, following the group's participation in its fair, the BCVS told John Bescoby that the group could count on their support if it ran foul of Section 28. A few months later, however, the committee noticed that the BCVS made no mention of gays when it organised an exhibition about minorities in Bath. They complained and the BCVS then invited Gay West to produce a newsletter on gay issues. The Campaign Committee put together a substantial dossier covering discrimination, prejudice and equal opportunities, isolation and coming out, Section 28 and schools, health and HIV/AIDS, lesbians, the need for legislation against discrimination in employment and housing, gay bereavement and Gay West. Under pressure in their own organisation, the BCVS organisers objected to some points on the origins of homosexuality but after further negotiation the dossier was published in the BCVS newsletter for May 1989 with the sentence "Sexuality develops within people quite naturally and independently", which negated theories of corruption or perversion. This incurred an adverse reaction from just one BCVS councillor.[416] In June 1989, the committee was told that the BCVS were keen to have a Gay West representative on their management committee and a committee member was duly elected at the BCVS AGM in July 1989. A month later, however, the committee again noted that there was no mention of Gay West in the BCVS's list of forthcoming workshops and its insert in the local free advertiser. The BCVS bulletin also published a homophobic letter, to which the group responded. On the other hand, when in 1990 BCVS arranged a community development conference aimed at bringing together various organisations involved in community work, the social worker organising it told Gay West that they were very keen the group should be involved. Shortly afterwards, there appears to have been an article on the group in a voluntary action supplement of the *Bath Advertiser.*

Following John Bescoby's resignation as Chair and changes in the personnel at BCVS, links weakened during the early 1990s. The Coffee Shop had to vacate the building altogether for several weeks in 1992 because of building works and was then asked to move to a less convenient room on the lower floor in 1993. In the meantime it found a venue with better disabled access at St. Michael's and over a period of time moved to that location, vacating the BCVS building for the last time in August 1993. There were no takers in response to BCVS's invitation to nominate a Gay West member for their executive committee in May 1992. The BCVS subscription was allowed to lapse in 1993 and although it was renewed in 1994 because "BCVS has lots of useful facilities like photocopying, and anyway it would be politic to continue membership" it lapsed again in 1995. It was renewed on that occasion, in 1998 and in 2000, after it had again lapsed, but relations with the BCVS were never as strong again as they had been in the 1980s.

During the 1980s and 1990s, Gay West also had close links with St. Marks Community Centre which was located in a redundant church in Widcombe, just outside Bath city centre. The group used the building for a number of its events including jumble sales, parties and the weekly aerobics session which ran for several years during the 1980s. St. Marks was run by a committee formed of representatives from the groups which used it. John Bescoby was keen that Gay West should raise its profile by having a representative and served on the committee in 1985. The group made donations to St. Marks and made sure it paid its subscriptions so that it would appear among the list of affiliated organisations.[417] The group's treasurer, Steve Cossey, also served as St. Marks's treasurer for many years.

In October 1989, the campaign committee noted that the Equal Opportunities Policy of the Bath Housing Advice Centre made no mention of lesbians and gay men, despite the problems some LGBT people experienced in finding private rented accommodation, inheriting council tenancies and obtaining endowment mortgages. When the committee raised these matters with the manager of the Centre, he agreed to add "sexual orientation" to their policy and said that he was anxious that lesbians and gay men should not feel inhibited in seeking help from the Centre. Two members of the committee met with the manager in January 1990 and he agreed to clarify the position regarding joint council tenancies and the succession of tenancies with Bath City Council and to contact the group when the Housing Advice Centre raised wider lesbian and gay issues with the City Council.

Gay West also developed close relations with the Citizens Advice Bureau in the late 1980s. In summer 1990, a committee member went to the Bath CAB's AGM and was told that they wanted to develop closer contact with the group. The CAB dealt with a number of gay-related enquiries and suggested involving the group in its training days.

In this way the group developed its links with civil society, which in turn responded. For example, in April 1982 while still Bath CHE, the group decided to donate £75 from the profits of its spring sale of goods donated by shops in Bath to a local special needs school and the school wrote back a few months later listing the musical instruments it had purchased. In 1986, Gay West donated £25 to a local newspaper appeal for funds to buy a minibus for a special needs school and the committee was pleased to see that the group was included in the list of donors.

Relations with the Media

Thanks to the success of the Bath Gay Awareness Group campaigns, Gay West was able to use the local press to advertise for members but it was much more wary of the media. The 1980s saw the worst excesses of unscrupulous tabloid journalism and the group generally preferred to keep a low profile. Media treatment of gays tended to be dominated by wider news agendas like the AIDS panic, murders of gay men and child pornography. In 1984 and again in 1989, Gay West continued a practice begun by Bath CHE by placing an advert in the Bath and Bristol papers around Remembrance Day, which read: "In memory of the tens of thousands of men and women who wore the badge of homosexuality in the gas chambers and concentration camps, who have no children to remember then [sic] and whom our history books forget."[418] Members of the group gave interviews on important issues such as AIDS but generally did not court publicity.[419] Consequently, when the committee heard in June 1994 that the Chair, Sid Roberts, had done an interview with the *Bath Chronicle* about lesbian and gay themes in soaps "to everyone's delighted astonishment, they published a positive article".[420]

Gay West also had little contact with the electronic media but in August 1988, two members of the group appeared on an HTV "The West This Week" programme about the backlash caused by Section 28. During 1994, the committee put a lot of work into preparing a public information broadcast to go out on HTV's Helpline programme. In the event, the company insisted that it should be broadcast after the 9 pm watershed and the two airings late at night in October or early November 1994 resulted in very few calls. The committee thought the restrictions excessive given the number of lesbian and gay issues appearing in popular prime-time programmes by that time. By 2001, however, a number of television producers were contacting the group to see if it could provide members to attend programmes on topics such as bisexuality. The short notice made this impractical for people who were working. In the early 2000s, Gay West set up its own website, which went live in 2002, giving the group a presence on the internet (www.gaywest.org.uk).

Gay West continued the tradition of trying to ensure that information was freely available for LGBT people locally, which had been established by the Bath group's campaign to get the public libraries to take *Gay News*. In 1991, the group contacted the Bath branch of Waterstone's bookshop and asked them to reinstate the display of GMP [Gay Men's Press] books, which the shop agreed to. During 1995–96, it conducted a lengthy correspondence with the firm, pressing them again to reinstate their separate LGBT book display in the Bath branch.[421] This was ultimately successful, although the display was soon abandoned again.[422]

Outreach

While Gay West took a cautious position in its relationship with the media, it tried to continue the outreach work begun by its predecessors, when members went to speak directly to outside organisations about homosexuality. This proved particularly contentious when the groups offered to talk to local schools. Both CHE Bristol and Bath Gay Awareness Group incorporated the CHE demand for better sex education in their constitutions and the same principle was implicit in Gay West's constitutional aim of providing help and support for gay people with problems and working towards obtaining equal treatment of gay people by the local community. In the 1970s, there was some receptiveness on the part of schools but as the issue of paedophilia was dramatised in the early 1980s through the PIE trials, this question became increasingly sensitive. When Bath CHE wrote to local headmasters offering to show the CHE tape/slide kit to sixth-formers, there was initially no response.[423] In 1983, however, two members of Gay West visited Ralph Allen School and showed the tape/slide show to a mixed audience of sixty staff and students. In December 1984, a team of three presented the show to a mixed audience of 50–60 sixth-formers at a comprehensive school near Bath. A question and answer session followed and one or two of the audience seemed rather anti-gay but everyone stayed for some minutes after the bell rang. "Quite a few of the audience were silent and it must be hoped that our message has not fallen on stony ground."[424] Gay West continued to do occasional outreach work as opportunities arose; for example, members of the group talked at Filton College, Bristol, in spring 1991 and again in November 1991.

7

AIDS, the Aled Richards Trust and Section 28

The two major events of the 1980s were the AIDS crisis and the campaign against Section 28. Both had repercussions for Gay West, directly in the short term and indirectly in the longer term. This section looks at how the group reacted to these two crises, which showed the limits of the civil society model.

HIV/AIDS

For gay men, the 1980s were dominated by AIDS. By chance, the formation of Gay West coincided with the start of the epidemic. The unexplained death of gay men in the United States was first reported in *Gay News* in November 1981.[425] The period between 1981 and 1985 has been characterised by the historian of AIDS in the UK as one of "policy from below", in which the initial response was one of self-help by AIDS missionaries.[426] These comprised gay men, who founded voluntary organisations such as the Terrence Higgins Trust and Body Positive, as well as clinicians and scientists who had early contact with the syndrome. It was only in 1985 that AIDS really began to impinge on the general public's consciousness and a mood of hysteria was whipped up by reports of a "gay plague" in the tabloid press. During 1986–87, the government developed a wartime response, driven by the fear that AIDS would spread into the general population. This fear receded after the May 1987 General Election and AIDS became more normalised as a chronic infection, with government policy focussed on health education and prevention work. Funds were ring-fenced and during the late 1980s and 1990s considerable sums were devoted to prevention work, some of which were channelled to organisations like the Terrence Higgins Trust, whose primary concern was with the needs of gay men. The AIDS crisis stimulated a new wave of gay activism, both in service provision to people with AIDS and in policy areas connected with the official response to the epidemic, such as the provision of health services, discrimination, testing for HIV, HIV/AIDS awareness and prevention work and the role of the pharmaceutical industry.[427]

Although much of this activity was concentrated in London, AIDS also had repercussions in the provinces. Bath was featured in the early publicity thanks to the courage of Bill Ayres, owner of the Underground club, who appeared in the national media while already suffering the effects of AIDS in order to warn people of the dangers posed by the disease. He died at the end of January 1986 aged 38.[428] Although not a member of Gay West, he had allowed it to use his club.[429] In 1985, four local men were reported to be suffering from the disease.[430] By June 1989, there were 154 people in Avon who had been given an HIV-positive test result. 15 of these had already died and 11 were living with AIDS. They comprised 25 gay/bisexual men and one woman with an unknown risk factor, ranging in age from 59 to 21, with a median age of 28/30.[431]

The first mention of AIDS in Gay West documentation occurs in the minutes of the General Meeting held in January 1983, recording that Bristol had one case.[432] From then on the group started to warn its members of the dangers posed by the virus and to support HIV/AIDS prevention work. This was largely due to the chairman for most of the period between 1983 and 1988, John Bescoby, who regularly visited the United States and had many friends in the gay community there. He witnessed at first hand the ravages of AIDS and described what was happening in the U.S. in letters which were published in the Diary, beginning with one entitled "The A.I.D.S. crisis in America", published in July 1983, and followed by others in the subsequent years.[433] Thereafter the newsletter published a number of articles on the subject, particularly when the first local cases resulted in an increase in media attention in 1985–86.[434]

The grief, anxiety and distress caused by AIDS were compounded in the early days by the homophobic treatment in much of the national press, particularly the tabloid newspapers. The local press also focussed on the subject, reporting in January 1985 that three Bath men and one Bristol man were being treated for the disease.[435] Members of Gay West immediately tried to combat the negative aspects of this publicity in a newspaper interview.[436] This was only partially successful, as a week later the *Bath Chronicle* published a serious balanced article on AIDS but headlined it: "It's gay plague! Story of a new terror".[437] Five days later, however, it published another article headlined simply "AIDS: official advice".[438] In March 1985, the Gay West newsletter advised members on how to react to the press hysteria about AIDS, concluding: "We have to treat this very seriously, not only form [sic] the health angle, but from the damaging effect that the ignorance and prejudice about AIDS may have on gay people in general." The same article also reported that the group had been approached by the District Medical Officer in Bath and two members of the committee had met with doctors at Bath's Royal United Hospital in February 1985.[439]

Local gay activists became increasingly alarmed that the sensationalist media reporting would provoke a backlash against gay people and decided to convene a group to combat this threat. The Gay Men's Health Network in Avon was set up at a meeting held on 20 February 1985, attended by representatives of Gay West, Labour Campaign for Lesbian and Gay Rights, Bristol University Gay Society, Bristol Gay Switchboard and others. The leading organiser was Charlie Beaton and, as well as the Gay West representatives, the group included several other former activists from CHE Bristol and Bath Gay Awareness Group, who had chosen not to join Gay West. The aims of the network were to provide information for gay men, offer support to AIDS sufferers, counter the homophobic hysteria in the press, keep the professional workers fully aware of gay needs and coordinate efforts using as far as possible the existing organisations.[440]

The group continued to meet monthly throughout 1985.[441] While concerned to sort out its line before speaking to the media, it began issuing press releases and publicised a meeting at the University Gaysoc with a speaker from the Terrence Higgins Trust, which was already planned for 22 March, to raise awareness of the dangers represented by AIDS and to discuss what action should be taken.[442] This meeting was restricted to gay men and lesbians and 65 were present.[443] The Network initially concentrated on making available factual information on AIDS and providing assistance to people with AIDS. It began to establish contact with professionals, attend seminars and consider the production of leaflets. Bristol Gay Switchboard acted as the main telephone contact and Gay West allowed its post box to be used, provided there was no mention of AIDS – an indication of the tense atmosphere of the times.[444] The gay men who started the group thought they were on their own but to their surprise, they found that other people shared their concerns. The group was soon joined by two women who were keen to help combat AIDS and had a galvanising effect on the original founders, making them realise that they should seek potential support from outside the gay ghetto and target their work towards everyone with HIV/AIDS.[445] The group started to give serious attention to fund-raising and in June 1985, it decided to establish a Trust for this purpose.[446] The Aled Richards Trust (ART), named after one of the first gay men to die of AIDS in the West of England, was formally launched at the Oasis Club on 5 November 1985.[447] The objects of the Trust agreed at the launch meeting were to promote the welfare of people suffering from AIDS; to alleviate physical, mental or financial deprivation; to sponsor, encourage and assist research; and to advance the education of the public, the medical and nursing professions, national and local public authorities, sufferers and their partners, dependents and relatives.[448]

The Trust's initial application to the Bristol & Weston Health Authority for a grant was rejected on the grounds that all funds had already been allocated but an application to the Department of Health and Social Security (DHSS) in early 1986 under the "Opportunities for Volunteering" scheme was more successful. This coincided with the "wartime response" period at national level. In February 1986, the Chief Medical Adviser of the South Western Regional Health Authority, prompted by an enquiry from the DHSS in London, phoned Bristol Gay Switchboard and then wrote to Charlie Beaton, asking to be informed when the Trust's planned telephone information service was established. He added that he was aware of much anxiety and concern by members of the public and thought that the development of a neutral but informative telephone service could do an enormous amount to assist in resolving unfounded fears.[449] The Chief Medical Adviser put Charlie Beaton in touch with the Health Authority's press officer who helped him with the press conference to launch the telephone service, which initially operated for two hours one night a week.[450]

The Trust had originally estimated the annual cost of providing a telephone service at £998 but the sums needed to respond to the AIDS crisis soon far surpassed this amount.[451] In 1986, the Trust was awarded a DHSS grant of £13,000 pa for three years, which allowed it to take on its first paid employee in order to recruit, train and administer the volunteers on which it depended.[452] In January 1987, it was awarded an annual grant of £40,000 for three years by the local District Health Authorities.[453] In April 1988, the Aled Richards Trust set up a Bath section, which was funded by a three year annual grant of £10,000 from Bath District Health Authority.[454] By June 1989, the Trust had 6 paid workers and 87 active volunteers, with 22 waiting for the next induction programme.[455] In November 1989, the Trust was awarded a grant of £45,000 pa for three years under the Department of Health's Section 64 Funding, which, with additional funding from other sources, allowed it to employ more paid workers, move to larger premises and expand its services.[456] By 1998–99, the Trust's income was £327,000, of which 76% came from statutory sources.[457]

Such levels of funding, ability to employ paid workers and access to senior public officials were unprecedented for local gay groups. In the context of a major public health crisis, the state turned to representatives of the voluntary sector who had the necessary knowledge and access to the people affected and had already shown themselves capable of organising an effective response. This allowed the Aled Richards Trust to provide a level of service which would have been impossible if it had had to rely on purely voluntary donations. At the same time, as the Trust organisers recognised when deciding to apply for a grant, statutory funding had major implications in terms of employing staff and acquiring premises. This was part of the general trend towards the professionalisation of social movements which occurred during the 1980s and 1990s.[458] Furthermore, AIDS did not just affect gay men. An early sign of this was the recognition that heterosexuals would not be comfortable with contacting Gay Switchboard, leading to the decision to set up its own phone-line.[459] As the Trust developed, it set up services for drug-users and later people from Africa, as well as special services targetted at out-gay men and the men who have sex with men in cottages and cruising grounds but do not identify as gay. Consequently, although LGBT activists had provided the initial stimulus for the foundation of the Trust and played a major role in its subsequent development, the Aled Richards Trust was not an exclusively gay organisation.

In the mid-1980s, activists nationally sought to counter the media hysteria about AIDS as a "gay plague" by stressing that it could affect heterosexuals as well but this had the result that much of the publicity failed to address the concerns and sexual practices of gay men. In the early 1990s, a process of "re-gaying" HIV/AIDS was started to ensure that safer sex information reached gay men, through voluntary organisations such as Gay Men Fighting Aids (GMFA) and statutory-funded gay men's projects set up across the country.[460] The ART set up a Gay Mens Health Forum, which held its first meeting in March 1992 with the aim of giving all members of the gay community an opportunity to air their views on the issues for gay men around HIV/AIDS.[461] At the same time, the Trust was commissioned by the three Bristol health districts to employ two outreach workers to work with men who had sex with men.[462] The Trust's Gay Men's Project started in 1992, covering Bristol and then extended its remit to cover Bath and West Wiltshire.[463] Bath and West Wiltshire NHS Trust set up its own Gay Mens Health Project and employed an outreach worker from early 1996 until February 1998, when responsibility was taken over by the ART's Gay Mens Project.[464] The Trust's Bath office received few calls and was closed in 2004.[465]

The ART's Gay Men's Project worked in partnership with the Community HIV AIDS Prevention Strategy (CHAPS), which was coordinated from London by the Terrence Higgins Trust. It ran the Outreach Crew of volunteers, who took the safer sex message to commercial venues, and Cruz, which did similar work at the outdoor cruising sites.[466] As well as the straightforward distribution of information and condoms, the project also carried out more long-range community development work, supporting groups such as Freedom Youth, Bristol Families & Friends Group, the Bristol Lesbian Gay & Bisexual Forum, and the Avon & Somerset Lesbian & Gay Policing Initiative, as well as producing information resources for men with learning difficulties and a lesbian and gay guide to the Bristol area (See Chapters 8 and 9 for more details).[467] Around 2000 the Project changed its name to Gay Men's Team. The Aled Richards Trust merged with the Terrence Higgins Trust in April 2000 and became THT West.

Like the rest of the gay scene, the Aled Richards Trust/THT West moved around Bristol as it grew bigger, starting with 1 Mark Lane and then moving in early summer 1989 to 54 Colston Street, both near the Centre, before taking over its present premises in 8–10 West Street in March 1992.[468] It was the first LGBT organisation to move into the Old Market/West Street area.[469]

Representatives of Gay West attended the early meetings of the Gay Men's Health Network in Avon. Gay West's chairperson, John Bescoby, was keen that Gay West should be represented on the Aled Richards Trust committee and Gay West committee members intermittently attended meetings of the Trust, such as the first AIDS Forum in January 1987, but dropped out of the organising committee.[470] Members of Gay West were involved in setting up and running the Bath section of the ART, which started a helpline based in Hetling Court in March 1989.[471] The resources needed to respond to a crisis on the scale of AIDS were effectively, however, beyond the scope of a purely voluntary group. The Gay West committee recognised this in March 1987, when it discussed a suggestion to start a group to provide help and support in dealing with the problems of Aids. It decided that it would be better to leave this to the trained volunteers of the Aled Richards Trust.

Nevertheless, Gay West supported the Trust by affiliating, making donations, encouraging its members to become supporting members and publicising the Trust's activities in the newsletter. In late 1989, it arranged a donation and collection for flowers for AIDS patients in the Bristol isolation hospital. The group also made donations to the Terrence Higgins Trust in London. Gay West took vigorous measures to raise the awareness of its own members about the risks of HIV/AIDS, including publishing frequent articles in the newsletter and selling condoms at the Coffee Shop. A former chairman of the group told how he had decided to take the HIV test and in June 1986, the newsletter reprinted a leaflet on safer sex produced by Scottish AIDS Monitor. A safer sex leaflet produced by Leeds Aids Advice was sent to all male members in 1988. In 1992, the group obtained some of the Terrence Higgins Trust's "Hot sex now" leaflets but had to distribute them at the Coffee Shop for fear of prosecution if they sent them through the post, a reflection of the continued political controversy caused by AIDS. Two ART workers regularly visited the Gay West Coffee Shop in Bath to give advice and distribute free condoms between September 1993 and May 1995, when the Area Health funding ended. Between October 2000 and October 2002, Gay West and the Terrence Higgins Trust West jointly ran a coffee shop in Weston-super-Mare and the group encouraged members to participate in the national Gay Men's Survey in 2001 and 2003.

As the care of people with AIDS and HIV/AIDS prevention work was taken over by specialised government-funded organisations, Gay West became essentially an interested bystander, concentrating on providing moral support and donations and on raising awareness. At least one member died of AIDS-related illness (ARC) and there may have been others but the group was not decimated in the way that some gay social circles were.[472]

Gay West and Section 28

As the Conservative government of Margaret Thatcher consolidated its hold on power during the 1980s and made clear that it had no interest in furthering gay rights, LGBT activists began to concentrate on working at the local level and developing links with the New Urban Left.[473] The initiatives which resulted from this marked the beginning of governmental efforts to provide services aimed at lesbian and gay citizens. In the short term, however, they were seized upon by the right-wing press and used to whip up a mood of anti-gay hysteria, most famously around the children's book *Jenny Lives with Eric and Martin* and the "Positive Images" project in the London Borough of Haringey. Following the third Conservative victory in the 1987 General Election, Conservative backbenchers introduced a last-minute amendment at the Committee stage of the Local Government Bill on 8 December 1987, which would forbid local authorities to "promote homosexuality or publish material for the promotion of homosexuality; .. promote the teaching in any maintained school of the acceptability of homosexuality as a pretended family relationship by the publication of such material or otherwise".[474] This clause, which affected both gay men and lesbians, provoked a howl of rage in the LGBT community and led to the launching of the anti-Section 28 campaign.[475]

Activists in Bristol, as elsewhere, reacted with anger to the proposed measure. A Bristol Arts Lobby and a Bristol Fight the Clause Campaign were set up, the latter holding campaign meetings in the Griffin pub. Gays and lesbians took part in the national campaign of protest, writing to and lobbying their MPS, and many went to the demonstrations in London on 9 January and Manchester on 20 February.[476] A crowded meeting at the

Watershed on 10 March discussed ways of fighting the clause and two days of local action were organised for 8–9 April. Activists put up banners on bridges over the roads leading into the city and protested when council workmen removed them. Other activists attracted public attention to their protest by jumping out of a pink closet set up in the main shopping area.[477] The Aled Richards Trust inadvertently contributed to the furore which led to Section 28 when one of its members gave a talk on AIDS to St. Brendan's Sixth-form College, a Catholic school, and left some explicit leaflets, which were intended for gay men. A shocked parent showed them to the Tory MP David Wilshire, a former leader of Wansdyke district council and one of the main proponents of the clause, who raised the issue in the Commons and told the press that the leaflet was "absolutely appalling".[478]

Section 28 caused a major crisis within Gay West and revealed divisions along both political and generational lines. The initial response of the Committee was decidedly muted. The clause does not seem to have been mentioned at all at the committee meeting on 13 December, five days after the clause was introduced but before its implications were widely appreciated. The Committee first discussed the issue at its meeting on 24 January 1988, when the Campaign Secretary said that it was important to revive the campaigning side of Gay West and urged it to get involved with an OLGA campaigning group being set up in Bristol. The meeting concluded that: "It was agreed that although Gay West was primarily a social group we needed to protect our interests and those of our members and that provision existed in the constitution for a campaigning section of the group under the Avon CHE name."[479] At subsequent meetings, the committee received further reports on the campaign and agreed to circulate information and to affiliate to the Stop the Clause Campaign in London.

Because of the extended deadlines and habitual double-issue for December/January, the earliest mention in the newsletter of the campaign to stop the clause came in the February 1988 issue. This contained two articles, one by the Campaign Secretary giving details of the national campaign against the clause and a lengthy description by the Editor, Andy Foyle, of the demonstration in London on 9 January 1988. The Diary of Events listed a Stop the Clause meeting at the Arnolfini/Watershed in Bristol on 1 February, observing: "This is not a Gay West organised event but one that we ought to support" and a Gay West campaign meeting on 9 February. The write-up for the latter stated: "Gay West is primarily a social group but in view of the importance of defending our rights and freedoms in view of recent legislation etc (eg Clause 27.) this meeting has been arranged in order for all GayWest members to get together to formulate a srategy [sic] to defend these rights before its too late!"[480] In the following issue for March

1988 a 2½ page report on the campaign meeting held on 9 February gave a list of actions decided on to oppose the measure, including organising a list and a telephone network of members who wanted to be kept informed about local demonstrations and meetings; the article gave a list of local MPs to write to and local radio and TV stations to phone, as well as urging members to join the local branch of OLGA and the Bristol Arts Lobby.[481] The rest of the issue was devoted to the usual social events. The April issue gave details of the protest march in Manchester on 20 February and the Stop the Clause March in London due to take place on 30 April as well as two local days of action in Bristol planned for 8–9 April.

Activists in the group clearly sensed the energising sense of anger raised by the clause, noting: "A bit of oppression seems to have worked wonders in some ways. Many people have come out and come together: the lesbian and gay community seems to be alive in a way it has not been for a decade; it is as though people feel, 'If not now, under these pressures, then when?'"[482] Nevertheless, some felt that the group was not doing enough to support the campaign. They noted that they had seen very few Gay West members on the demonstrations and felt that, under the terms of the group's constitution, it should have been organising coaches to take people to the demonstrations and educating its membership about political events which affect lesbians and gays.[483]

Reflecting at the end of the campaign on what had happened, some activists thought that the committee had been too complacent and had not done enough to protest about the clause. The newsletter editor, Andy Foyle, in particular, felt so strongly that he included a strongly worded letter of condemnation and three blank pages in the May 1988 issue as a sign of protest. The rest of the committee objected, arguing that he did not have the right to use the diary in this way and after discussion he agreed to retrieve the proofs from the printers and make extensive amendments. The May issue appeared with a rather rough appearance and an open personal letter from Andy Foyle addressed to the committee and membership which stated:

> Over the seemingly eternal issue of Clause 28, the group has taken very little concerted action. The campaign group has made attempts to ensure that the membership is aware of what is happening and what it may mean, but I believe there has been little will on the part of the committee to see that these attempts are effective. Much could have been done – letters to MP's and others in places of influence, more active involvement in local groups which have formed to fight the Bill and to monitor its effects; events could have been held to raise funds in support of the national Stop the Clause group, contacts made with local council

and union officials, maybe even hosting public meetings in Bristol and Bath. [...] Sadly for many, there seems to be an unwillingness to face the political issues before us. [...] The most important and far reaching reform in the law for twenty years has passed us by. May we hope that we can at least learn some useful lesson from the past months; being just 'a social group' is no longer enough.[484]

This sparked off a lively correspondence from members which continued through the next five issues. One member thought that being just a social group was enough: "I do not wish to belong to a politically motivated group who (sic) by its very nature would be seen to support the left wing gay rights lobby whose extreme actions only strengthen prejudice against the gay community."[485] Another letter praised the editor for his courageous stand. A correspondent in the following issue claimed that "the recent influx into Gay West of younger and more politically aware lesbians and gays has shifted the group's centre of gravity away from the 'tea and scones' tendency" and while he appreciated that "many self-confessed Tories are doing valuable outreach work", he thought that "the committee should assist rather than obstruct those who want to do more politically."[486]

The debate reflected political differences within the group. Some of the key members of the committee were in other respects sympathetic to the policies of the Conservative government. One committee member was noted for his personal devotion to Mrs Thatcher. The chairman, John Bescoby, who worked hard at developing the group's links with other LGBT and voluntary sector organisations, had no liking for left-wing politics. Commenting on the motions passed at a meeting of the Legislation for Lesbian and Gay Rights Campaign in summer 1987, he told the Committee that he "was sorry to see that most of the motions were overtly party political which was not what we had hoped the Campaign would be" and at the AGM in September 1987, he

commented that there were a wide range of opinions amongst the 249 members but that the group had remained free of party political manoeuvrings and united in our main concern to promote the interests of gay men and women. John referred to the conflicting pressures of those who favoured more involvement in gay politics and those who saw the group as primarily social.[487]

John Bescoby was abroad for much of the time that Section 28 was under discussion in Parliament but his views were influential. Another committee member was Bob Osborne who had the previous year had to fight a battle to retain his job as the Conservative local agent and who, although committed to gay rights, objected to local government involvement in LGBT activities on philosophical grounds.[488] There was also a generational difference, with older members taking a more cautious stance while younger ones, for whom this was a catalytic experience, wanted more active campaigning. There were, however, exceptions on both sides.

Thus, personal and political leanings and an awareness of the long tension between campaigning and social activities in the group's past, inclined the majority of the Committee to caution. They seem, however, to have underestimated the sheer amount of anger amongst lesbians and gay men generated by the government's attempt to turn the clock back on gay rights. Given the urgency due to the parliamentary timetable, the opposition to Section 28 was necessarily confrontational and based on street demonstrations, dramatic protests and left-wing discourse.

The Committee did not make an official response to the criticism. The committee minutes noted that members had been informed of meetings arranged by the Stop the Clause group and that Gay West had paid for advertising for their meeting but accepted that Gay West had not organised a meeting itself.[489] In the aftermath of the row over the Section 28 campaign, two members of the committee set out their different viewpoints in the newsletter. John Pritchett, himself an experienced campaigner, wrote: "I believe quite firmly that Gay West must remain as a social group, otherwise we shall cease to exist as we watch our membership slowly drift away. Campaigning does not have to be all marching and flag waving, and the very existence of Gay West within the local community, and our activities and the contacts that we build up within that community are all campaigning in the widest sense of the word."[490] The Editor, Andy Foyle, accepted that not everyone had to be involved in campaigning and to speak out:

> But surely, the advantage of being part of a group is that the group has power to speak out where the individual voice would be lost. So whilst I don't argue that a 'public stance' is an integral part of being gay, I do believe that it is OTHERS who make a public issue of our sexuality when they legislate against us, and it is for that reason that we ought to use the power of a group to act where an individual cannot be effective.[491]

Andy Foyle based his criticism of the committee's inaction on the argument that the group's constitution placed a duty on those who ran it to provide educational material for the benefit of the gay community and to work locally to promote the principle of absolute equality before the law for homosexuals.[492] He also argued that this constitutional provision needed strengthening and the Committee agreed to make the necessary revisions. The outcome of this debate was a number of amendments to the Constitution passed at the AGM in September 1988 which led to the setting up of a strengthened Gay West Campaign Committee. The debate shows how, in sometimes unexpected ways, Section 28 united the LGBT movement and re-energised political activism.

Soon after the AGM, an issue arose when the headmaster of a local secondary school in Keynsham banned the performance of a play by the Avon Touring Theatre Company on the grounds that the portrayal of a gay character might infringe Section 28. The Campaign Secretary was keen to turn this into the first test case in the country but the NCCL declined to take it up on the grounds that it would not set a reliable precedent. [493] The affair nevertheless made headlines in the local and theatrical press.[494] Bristol West Labour Party wrote to the press condemning Section 28, while it soon emerged that a youth group near Bath, consisting of 12 to 18 year olds, had seen the play and made no adverse comments.[495] The club leader remarked: "It never entered our heads that there would be a problem."

By the middle of 1989 it was becoming evident that Section 28 had backfired on the government. The Diary Editor, Bob Osborne, commented under the heading "Whatever happened to Section 28?" that the legislation seemed to have made little difference. "Does this mean the Government has made a complete fool of itself by introducing a [sic] unworkable and unnecessary piece of legislation?" It was difficult to see whether a slow trend was building up in interpreting the law but:

> What I do believe is that Section 28 has done something the Government never even thought of; it created an issue which virtually every gay person could, or should, have united in opposition to. CHE and OLGA stopped discussing whether to merge and started organising against the Clause [...] Stop the Clause groups sprang up around the country, never have I seen so many people in Bath and Bristol at a pro-gay meeting as I saw at the Arnolfini last February. Gay West Campaign Committee, having been in a deep coma for some considerable time, suddenly sprang into life and started doing things.[496]

The Campaign Committee held its inaugural meeting in December 1988, attracting 16 people, more than expected. Announcing the meeting in the newsletter, the new Campaign Secretary, Diesel Balaam, wrote:

Gay West is, and will continue to be, primarily a social group. But there is now a general recognition of the fact that the collective situation of gay women and men has changed markedly over the last few years, and that we need an efficient well-coordinated group of volunteers prepared to take up and respond quickly to local and national issues as they arise. To those who are still opposed to the idea of campaigning I should like to say two things. 1) The limited freedoms we enjoy in this country – including the right to belong to Gay West – were won by men and women who were prepared to fight for their freedoms. Most gay people in the world have no freedom at all, so we owe it to them, as well as to ourselves, to make sure that our [sic] are not taken away. 2) A recent survey of social attitudes showed that we are facing a high tide of homophobia [...]. If we don't look after each other no-one else will.[497]

The Campaign Committee set to work on a variety of local and national issues, including writing to local council candidates, questioning the equal opportunities policy of Bath Housing Advice Centre, with the result that they were amended to include LGBT people, and lobbying the Press Council to include lesbian and gay issues in its code of conduct. Members of the Campaign Committee held a number of meetings with Chris Patten, the M.P. for Bath, on the subjects of police entrapment, the age of consent and the continued illegality of homosexuality in the Isle of Man. Prior to the 1992 General Election, the newsletter published an article by Diesel Balaam, discussing in a critical but balanced way the attitudes of the main parties towards issues of concern to lesbians and gays and assessing what they might do if they came to power.[498]

After a fourth Conservative victory in 1992, however, a feeling that nothing was going to change set in and energy began to dissipate. Meetings of the Campaign Committee were suspended until September. A new Campaign Co-ordinator continued writing to and lobbying local MPs on the age of consent but resigned in November 1992, complaining that campaign issues had not been printed in the newsletter. The national campaign to reduce the age of consent, which culminated in a parliamentary vote in February 1994, reinvigorated local activists. Berkeley became Campaign Coordinator in September 1993 and breathed new life into campaigning (see Chapters 8 and 9). Manuel Gosano, a Gay West member and coordinator of Bristol Switchboard, who had been writing to his local MP, William Waldegrave, then a cabinet minister, for years, went to see him at his surgery about the age of consent in January 1994. Waldegrave said that he planned to vote for a compromise age of 18, so Manuel pointed out some drawbacks such as the lack of access to important information like safer sex, the possibility that police would start prosecuting men under 18 and the long-term psychological damage to young men who are considered inferior to their peers.[499] When it came to the vote, Waldegrave opted for 16, attributing his change of mind to the powerful speeches of some of his colleagues. He said that apart from the philosophical question of whether the law ought to interfere in private behaviour, he asked himself whether, if he found his sixteen-year-old son in bed with another man, he would call the police. His reply was that of course he would not.[500]

The June 1994 newsletter, prepared after John Smith's death and before his successor was decided, printed extracts from Tony Blair's speech in Parliament supporting an equal age of consent and condemning discrimination, commenting: "Perhaps a 'friend in the camp' if not a 'camp friend', but certainly an ally, not afraid to speak his mind, with a knowledgeable and informed opinion – maybe common-sense and common equality may yet be given birth by the labour party – only time will tell!!"[501] In 1997, as a new era opened with the victory of New Labour, the editor commented:

> Attitudes towards gay people are changing, this is well demonstrated with the election of three out gay MPs in the recent general election and the appointment of an out gay minister of state. This is a positive move towards wider public acceptance and equality. However, attitudes within the gay community must also change. So many gay men and women play the victim, often imagining prejudice where none exists hiding in their closets with the doors firmly bolted. I'm not saying that gay people do not face prejudice but there is a danger that this card can be over-played. We should build on the positive not dwell on the negative.[502]

8

Gay West and Bristol in the 1990s/2000s

The massive changes at the international and national level during the 1980s were reflected in local developments in the 1990s. The social conservatism which had been allied with economic liberalism under Margaret Thatcher gradually gave way to a more liberal attitude towards sexual matters, propelled by the tide of consumerism which had been unleashed by neo-liberalism. Shopping, long considered a gay speciality for those who could afford it, became the new religion. Westminster eventually followed where the High Street led. As these changes were consolidated during the 1990s, two technological innovations, the internet and mobile phones, had a major impact on LGBT life, offering access to information and personal contacts on a hitherto unprecedented scale.

The LGBT movement also took on a new lease of life at national level. As a result of the defeat over Section 28, many activists saw the need for a professional lobbying organisation, which would be able to exercise influence amongst MPs and government ministers in the corridors of power. Stonewall was organised in early 1989 by, among others, actors Ian McKellen and Michael Cashman, who had led the Arts opposition to Section 28.[503] It was a professional lobby group run by a management committee which aimed to press for lesbian and gay rights by working closely with parliamentarians and other decision-makers. As well as legal equality, it has also aimed to combat other forms of discrimination, particularly in employment and education. Despite its American-inspired name, it was in many ways the successor to the Homosexual Law Reform Society of the 1960s.

Outrage! was set up in London in May 1990 following a spate of unsolved murders of gay men and adopted many of the radical tactics of GLF and the more recent American ACT-UP group, such as marches, demos and zaps.[504] In part, it was a reaction by queer activists to the perceived lack of democratic accountability of Stonewall and it used media-savvy tactics of non-violent direct action to protest against the widespread continuing homophobia in the police, churches, Parliament and the media. Its most high profile member was Peter Tatchell. Despite friction between the two groups, together they succeeded in placing LGBT issues on the national political agenda, concentrating initially on the question of a lower and equal age of consent.

These new organisations encountered an atmosphere in which both official thinking and public opinion were beginning to change. The public health crisis provoked by AIDS brought AIDS activists into regular contact with public officials and the resulting HIV/AIDS prevention awareness campaigns led to a public discussion of same-sex sexual practices which would have been unimaginable a few years earlier. From the late 1980s onwards, public opinion became noticeably more tolerant of homosexuality.[505] Chris Smith came out as the first openly-gay MP at a demonstration in Rugby in 1984 and held his seat in subsequent general elections. Union activists secured a greater trade union commitment to combat discrimination, particularly as a result of lesbian and gay support for the miners during the bitter strike of 1984–85, and the Labour Campaign for Lesbian and Gay Rights began to mobilise opinion in Labour constituency parties, leading to the passing of motions supporting equal rights for lesbians and gay men at the 1985 Trades Union Congress and Labour Party conferences. At the 1986 Labour Party conference, a wide-ranging gay rights motion was passed with a 79% majority, which was enough to ensure the inclusion of a commitment that lesbians and gay men would not be discriminated against in the party's 1987 election manifesto. The parliamentary Labour Party took longer to convince and initially were disinclined to oppose Section 28 for fear of being identified with the "loony left". The wave of protest against Section 28 led to a change of heart and the parliamentary leadership then came out against the measure. It also cautiously became more supportive of lesbian and gay rights in general, although always with a keen awareness of the electoral consequences.[506]

The Conservative government of John Major also signalled a greater receptiveness to LGBT issues by allowing a free vote on reducing the age of consent. Following a passionate campaign and debate, the decision of Parliament to reduce the age to 18 rather than legislate full equality at 16, was regarded as a defeat by activists. Nevertheless, this marked the first significant change to the 1967 Act.[507] During this debate, Tony Blair made an impassioned speech in favour of lesbian and gay equality, which foreshadowed the far-reaching reforms carried out by the New Labour government elected in May 1997. Despite a bitter rearguard action by opponents in the House of Lords, the government succeeded in passing a series of measures which included an equal age of consent at 16 (2000), the lifting of the ban on lesbians and gays in the Armed Forces (2000), the right to adopt children (2002), the ban on homophobic discrimination in the workplace (2003), the final repeal of Section 28 (2003), the introduction of civil partnerships (2005), the outlawing of discrimination in the provision of goods and services (2006), making homophobia a hate crime (2008) and the recognition of lesbian fertility rights (2008).[508]

These changes at the national level were accompanied and often preceded by changes at the local level. This chapter looks at the changes in the local environment and the effect which these have had on Gay West since 1990.

Bristol in the 1990s: New Opportunities

The history of Gay West since 1990 can best be understood in the context of developments in Bristol, which themselves reflected the wider global and national changes. Two major developments occurred, one affecting the commercial scene and the other the voluntary movement, starting in the late 1980s and gathering pace in the 1990s.[509]

The commercial scene had remained largely unchanged since the early 1970s but in mid-1987, the Griffin opened at 41 Colston Street. This was the first of a more modern, openly-gay style of pub and was followed in summer 1992 by the Queen's Shilling (later Queenshilling or Q/-) at 9 Frogmore St. and in spring 1997 by the Pineapple at 37 St. George's Rd. The club scene also expanded, with new clubs such as Just and a succession of other venues which opened, flourished for a while and then closed again. There was also an increasing number of clubs, particularly for women, which functioned once a week or once a month, such as Hint of Pink and Lick at Lakota. The pubs and clubs which had dominated the scene since the 1970s gradually disappeared, with the Oasis and Michael's Restaurant closing down around 1993/94 and Club 49 around 1996/97, while the Elephant managed to make it into the 2000s before closing. Just Club opened at the end of 1994 and was intended to fill the gap in the market left by the closure of the Oasis. Located at 1 Fiennes Court off Fairfax Street in the city centre, by coincidence it was situated in the premises previously occupied by a lesbian club, the Scarlet Coat. It closed in April 1999 when developers bought out the lease.[510]

Following the lead of the Aled Richards Trust in 1992, a whole series of new gay commercial ventures started opening in the Old Market/West Street area, beginning with the Cottage (now Village) Sauna in 1996, the Friends of Dorothy internet café in 1997 and Castro's in 1998.[511] Further pubs and clubs followed and began to market themselves as Bristol's gay village, despite the opposition of the local vicar, who was the brother of the anti-gay Conservative politician, Anne Widdecombe.[512] In contrast to Manchester, where the Canal Street Gay Village developed around a pre-existing gay scene and was supported by Manchester City Council as part of the city's regeneration project, the Bristol gay village represented the colonisation by entrepreneurs of a new area where developers were keen to boost low property values and there was little encouragement by Bristol City Council.[513] The commercial scene in Bath also expanded, albeit on a smaller scale, with the opening of the Bath Tap in 1996 and Mandalyn's in 2002, while the Garrick's Head, which had been a gay pub practically since the time that Garrick trod the boards, finally managed to transform itself into a completely straight establishment at the end of 1997 after a change in management.

As detailed in Chapter 5, two new social groups were set up in 1990, 3Ms and 3Cs, which initially were seen as potential competitors to Gay West. Meanwhile, LGBT activists in the voluntary sector began to mobilise funding from public sources in the form of grants and support for paid staff, which provided the resources needed to carry out projects far in excess of anything that could be achieved on the basis of personal subscriptions and the proceeds of jumble sales. There were three main sources of public funding: health trusts, the National Lottery and local councils. The health trusts channelled money into LGBT-oriented organisations in fulfillment of their remit to raise awareness of sexual health matters and prevent the spread of HIV and other sexually-transmitted diseases. The National Lottery was interested in combatting social exclusion and had included lesbians and gays among their priority groups. Local councils were constrained by uncertainty over the scope of Section 28 but increasingly saw lesbians and gays as disadvantaged sections of the community which would benefit from having access to organisations attuned to their needs. The net result of these changes was a growing number of groups with specialised remits.

A prime instigator in much of this activity was Gay West's Campaign Coordinator, Berkeley, who later worked for the Aled Richards Trust.[514] Berkeley represented a new generation of gay activist. Born in Bristol, he had come out at the time of the Section 28 campaign. Eighteen months living in Sydney, Australia between 1988 and 1990 was like a vision of utopia, showing him what a difference equal rights legislation could make. Returning to the UK he threw himself into gay activism in London during 1991–92, joining Act-Up, Outrage! and helping to organise the London Pride event. He then moved back to Bristol and used the skills he had acquired in London to shake up the local scene, setting up the Bristol branch of Outrage! with another local man and later reviving the gay festival as Pride West. He also worked as a volunteer on Switchboard and joined Gay West, initially as a social outlet. When a vacancy arose on the committee, he became the Campaign Coordinator in September 1993. In contrast with the earlier generation of activists, who had generally combined campaigning with other paid employment, Berkeley saw gay community development as a career path. In January 1995, he started work as a paid member of the staff for the Aled Richards Trust, where he was the coordinator of the Gay Mens Team and helped set up the Freedom Youth group, giving up his other activities to avoid a conflict of interest.[515]

Outrage! Bristol was set up in early 1992 as a non-violent, direct-action group fighting homophobia following the model of the London Outrage! and held its first meeting in March 1992.[516] Its main activities during 1992 were leafleting a school in Kingswood, holding a protest outside Clerical Medical's offices in Bristol against the company's refusal to include sexual orientation in their equal opportunities policy, letter-writing to schools and a kiss-in in the Broadmead shopping centre. Its chief spokesperson addressed the first Gay West Speaker Evening in January 1993.[517]

Pride West was created as a new organisation in autumn 1993, with the aim of planning a lesbian and gay festival in Avon in June 1994. This continued the tradition begun by earlier festivals under the names of Bristol Gay Festival and Avon Pride. Berkeley was the chair and other Outrage! Bristol activists also became involved with the organisation.[518] Pride West held festivals in 1994, 1995 and 1996, together with a number of other events such as Winter Pride in December 1995.[519] Pride festivals continued to be held intermittently in Bristol, with events in 1999, 2001 and 2010, as well as a number of Mardi Gras celebrations held in the early 2000s.[520] In 1995, the Lord Mayor of Bristol opened the festival in what was believed to be the first official opening of any British Pride event by a civic leader.[521] In August 2010, the highlight of Pride Bristol was a festival day in Castle Park in the historic centre of the city, with tents and stalls from a wide range of commercial and voluntary organisations, followed by late night parties in the main commercial venues.[522] In 1988, 1994–95 and 2010, the festival included a march through the city centre. The Pride West website offers one of the main online guides to the city's LGBT scene.[523]

The voluntary sector in Bristol was dominated by the Aled Richards Trust. Starting with an annual grant of some £13,000 in 1986, by 1998/99 it had a turnover of £327,000, of which three-quarters came from statutory income and 60% went on paid staff, who coordinated the volunteers.[524] The Trust had a number of different constituencies, including drug users and people from Africa, but gay men remained one of its main concerns. The Trust's Gay Men's Project (later Gay Men's Team), set up in 1992, supported a range of services as part of their work on community development.[525] These included Freedom Youth (for under-25s), Cruz (outreach work distributing condoms and advice at outdoor cruising sites), the Avon & Somerset Lesbian & Gay Policing Initiative (see Chapter 9), the distribution of condoms and information in indoor commercial venues through the Outreach Crew, CHAPS (a national campaign to reduce the incidence of HIV infection among gay and bisexual men), the Bristol Families & Friends Group and the production of a gay guide to Bristol and Bath, as well as counselling, buddying, grants to relieve individual hardship and so on. After merging with other HIV/AIDS organisations and becoming the Terrence Higgins Trust West, the organisation was instrumental in securing a large Big Lottery Fund grant, which enabled the Norah Fry Research Centre at the University of Bristol to carry out a research project on LGBT people with learning difficulties, published under the title *Secret Loves, Hidden Lives?*[526]

The relationship with the local councils began in the early 1980s when gay activists started pressing them to extend their equal opportunities policies to cover LGBT employees. Activists adopted a parallel approach comprising both pressure from trade unions and support from sympathetic councillors.[527] Initially, Avon County Council proved more amenable and included sexual orientation in its equal opportunities policy around 1982 (see Chapter 2). Bristol City Council was less responsive and it was some years later before it followed suit. At this time, gay activists did not even consider asking for council funding.[528] In the later 1980s, however, following the precedent set by the Greater London Council, local councils began to make small grants to LGBT groups and initiatives, provoking a backlash from right-wingers. In Bristol, plans to include homosexuals among groups prioritised for urban aid in 1986, a grant of £1,000 for a Lesbian Day of Celebration in 1987, a grant of £200 to the Avon Pride Castle Green Collective for the 1988 Avon Pride and a gay prejudice awareness course for councillors and staff were all attacked by Conservative councillors and defended by pro-gay letter-writers in the press.[529] Similar protests arose when Avon County Council gave a grant to the Bristol Young Lesbian Group in 1991.[530] In 1995 Avon County Council awarded the Bristol Young Lesbian and Bisexual Group a grant of around £2,000. The Tory councillors voted against the grant and there was a hostile campaign in the press.[531] Pride West was unsuccessful in applications to Avon County and Bristol City Councils for two years but was then successful in an application to Bristol City Council's Leisure Services Arts Development Committee. This grant also came under attack from Tory councillors.[532]

The Bristol Lesbian, Gay & Bisexual Forum was established in October 1994, initially to press Bristol City Council to adopt an Equal Opportunities Policy to include sexual orientation when it took over functions from the soon-to-be disbanded Avon County Council.[533] Once this had been successfully achieved, it became an advisory and consultative body representing LGB interests, mainly to Bristol City Council and other local authorities but also to statutory and voluntary organisations in general. It held its first Open Forum meeting and AGM in Bristol in March 1995 and introduced its manifesto, calling for equal civil and legal rights and a change in the attitudes of society, at a meeting in June 1996 at which Angela Mason, the Executive Director of Stonewall, was the guest speaker.[534]

The Forum drew up a Five Year Plan covering the period up to 2002 in order to receive funding from the Council and was due to receive £2,000 in 1998/1999.[535] In 1998, a survey was carried out by the University of the West of England on behalf of the Forum to assess the views of gays and lesbians in Bristol on the services they received from the Council. Some activists thought that the survey was badly designed and it had a poor response rate but nevertheless the resulting report, *Second Best Value*, was able to highlight some of the discrimination faced by LGB people in Bristol in the areas of health, education, social services, housing, young people and the police.[536] In 2000, the Forum negotiated a Compact with Bristol City Council, which aimed to work towards equality of access to services and resources controlled by the City Council, promote understanding and respect for the LGB community and empower LGB citizens to become more actively involved in community life.[537] In 2004, the City Council in conjunction with the Forum published a 145 page guide to LGBT and gay-friendly organisations in the city.[538] In 2010 the Forum continued as a voluntary organisation and registered charity, with two part-time members of staff and a newsletter, *Outburst: Voices from Bristol's LGB Community*. The Forum acts as the main intermediary between the City Council and LGBT organisations in the city.[539]

A series of new groups were organised during this period, particularly aimed at helping young people. The Bristol Lesbian and Gay Youth Group was formed in 1986.[540] The Young Lesbian Group (for women under 25) was set up in early 1992.[541] Freedom Youth was started in July 1995 as a youth group for lesbians, gay men and bisexuals, plus those coming to terms with their sexuality, who were under 25. It met every Tuesday evening in the Aled Richards Trust building in Bristol. Its aims were to challenge the isolation facing young people by building a positive self identity, provide a safe place for young people to meet and look at a range of issues including coming out, safer sex, families, education, employment and housing, and provide an alternative to the commercial gay scene.[542] In December 1995, Freedom Youth merged with the Bristol Young Lesbian and Bisexual Group to form Freedom (later Freedom Youth again) and in June 1996 was awarded a lottery grant of £159,000 to develop its work over the following three years, to include a full-time worker, a phone line and a housing project. A chance comment during a newspaper interview mentioning a barbecue as one of the social activities planned for the group led to hostile headlines in the *Daily Mail*.[543] In 1998, Freedom Youth was running three sessions a week, two of which were in partnership with the Aled Richards Trust and the Gay Men's Project.[544] The funding ended in 1999 but the group continued as a voluntary sector project for several years by offering a weekly drop-in service, with funding from Bristol City Council's Young People's Services. In November 2005, it was taken over by the Young People's Services inclusion team and is now statutory funded and part of mainstream youth services. Its aims are to reduce the isolation felt by young lesbians, gay men and bisexuals, to raise young people's self-esteem and develop a positive identity, and to challenge homophobia and heterosexism within an environment of equal opportunities.[545]

In October 1996, an open meeting was called to consider organising a gay youth group in Bath.[546] In 1998 a Freedom group was set up in the city and this started holding weekly meetings from October 1998. Funding came from Bath and North East Somerset Youth and Community service and the National Lottery Charities Board and the group was a partnership between Freedom Youth, Off the Record (Bath) and the Aled Richards Trust Gay Men's Health Project.[547]

In August 1996, a group called Outreach started meeting for coffee evenings in Yate, a satellite town just north of Bristol, initially monthly and soon afterwards fortnightly. The first meeting attracted six men and four women, ranging in age from 17 to early forties.[548] Members of the group started Outreach Community in March 1998 and successfully pressed South Gloucestershire Council (one of the unitary authorities created after the abolition of Avon County Council in 1996) to make the *Pink Paper* (later *Fyne Times*) available in all libraries, as well as to provide a gay-friendly venue and a youth group.[549] In mid-1997, a related group called South Gloucestershire Lesbian, Gay & Bisexual Community Group received a grant of £150 from South Gloucestershire Council.[550] The South Gloucestershire Lesbian Gay & Bisexual Forum, similar to the Bristol Forum, was set up in 2000.[551] For a time during the 2000s there was a self-organised group for young LGB people called Purple Turnips, which was supported by South Gloucestershire Council youth workers.[552]

Other groups were set up to help particular categories of LGBT people. The Bristol Bisexual Support Group was re-launched in late 1995.[553] Bristol Families & Friends was set up in January 1997 as a support group for the families and friends of lesbians, gay men and bisexuals while GLAFF (Gay & Lesbian Alcohol-Free Friends) is a support group for recovering alcoholics.[554] The Bristol Gay Men's Chorus was founded in March 1992 by a member of Gay West and lasted for seven years.[555] It was followed later by another choir, SingOut Bristol.[556] At the end of 2002, there was a whole range of groups catering for lesbians: Pink Herrings, Women Live, Women Out Walking, Women-Out-West, Bath Women's Social Group, Women's Bisexual Group, ELSIEE (Especially for Lesbians who Socialise in the Early Evenings) and Pink Prom discos, as well as the long-running nationwide lesbian organisation, KENRIC.[557] Other groups which started during the 2000s were directed towards particular recreations and sports, such as Outwest (line dancing), Bristol Bisons (rugby) Bristol Panthers (football) and CycleOut Bristol.[558] Besides these groups, there were the social groups 3Ms and 3Cs (which merged in 2010 to form Gays Meeting Gays or GMG South West), and local branches of national organisations such as the Gay Outdoor Club (GOC), the Metropolitan Community Church (MCC) and the Lesbian & Gay Christian Movement (LGCM). The University of Bristol's Gaysoc was now the LGBTsoc.[559] The Bristol Lesbian & Gay Switchboard, which started in 1975 and continued to be run on a voluntary basis, still found a role providing help and advice in the age of the internet,

The commercial sector also formed associations. The Bristol Triangle was set up in October 1995 as a group of independent pub and club owners, with the aim of raising the profile of gay life in Bristol by working together jointly to promote their businesses. Their first project was to produce a free map and guide to identify the location of each member's premises, together with a listing of other gay and gay-friendly organisations in the city.[560]

Gay West in the 1990s and Early 2000s

Consequently, by the turn of the century, the environment in which Gay West operated was very different from when it was formed twenty years earlier. The developments in Bristol outlined above, together with the all-pervasive presence of the internet, had significant repercussions for the group. Gay West publicised the new groups in its newsletter and generally welcomed their appearance. In the longer term, however they posed a problem for the group. While the young people who were Freedom Youth's main target were unlikely to have been interested in Gay West, with its image as a group for older men, the proliferation of specialised groups and

158

Halloween Party, 1990s.
Photo: Vince Baughan,
Julian Vagg.

the growing segmentation of the gay scene may have siphoned off some of its potential membership. It placed a question mark over the role of a general-purpose social group, which appeared to be becoming marginalised in an increasingly diverse and fragmented environment. Successive committees struggled to come to terms with the new situation over the following years.

In May 1991, the former Campaign Coordinator wrote to the newsletter urging the committee to think about the consequences of

> GayWest's membership escalating to dizzying new heights. [...] With improved links between GayWest and groups like Lesbian Line and 3M's, as well as our continuing support for Switchboard and ART, GayWest can legitimately claim to be a kind of umbrella organisation for local lesbians and gay men, at the sharp end of the local gay community. When issues relevant to lesbians and gay men crop up in local government and in the press, we should demand that our voice be heard – after all, with 300+ members we now carry considerable authority and clout.

He even mentioned the possibility of taking on a paid worker.[561]

This proved to be the proverbial pride before the fall. Gay West entered the 1990s on a high but as the decade progressed it began to falter. Membership peaked at 404 in January 1992 and then began a slow decline, fluctuating around 250–300 for most of the 1990s, before beginning a sharper decline in 1999. In April 2002 it fell below 100 and although it recovered slightly, from April 2004 onwards it remained around the 80–90 mark. During the 1990s, the group turned in on itself, concentrating on trying to appeal to younger people and those who were just coming out while allowing its links with wider civil society to wither.[562] This tended to isolate the group at a time when new groups and commercial establishments were springing up in Bristol, offering expanded social opportunities, and new channels for political dialogue were also opening up. The result was serious worries about the group's long-term viability. The committee became increasingly alarmed and despondent. In September 1993, a member asked "Is Gay West dying", citing poor attendances at events and Coffee Shop, a shortage of people prepared to serve on the committee and a perceived lack of events. A few months later, the same member criticised those who ran down Coffee Shop:

> Gay West is, potentially at least, a good thing. It is the only group in the area that has a comprehensive and serious aim. It is not just a social group. Gay West is a political force with powerful lobbying potential. It is a counselling and support group. And it is also the only group that promotes equality not only between gays and straights, but also between men and women. This makes Gay West the area's most important group, and Coffee Shop is Gay West's flag ship. It is a regular point of contact for established members, new members, and non-members (eg. the recent safe sex promotion people). If members are dissatisfied with what Gay West is, then they should get off their arses, stop whining and do something positive to change the situation.[563]

The number of social events fell off in the late 1990s. In May 1998, the chairperson and the events coordinator lamented that fewer members were coming forward to host events and those events which were put on were getting a low response in terms of turnout. By July 1999 the social secretary was in despair at the lack of response to organised events. In October 2000 the newsletter wondered whether Gay West was running on empty. By April 2001 the newsletter was asking whether it was the beginning of the end. There was an urgent need for volunteers to run the Rainbow Cafe, events were in crisis because very few people were coming forward to host them and attendance at these events had dropped considerably; no-one had come forward to replace the departing editor and the secretary had also resigned.

In 1998, the group suffered two blows which significantly reduced its profile amongst local LGBT people.[564] During 1996 and 1997, Gay West organised monthly POSH discos in the 1805 Rooms at the Bath Theatre Royal which proved both popular and profitable, allowing the group to make donations of £1,000 to the Bristol Switchboard and £500 to the Stonewall Equality 2000 initiative (see Chapter 9 for a history of the discos).[565] The discos came to a stop in March 1998 amidst some confusion over a rival disco of the same name and recrimination over some tickets destroyed by the Garrick's Head management.[566] Later the same year, problems in the organisation of London Pride led to the postponement of the planned festival and Gay West was forced to cancel its coach booking, losing its deposit in the process.[567] The next year, for the first time in many years, it did not lay on any coaches to take people to the London Pride march.[568] Both discos and coaches had been popular with local LGBT people who were not members and with their demise Gay West lost two valuable sources of publicity.

The group tried to console itself with the thought that it was the victim of its own success:

> It is the nature of groups like GayWest to go through phases as members come and go, and people's needs change. I strongly believe there is a valid role for GayWest to play in this community, even if the group needs to decide what that role is for the future. Declining membership may in part be due to the group's success. We aim to provide support and social life – both are now more freely available elsewhere, thanks to the campaigning success of lesbian/gay groups nationwide.[569]

Two factors seem to have saved Gay West from collapse during this period. On the one hand, its formal structure, with its regular pattern of committee meetings, newsletters and so on, gave those who wanted to keep it going something around which to focus their energies. Members of the committee worked hard to find a new direction for the group and Paul Green, who became Chair in 2004, introduced new business concepts of forward planning as well as improving publicity and fund-raising. At the same time, the Saturday morning Rainbow Cafe in Bath continued to attract a regular attendance. The dependability of its functioning, the ease and informality of access and the other leisure and retail facilities offered by the city of Bath for a day out made it an ideal forum to create and maintain friendship networks, particularly for a generation for whom Facebook and MySpace were alien experiences. Membership of the group stabilised at around 80 and the number of people coming to the Rainbow Cafe (not all of whom were formal members) at around 30.

Despite its problems, Gay West continued to look for new opportunities and to make new openings into civil society. In late 2000, it ran a stand at the New Ideas Fair in the Somerset town of Frome.

> Having set up, we awaited the public invasion. I'd been told I was being quite brave doing this in Frome, as its not known for being Gay friendly, so we waited with baited breath for the bigoted remarks. I am pleased to say we encountered nothing derogatory, in fact within minutes of it starting we were congratulated on being there. The whole day was fantastic, many, many people were interested in the stand, they bought the GayWest magazines and asked about membership.[570]

In April 2004, Age Concern, the owners of the premises where the Saturday Rainbow Cafe is held, asked for an increase in room hire which would have nearly doubled the rent in less than two years. This would have destroyed the financial viability of the Cafe and so the committee arranged a small deputation of the group's older regulars to ask the Age Concern manager to reconsider. She in turn was surprised to discover that some homosexuals also fell within the remit of her organisation. She promptly rescinded the rent rise and arranged for relevant Age Concern leaflets to be made available for group members.

Despite its internal difficulties and the weakening of its links with other voluntary groups, as the 1990s progressed, Gay West found increasing official recognition from public bodies. In Bath, the group had had little contact with the local authority apart from its lobbying activities at election times. The main exception was the public library service. Although the Bath Gay Awareness Group's repeated attempts to get the public libraries to stock *Gay News* only reached a successful conclusion in 1981, as far back as 1972, the Director of Bath Municipal Libraries had offered to include the group in the Directory of Local Societies, maintained by the Reference Library.[571] In March 1987, a meeting was held with representatives of Avon Libraries, who said they were looking into ways of getting more gay books into libraries and encouraged Gay West to ask local libraries to display the group advert. Contact with the libraries was maintained over the following years. By the mid 1990s, however, public bodies were regularly approaching the group. In August 1996, Bath & North East Somerset Council sent the group a note inviting it to a public meeting on the environment while Bath University wrote about some of its gay students who might need support during their course. In August 1997 Bath College of Higher Education invited Gay West to exhibit at their Freshers' Fair and in September 1999, the City of Bath College invited the group to attend its end of year prize giving. Bath University regularly sent its vacancy notices in the early 2000s as a sign of its commitment to equal opportunities.

From 1 July 2002 Bath & North East Somerset council set up a register, which allowed gay and lesbian partnerships to be officially recognised at the Registry Office.[572] This was three years before legislation instituting civil partnerships was passed at the national level and so would not have the legal force of marriage, although it would help with inheritance tax and registering next of kin. The initiative in this case came from a city councillor and was supported by the Students Union and Bath's Metropolitan Community Church. There was the predictable opposition from local churches. Gay West welcomed the initiative in its magazine but was not directly involved, although a couple of committee members attended a meeting on civil partnerships in the Bristol Council House in 2005.[573]

In 2002, Gay West received the ultimate accolade when it was invited to nominate a representative to take part in a reception for voluntary groups at the Guildhall during the Queen's Golden Jubilee visit to Bath. The committee chose Ernie Everest, the long-serving host of the Rainbow Cafe, as the group's representative. In the event, Ernie Everest met Prince Philip rather than the Queen during the reception on 2 May 2002.[574] The Prince asked what Gay West was and when told that it was a gay and lesbian social group which met in Bath, replied "Oh!" and walked on. Perhaps the late Queen Mother might have shown more empathy.

Local organisations also honoured the group. In July 2007, the Living Springs Metropolitan Community Church decided to give its annual community award to Gay West to acknowledge its charitable work on its 25th anniversary. The award was presented to the Chair, Paul Green, by the lady Mayor of Bath and reported in the local paper.[575]

In 2011, Gay West is still very much alive and thriving. Its social programme is much reduced compared with the 1980s and it is now one of a multiplicity of groups in the area. Nevertheless, week in week out, it continues to hold its Rainbow Cafe every Saturday morning in the centre of Bath, attracting about 20–30 people most weeks, and it organises occasional social events, such as theatre visits, pub evenings, outings, picnics and walks. The committee continues to look for new opportunities and the group sees a role for itself as a source of friends for those have tired of the clubbing scene.[576] In an increasingly fragmented scene, Gay West has found a niche as a group for older gay men, since most of those who come to the Rainbow Cafe are over 50, although the committee is generally younger. Some of these are long-time members of the group but others have been

Gay West's Rainbow Cafe in March 2009. Photo: Robert Howes.

introduced to it more recently.

As with other organisations patronised mainly by the older generation, concern is sometimes expressed that the group will disappear as this cohort dies out. It is suggested that young people do not often attend, in part because they prefer socialising with their own age group and in part because they now tend to form friendships and seek sexual partners through internet sites such as Gaydar, Facebook, etc. The idea of voluntary groups and physically meeting people face-to-face is said no longer to correspond to their everyday experience. This may turn out to be true but ageing is a dynamic process: people's interests and expectations change as they grow older. There are now three generations of gay men and women who have lived with the experience of the LGBT movement and more will follow. It remains to be seen whether voluntary groups are inextricably linked with the outlook on life of the generations which grew up with them or whether, as the internet generation grows older, such groups will start to appeal to them as well. Gay West has so far shown a remarkable ability to reinvent itself and to adapt to changed circumstances. As the country faces financial retrenchment in the aftermath of the banking crisis of 2008 and the 2010 general election, voluntary groups such as Gay West may well have a new role to play in the future.

9

Civil Society and Community

A theme running through the preceding chapters has been the tension between campaigning and social activities. Social activities were popular but to many politically-minded activists they seemed irrelevant in the face of the urgent need to combat deep-rooted homophobia. On the other hand, the number of people willing to become involved in campaigning was tiny and the energy generated in moments of crisis proved difficult to sustain for very long. With the benefit of hindsight, however, this conflict seems less stark, as in the longer run both aspects of the LGBT movement helped to create a space for lesbian and gay people in local civil society. This process will be illustrated by two case studies – the history of Gay West discos and the Policing Initiative – which together illustrate some of the strengths and limitations of the civil society model.

Disco Fever

A central argument of this book has been that, in searching for space to run its social activities, Gay West helped to create a LGBT presence in local civil society. This is nowhere more clearly demonstrated than in the group's perennial struggle to put on discos. Mention the subject of discos to anyone who has been involved in running Gay West and eyes roll heavenward. The organisation of discos was one of the most fraught areas with which the group became involved and the committee minutes regularly record discussions of the problems which they raised. Yet they provide a good example of the way in which the group's pursuit of social activities had ramifications, often unintended, on its relations with the other areas of society, including the state and the market.

The discos were mostly held in Bath and offered a valuable opportunity to the group since, with a couple of short-lived exceptions, the city has not been able to support a commercial gay club. Discos were, when profitable, a means of raising funds and increased the group's profile amongst the local LGBT community. They were however beset with problems including the difficulty of finding a suitable venue at a reasonable price, opposition from homophobic landlords, councillors and members of staff, licensing restrictions, DJs who arrived late, financial rip-offs, fickle audiences and occasional physical altercations. Not to mention disagreements over which music to play. Nevertheless, when a successful combination was achieved, the discos were very popular events.

Bath Gay Awareness Group held its first disco at the Regency on Saturday 29 September 1973 but a couple of months later were again looking for a pub where they could hold a disco. In a comment to be repeated many times in the future, the newsletter noted "Once again we're having difficulty in finding a suitable venue."[577] CHE Bristol also held a number of discos on the Lochiel floating pub in 1981 but the saga of the Gay West discos really began in 1979 in Bath. On 5 January 1979, the group held a disco in the basement of Century House, the Labour Party headquarters in Pierrepont Street, with over 100 people present, while over 200 came to the third disco on 6 July 1979, producing a profit of £37.[578] Discos were held in Century House at roughly quarterly intervals for the next two and a half years but in October 1981 the magistrates revoked the premises' late night licence because of complaints by neighbours about the noise (from other live music shows).[579] Meanwhile, the group had found a new venue when they were invited by the owners to hold a disco at the Cascades Club in the nearby town of Trowbridge. The first disco was held on 30 August 1981, followed by another on 10 January 1982.[580] These were Sundays, when there were few customers for straight discos. A number of discos were held at this venue, including one featuring a roadshow put on by the Zipper stores chain in May 1982, which attracted 244 people and produced a healthy profit of over £300.[581] These discos were so popular that for a while the group organised a coach from Bath to take people across to Trowbridge. In April 1983, however, the disco had to be cancelled when the police opposed a Sunday licence.[582]

Over the years a number of venues were used including Walcot Village Hall (1984–1986), Bath Sports and Leisure Centre (1985–1986, 1991), Royal York Hotel (1987–1988), Fernley Hotel (1988), St. James Vaults (1989–1990), University of Bath (1990–1991), Weston Hotel, Bath (1993) and the 1805 Rooms in the Theatre Royal, Bath (1995–1998, called POSH discos from February 1996).

There was uproar at Walcot Village Hall in September 1984, when some local youths invaded the hall and the police had to be called, leading many of the disco-goers to make a hurried departure.[583] The committee tried to tighten up security arrangements at future discos. The newsletter pointed out that such incidents were fairly common at straight discos, although the exception at gay ones, and commented:

> If we let this sort of thing beat us we may as well give up totally any concept of a gay community – we have to fight for what we want – we must be prepared to experience difficulties but we must not turn away from them – we must overcome them. If we stop having discos at Walcot, or if people will not attend discos at Walcot, then these mindless idiots have won and we will deserve the contempt that society eagerly heaps on us at every given opportunity.[584]

In the event, further discos were held at Walcot without incident.

In February 1985, the group held a Valentine's disco at the Bath Leisure Centre. This was marred by the failure to apply for a bar licence extension and the committee agreed to register a complaint about the attitude of the caretaker.[585] When it booked another disco in the Leisure Centre in June 1985, it was told that "there must be no publicity, the event must be properly stewarded and guests should not cause offence to the public or staff. The management also accepts no responsibility for its staffs' personal opinions."[586] Although the committee considered the Centre's letter offensive, it decided to ignore it on this occasion for fear of jeopardising the booking. In the event, the disco went off successfully, with a friendly response from the staff in the absence of the caretaker.[587] In 1990, however, when the group tried to book another disco at the same venue and was refused, it decided to contest the matter. The Assistant Director of Leisure Services told the group that they could not envisage circumstances in which it would be considered proper to accept a booking from Gay West and was backed by the Director of Leisure Services and the Chairman of the Council's Spa and Recreation Committee. The group then approached other councillors and publicised the issue in the local press. The councillors saw this as an example of discrimination and the committee ended by supporting the hire of the hall unanimously. The disco was held in February 1991 in a good atmosphere and one of the councillors, calling in to check that everything was alright, asked to be contacted if there was any problem with the staff.[588]

Gay West also encountered difficulties with the private sector. In 1986, it found a suitable venue at Bath City Football Club but the chairman would not accept a booking.[589] The following year, it discovered the Irving Suite in the Royal York Hotel, whose decor was described as "high camp gone to seed". In other respects this was an ideal location as it was central, relatively cheap "and perhaps the most startling of all: being a gay group didn't seem to be an issue."[590] The group held a number of discos there but when the hotel closed the suite for redecoration, it realised that it would be unable to pay the higher charges when the rooms reopened and would have to look for a new venue.

It found one in the Fernley Hotel, which was advertising its Salad Bar as a gay bar. A number of Gay West discos were held here in the early summer of 1988. The newsletter describes what then happened when Gay West members arrived to set up the July disco:

> When we were confronted with a bar already well peopled at 8.45, we thought it odd. Odder still when a member of the public, already sat drinking, came up to inform us that 'the regulars' had all decided that they were not going to pay the entry charge. All were seemingly quite happy though, to enjoy the disco. There followed a miserable hour and a half, during which we were dictated to by, not the manager, not the bar staff, but the 'doorman', who threatened amongst other things to punch me in the face and to stick his fingers rather forcibly into a place where fingers really don't belong. The hotel management, as they are wont to do, did a communal disappearing act. (Where do they all go, when being paid to manage?) The upshot was, we were forcibly barred from charging entry to anyone the doorman liked the look of. Which meant most people coming in. That in turn meant that those who did pay wer[e] justifiably upset to see others get in for nowt, and that by 10pm, we had a bar two thirds full, and takings of about £20 to cover costs of £95. We returned all the door takings to those who had paid (or we did as far as we could tell), and left. The Hotel agreed to pay the DJ and run the disco for the evening. They very quickly organised a pint pot full of change and someone at the door to take money! Future discos are being run by the Fernley; I hope that those who do not belong to Gay West, are happy to go to its discos, and who accuse us of being 'money-grabbing' are also happy to pay their money into the bank account of a wealthy hotel-owner rather than to an organisation which uses profit from events like discos to make donations to Aled Richards Trust, Gay Switchboard, and numerous other local and national lesbian and gay organisations. They're welcome to it![591]

The POSH discos which the group held regularly in the Theatre Royal's 1805 Rooms from May 1995 to July 1997 were very popular but also ended in some confusion, when a rival disco with the same name started in December 1997. At this time, the Garrick's Head, where many LGBT

Gay West garden party, Chipping Sodbury, July 2010. Photo: Robert Howes.

people used to have a drink before attending the discos, was deliberately trying to become a straight pub, after a change in management.[592] On 28 March 1998, Gay West held a POSH disco which produced £141 profit but the committee was angered to learn that the manager of the Garrick's Head had torn up the tickets the pub had been given to sell. This seems to have been the final straw, as the group did not organise any more discos after that.

Policing Initiative

The Avon & Somerset Lesbian and Gay Policing Initiative, which ran from 1994 to 2004, encapsulated many of the changes which occurred in the 1990s. The aim was to improve relations between the police and LGBT people and the main issues which it dealt with were: 1) policing cottages and cruising areas; 2) training police officers in the handling of LGBT issues; and 3) encouraging members of the LGBT community to report homophobic attacks. The Policing Initiative involved the arm of the state with which gay men in particular have had the most conflictual relationship, not only in this country but across the world, and indeed across the centuries. It covered, on the one hand, cottaging and cruising, the age-old subculture of searching for quick anonymous sexual gratification on the margins of society, and on the other, human rights in the form of personal security and respect for privacy, the banner under which lesbian and gay rights have largely been secured in western democracies. The issues covered also involved the relationship between gays and society in general, ranging from complaints over public sex to homophobic abuse and assaults. The Initiative stood at the intersection of national and local politics, illustrating the long-term repercussions of AIDS and Section 28. The people who took the Policing Initiative forward represented a coalition of long-term gay activists, members of the Aled Richards Trust who had become familiar with the issues of public sex through their outreach HIV/AIDS prevention work with the "men who have sex with men" in cottages and cruising areas, two out-gay police constables, an empathetic community liaison officer and senior police managers who wanted to modernise the force's methods in the face of the increasingly diverse society which they were expected to police. The Policing Initiative represented the culmination of years of campaigning which had begun in the 1970s, with openly-gay activists accepted as authoritative negotiating partners by senior representatives of public bodies. At the same time, it revealed some of the limits of involvement with the state.

While Gay West as an organisation played no part in party politics, it had a major role in the events which led up to the formation of the Policing Initiative. Although cottaging and cruising in public sex environments was only one of the matters discussed by the Policing Initiative, historically it was the issue which most frequently involved gay men with the police. As a custom, it long predated the organised gay movement and it continued unabated after the change in the law in 1967. The 1967 Sexual Offences Act clarified and tightened up the law on public sexual behaviour and, as a result, convictions for indecency doubled during the early 1970s. It was therefore an issue which concerned many gay men (to the despair of lesbians) but opinions on this contentious subject varied. The debate occasionally surfaced in the newsletters of Gay West and its predecessors. In 1974, an article in CHE Bristol's *Chewssheet* described a rather dispiriting visit to the Exeter gay scene, which then consisted mainly of cottages and a very few gay pubs. There were some complaints, apparently from women, and in a following issue the convenor defended the article: "However swordid [sic] these may appear, the fact remains that they exist – in the absence of something better. One should not attempt to hide facts 'beneath carpets'."[593] The Bath group, on the other hand, treated the subject more lightly, leading a report in 1973 on council plans to demolish the much-frequented convenience in Royal Victoria Park with the headline: "Watering place to stop Trading".[594]

The debate was reignited in July 1990 when a correspondent wrote to the Gay West newsletter condemning gays who insisted that they should be free to solicit for sex and indulge in sexual activity in public lavatories without police interference. "'Cottaging' is a stigma that the gay community could well do without. Nothing does more to reinforce the belief that gayness is a sexual deviation rather than a way of life."[595] In subsequent issues, correspondents pointed out that the general public would hardly be aware of cottaging if it were not for the police need to boost their arrest figures and the lurid media reporting, while for many married gay men and bisexuals, cottaging was seen as the only viable form of low profile contact and for young emergent gays it seemed the natural place to meet others. Another correspondent argued that cottaging was indefensible where there were meeting places for gays but it provided for the needs of the frustrated in towns and villages where there were no gay centres. In reply to this point, further correspondents entered the debate. One pointed out that some of the commercial establishments in Bristol "would drive anyone to cottaging as a welcome relief. [...] Or am I the only one who finds the 'scene' intimidating and unwelcoming." He didn't feel that people should be forced to conform to what is deemed to be respectable behaviour and noted that for some people cottaging is their only outlet.[596] Another correspondent observed that not everyone had access to commercial venues because of age restrictions or cost; instead of deploring cottaging, people should campaign against those laws which made public displays of affection between gays so risky.

The committee tried to warn people of the risks involved. In 1982, the group's short-lived magazine, *Gaylink*, published a tongue-in-cheek description of cottaging followed by a warning of the serious legal and sexual health risks involved.[597] In November 1984, the newsletter commented on two recent cottaging cases in Bristol and editorial comment in the *Bristol Evening Post* condemning the waste of police time involved in spying in toilets. At the end of 1987, two men described the traumatic effect when one of them was arrested while innocently using the toilet facilities in a Bristol department store and gave advice on what to do in similar circumstances. In September 1988, the newsletter warned readers that the public toilets at Kington Langley near Chippenham had become quite notorious for the number of arrests and advised those interested in cottaging to give the place a miss for a long time. It appeared that this was part of a national clampdown and there were widespread reports of arrests in Bristol, Bath, Chippenham, Cheltenham and the Exeter area. The Chairman, John Bescoby, reminded people at the weekly Coffee Shops of the dangers but even this was contentious. Some accused him of moralising, with one person even asking him not to mention the subject. John Pritchett defended his action, pointing out that John Bescoby had given help in many cases of arrest. "The only purpose for making announcements at Coffee Shop is to ensure that as many people as possible know of the dangers, so that they can then make an informed decision on the way they will behave. If individuals are still prepared to take the risk, that is their choice. But we do have a duty to pass on such information when we get it."[598] In November 1992, the newsletter warned of incidents of queer-bashing on Durdham Downs; in March 1993, it alerted cottagers in Bristol about an extortionist posing as a policeman and in September 1995, about a thief operating in the Bristol area.

Whatever people's views on the rights and wrongs of cottaging, most gays were united in revulsion at the methods used by the police to make arrests and the subsequent press publicity, which often inflicted damage on the defendants out of all proportion to the trivial penalties imposed by the courts, in terms of social disgrace, broken family relationships, lost jobs and even suicide. As the number of arrests rose sharply in the early 1970s, gay activists at the national level began to protest at police tactics, which seem to have been in general use across the country, and at the biased press reporting.[599] In a case involving the Marlborough Lane convenience in Bath in April 1977, a policeman told the court "how he kept watch in the roof of the lavatories and dropped a note through a grill to let colleagues know when to pounce."[600] In 1982, a policeman arrested a man in the toilets at Lawrence Hill, Bristol after watching from the roof.[601]

The publicity given to these police tactics proved increasingly counter-productive. A Bath resident wrote to the *Chronicle* in 1979 to say that she was

> astounded that in these times, when violent crime is increasing and vandalism has reached epidemic proportions, the police have nothing better to do than watch public toilets in our parks, to trap those unfortunate people our society forces, through its prejudice, to use such places to catch their fleeting moments of happiness. Homosexuality is not a crime and it is high time that this aspect of the law was changed too. Its enforcement now merely sustains the widespread prejudice which still exists, yet highlights the persecution which homosexuals suffer from all sections of society [602]

The Bath group assembled a collection of newspaper cuttings on the sad litany of court cases in the late 1970s and early 1980s, and condemned the local paper for publishing the full addresses of the accused.[603] In July

1991, the newsletter republished verbatim two reports from the *Western Daily Press* and the *Bristol Evening Post* about men arrested on the Downs, including their names and addresses. This provoked a flurry of outraged letters from members protesting at the publication of the names and addresses and accusing the Diary of adopting the same position as the tabloid press. The diary editor defended himself, saying his intention was to highlight the homophobia in the biased reporting of journalists. He had written to the two newspapers concerned and the Press Complaints Commission and he advised the correspondents to do the same rather than venting their disgust on him.

Activists in Bristol took a more direct approach. One of CHE Bristol's last actions was to produce a leaflet warning cottagers about police tactics and giving advice on what to do if arrested.[604] Gay West agreed to distribute it at its meetings. In July 1983, incensed at reports in the local press that male prostitutes were operating at a cruising site off the Portway and that a councillor was collecting car numbers and passing them on to the police, Bristol activists organised a protest "picnic" at the site and, quoting the headline in the *Bristol Evening Post*, displayed signs proclaiming themselves "men of vice".[605] Three years later, following a similar press campaign, they had a meeting with the police superintendent responsible for community involvement, at which they tried to ascertain current police policy relating to gay activity in public conveniences, particularly the use of entrapment and agents provocateurs. They suggested an alternative method of policing conveniences based on regular uniformed policing and a policy of issuing cautions. They also asked for a meeting with someone responsible for police training but nothing further came of this at the time. [606]

Both the Bristol and Bath groups, as well as others, attempted to establish a dialogue with the police. In 1973, Bristol University's Gay Student Society tried to organise a talk on "Homosexuals and the police" but the Bristol police refused to provide a speaker on this topic.[607] In 1978, Bristol CHE wrote to the Police Community Relations Officer offering three dates for a speaker. The offer was turned down by the police and the group decided not to proceed further with this contact for the time being.[608] Bath CHE had a meeting with the local community relations officers in 1982, at which surveillance of public toilets and police training were discussed.[609] Gay West also tried to make contact with the Bath Police and despite an initial refusal, decided to try again in November 1987, following the appointment of a new Superintendent. The Community Involvement Officer was prepared to attend a public meeting to discuss the role of the police force and the gay community and so in July 1988 the committee asked for specific examples of problem areas and personal experiences of the police treatment of lesbians and gays in Bath, but nothing more seems to have come of this. Suspicion of the police revived again in 1990 during the police investigation into the murder of Keith Burgess, a Bristol gay man, in December 1989. Gay West was approached by the police for assistance and urged its members to help but advised utmost caution in what information they gave. This was because of unconfirmed reports that police had used information gathered in connection with this murder to further harass, intimidate and arrest gay men.[610]

The Policing Initiative which emerged in 1994 was an unexpected by-product of Section 28. Gay West had revived its Campaign Committee in the aftermath of the Section 28 campaign and new life was breathed into campaigning when Berkeley joined in September 1993. Berkeley had had experience of negotiating with the police as an Outrage! activist in London and, in his role as Gay West's Campaign Coordinator, he wrote a letter to the Avon & Somerset police about liaison arrangements on 1 February 1994. This time the approach was favourably received by the police and arrangements were set in hand during the rest of the year to set up liaison on a formal basis.

The change in police attitudes towards gay issues had a number of causes. The ideas of John Alderson, former chief of Devon and Cornwall police, the Scarman Report into the Brixton riots of 1981, and subsequent research and policy initiatives had led more forward-thinking police officers to adopt new ideas of community and problem-oriented policing, which were later given further prominence by the repercussions of the MacPherson Report (1999) into the racist murder of the black teenager Stephen Lawrence.[611] Another element in the equation was the Lesbian and Gay Police Association (LAGPA, now Gay Police Association). This was formed in summer 1990 by lesbian and gay police officers and initially worked to press for equal opportunities policies in the police force and to offer advice and support to lesbians and gay men working in the police service. By 1993, around two thirds of the forces in England and Wales had included "sexual orientation" in their equal opportunities policy statement and the association then turned its attention towards its third aim, to work towards better relations between the police service and the lesbian and gay community.[612] Two out-gay local police constables made important contributions to the Policing Initiative. The Avon & Somerset Policing Initiative was not the first such venture in the country and it was able to draw on the experience of earlier projects in London, Manchester and Leicester. Nevertheless, it was a pioneering project and two reports by HM Inspector of Constabulary referred to it with approval.[613]

Following up Berkeley's initial approach, members of Gay West met with police officers on 10 March 1994 and agreed to form a group and meet regularly.[614] A public meeting on policing the lesbian and gay communities was convened at the Watershed in Bristol on 11 April and the inaugural liaison meeting was held on 7 November 1994. Aims, objectives and terms of reference were agreed at the meeting on 5 December 1994 and from then on meetings were held regularly at monthly and later quarterly intervals. The community side (as the lesbian and gay members were referred to) held its own separate meetings to discuss what topics it wanted to raise and various sub groups were set up from time to time. The Initiative held a number of meetings with Assistant Chief Constable Terry Grange, who took a particular interest in it and lent his authority to give its views more influence with other police officers. He later became the Association of Chief Police Officers member with responsibility for LGBT liaison issues. The day-to-day arrangements on the police side were carried out by a community relations officer. On the LGBT or community side, the main representatives were a member of staff and a volunteer from the Aled Richards Trust, a union representative, the owner of Just nightclub, and a member of Gay West who was also the administrator of Bristol Lesbian and Gay Switchboard. The chair of Gay West did not usually attend but sent his apologies. The Policing Initiative adopted a formal constitution in September 1998, with the aim of applying for funding.[615]

Meetings were held at a variety of venues, including the Aled Richards Trust, police HQ at Portishead, individual police stations, the Council House in Bristol, gay pubs and clubs, and community centres in the Bristol suburbs. Most meetings were held in Bristol but some took place in Bath and other places in Somerset. The main issues covered by the Policing Initiative were policing cottages and cruising areas; training of police officers about LGBT issues; encouraging members of the LGBT community to report homophobic harassment and attacks; improving the exchange of information between the police and LGBT people through liaison arrangements; and setting up a support network for the survivors of homophobic crime.

The most contentious question was the policing of cottages and cruising grounds. The press release announcing the launch of the Initiative was overshadowed by a high-profile raid by local police on the cruising site at Tog Hill in which two men were arrested.[616] Members of the Initiative went to Kingswood police station, the district responsible, to discuss alternative measures.[617] In June 1995, the local press reported that a councillor was collecting signatures from local residents on a petition calling for the closure of the toilet at Horfield.[618] Berkeley wrote to the council committee responsible refuting the more lurid accusations of male prostitutes and child abuse, and the committee agreed to keep the conveniences open during the daytime.[619]

The Initiative proposed a variety of measures which would lead to less heavy-handed policing, including putting up notices and moving men on without arresting them ("Zip up and go"). Cottages and cruising sites were referred to in official documents as Public Sex Environments (PSEs) in an attempt to neutralise some of the emotion surrounding the subject. Nevertheless, it took time for the message to get through to local stations. In July 1996, the Community Side expressed deep concern about the Bath Police conducting a covert observation operation at Sydney Gardens and Rainbow Wood without any prior discussion. "It was felt that such observation is costly and pointless because the issues are the same for every PSE and actions that lead to arrests simply bring the problem disproportionately on a few individuals and only acts to move the, so called, public nuisance to another site."[620]

The experience gained was eventually incorporated into official policy. In February 1998, one of the out-gay policemen produced a paper on Public Sex Environments, setting out the background and suggesting a four-stage approach which concentrated on minimising the public nuisance aspect of the practice.[621] After some re-writing, this was circulated for comment within the police and by the community side.[622] The proposals on PSEs were incorporated into the draft Force Procedural Guide on Homophobic Incidents, which, with some amendments from the community side, notably raising the required level of authorisation for the use of plain clothes officers from District Commander to Assistant Chief Constable rank, then became Force policy.[623]

The policy defined a homophobic incident as any incident which it appeared to the victim, investigating officer or any other person to be motivated by homophobia, that is the irrational fear or hatred of lesbians and gay men; stated that if these incidents were handled insensitively or unprofessionally, they would reinforce the apprehension and mistrust felt by the lesbian, gay and bisexual communities; and set out procedures for dealing with homophobic incidents. On policing Public Sex Environments, the policy adopted a staged approach, recommending a range of tactics which included displaying warning notices, providing attendants, making lighting and other structural alterations, approaching gay community groups and gay media for co-operation and advice, and deterring illegal activity at times which gave rise to complaints. If these initial steps proved ineffective, then other options could be used such as uniform officers in high profile operations, giving people verbal warnings combined with warning notices and setting up a group of neighbours/residents and gay groups to facilitate discussion. The policy responded to some of the major criticisms

176

of earlier police tactics by providing that the use of plain clothes officers could only take place if authorised by an Assistant Chief Constable and the officer in charge should be able to demonstrate that the preliminary steps outlined above had been taken. Care was to be taken not to breach Home Office guidelines on agents provocateurs, officers should work in pairs, should not incite actions which would render a person liable to arrest and should endeavour to obtain independent witnesses. No one should be arrested on account of behaviour towards the officers except in extreme cases, consideration should be given to the use of cautions for first time offenders and officers could refer men to counselling and support services, such as the local Gay Men's Project. The policy was later updated while substantially retaining these provisions.

The subject of gay sex in public continues to be a contentious issue which easily raises negative emotions amongst the public. In October 2007, four Avonmouth firefighters were disciplined after driving their fire engine around the gay cruising area on the Downs and shining their torches into the bushes. This was publicised at the same time that Avon Fire and Rescue Service was hosting a conference on LGBT Equality in the Fire Service. As a result of the disciplinary action, the fire chief received more than 300 abusive emails and a death threat but stuck to his position.[624] On the other hand, a former gay activist who frequents cruising sites told me that he sometimes returns in the daytime with bin bags and clears up the mess because he doesn't see why the general public should be exposed to the evidence. Old habits of public service die hard!

There was one element in these discussions which has had major implications for the development of the city. The community side aired the idea of "zones of tolerance" in out-of-the-way areas where gay men could engage in public sex without fear of arrest but the police said that they could not condone breaches of the law and this suggestion was not pursued. However, when someone later half-heartedly suggested the creation of a sauna as a way of reducing public sex, the community side was surprised when both the council and the police took the suggestion seriously and this led to the opening of the Cottage Sauna in Old Market in 1996.[625] This was the first commercial establishment to open in the area which in the 2000s became Bristol's "gay village".

The question of Public Sex Environments was closely linked to that of homophobic hate crime. Gay activists in the Policing Initiative raised the question of stones being thrown at cars on the Downs and the police became increasingly aware that while men frequenting these sites may have been committing minor offences, they were also the victims of serious crimes of violence, which usually went unreported because the victim

Marlborough Lane convenience, Bath, scene of many arrests, photographed in 1985 shortly before its demolition. Photo: Robert Howes.

feared the consequences of making a complaint to the police. The danger surrounding these sites was tragically illustrated when a married man was murdered at a notorious cottage in Weston-super-Mare in October 1998.[626] The community side pressed the police for the monitoring of homophobic crimes and this was introduced from October 1996. This entailed the definition of what constituted a homophobic crime. The Initiative also tried to encourage the reporting of homophobic harassment and assaults, piloting a third-party reporting form to permit anonymous reporting of incidents and promoting a "Your Shout!" poster campaign in 2000–01. The liaison meetings were also intended to help this and in March 2001, the police started a weekly advice surgery in the Pineapple pub. These activities fed into the Community Safety Partnership programme introduced by the New Labour government and the Policing Initiative tried to ensure that LGBT issues were included in the strategies drawn up by each of the local authorities in the Avon & Somerset area.[627]

Gay activists found that the senior police officers were keen to support the Initiative and felt that the main difficulty would be changing the attitudes of the rank-and-file police. The Community Affairs police representative observed that this was a subject that was highly emotive and one that a number of people, particularly police officers, found difficult to come to terms with.[628] At a meeting on 1 May 1997, ACC Terry Grange agreed to build sexual equality training into the probationary training programme.[629] The community side was later invited to participate in consultation on training and some of them became heavily involved in the delivery of training.[630] The Assistant Chief Constable also agreed to develop the system of liaison officers and by September 1996 there was a published list of district liaison officers.

The Initiative was not all plain sailing. The community side regularly monitored informal reports about police activities and raised questions when LGBT people were affected. In March 1997, a member of the Initiative wrote a sharp letter to the Chief Constable of Gwent about a raid on the Greenhouse Health Club in Newport, which led to the setting up of a Policing Initiative in Gwent.[631] In 1999–2000 they complained about the prosecution of a man for possession of a pornographic video, where there were serious allegations about the behaviour of a police officer and the magistrates conducting the case.[632] There were also difficulties in overcoming the suspicions amongst LGBT people. Repeated attempts to get lesbians involved came to nothing, as women recalled an incident ten years earlier when some lesbians leaving a Bristol club had been seriously assaulted and the police in the area had refused to give them any help.[633] The liaison meetings also failed to attract many LGBT people, for example a meeting held in the Bath Tap in February 2000 was poorly attended.[634] The group used the strap-line "Action against Homophobic Hate Crime" in 2001 and then adopted this as its name in order to make its role clearer. One of the reasons why the Initiative was eventually wound up was the lack of LGBT volunteers as well as a change in police priorities. This led to the decision to dissolve the Initiative in 2004, although some of its work has been taken up by the Bristol LGB Forum.[635]

The new approach to policing was publicised through the Gay West newsletter, which regularly printed reports about the Initiative. A policeman who was a member informed the committee in early 1992 that the Avon & Somerset force's equal opportunities policy did not include sexual orientation but by June that year the newsletter was reporting that sexual orientation had been included in the policy. In May 1995 the newsletter printed a notice from the Police Liaison Committee listing cottages and cruising sites where police activity could be increased following complaints. In August 1996 the diary published a cruising alert from the Policing Initiative regarding complaints about illegal activities taking place in two areas in Bath. "The Avon & Somerset constabulary believes in the right of all persons to live their life without fear and intimidation, however they have a legal obligation to respond to complaints from members of the public."[636] The outreach worker employed by the Bath Gay Men's Project told the committee that the police were merely warning people and handing out leaflets rather than making arrests.[637] Police community officers regularly visited the Rainbow Cafe during the later 1990s, giving a human face to the liaison arrangements.

In the later 2000s, the questions of LGBT equality and homophobia became subsumed into the wider issues of diversity and hate crimes affecting a range of minorities, now given national legislative force. In 2010, the Diversity section of the Avon & Somerset Constabulary website specifically listed "Sexual Orientation" as one of the six strands of diversity and detailed the measures the force had in place to promote sexual orientation equality. [638] These included a commitment to deal promptly and effectively with reported incidents of homophobia, providing a forum to engage with local LGB communities, supporting the employment and career development of gay and lesbian members of staff, training police officers in diversity issues and monitoring the impact of equality policies. The force was a Stonewall Diversity Champion. Compared with the attitudes shown twenty years earlier, this represents a major acknowledgment of LGBT needs.[639]

Limits of Civil Society

The saga of the discos and the development of the Policing Initiative illustrate both the strengths and the weaknesses of a pure civil society model. As Jürgen Habermas noted: "Civil society can directly transform only itself, and it can have at most an indirect effect on the self-transformation of the political system."[640] Working in civil society was productive when there were few political opportunities but ultimately, a point was reached when it was necessary to engage with the state. On the one hand, given that Bath could not support a gay centre like Bristol's, Gay West was forced to seek other premises to hold its discos, which were its most popular social activity. This brought it into contact not only with the owners and managers of a series of commercial clubs, hotels, meeting halls and local authority premises but also their bar staff and auxiliary workers. While it encountered examples of commercial opportunism and flagrant homophobia – and protested where possible, it also found acceptance and a welcome from many other people, who were able to see lesbians and gay men as ordinary people engaged in the normal round of socialising.

On the other hand, Gay West was also instrumental in launching the Policing Initiative, having long shown an awareness of the problems surrounding cottaging and a desire to improve relations with the police. As with the Gay Men's Health Network in Avon/Aled Richards Trust, Gay West members attended the early meetings and the group's name helped to boost the representativeness of the activists who took the Initiative forward. The chief instigator, Berkeley, started the process in his capacity as Gay West's Campaign Co-ordinator, a role which itself derived from the protests of earlier activists against the group's failure to respond to Section 28. However, as with the Aled Richards Trust, once the initiative was up and running, Gay West largely withdrew and maintained a watching brief. Whether through lack of inclination or lack of time, the Gay West committee did not get involved in the long-term management of projects. The activists who formed the community side on the Policing Initiative and remained deeply involved were those who had a direct practical interest in relations between the police and LGBT people. These came from the pure voluntary sector (the coordinator of Switchboard, which received calls from people who had come into contact with the police), the publicly-funded voluntary sector (the two representatives of the Aled Richards Trust, whose outreach work in cruising areas made them aware of the issues involved), the commercial sector (the night-club owner) and trade unions (the Unison representative). The ART and union representatives were used to negotiating with public bodies on LGBT issues because of their working experience.

This repeated pattern suggests that no one organisation, particularly one relying entirely on voluntary members, can represent all the interests of a population as diverse as the LGBT one. Rather, it confirms the distinction made by Byrne between protest movements and social movements, or, in management jargon, between project management and service delivery. The Policing Initiative had a political dimension because it was aimed at altering specific areas of public policy. It seized a political opportunity but had a finite life-span. Gay West's social activities, on the other hand, were ongoing and had a cultural impact. They provided an entry point into the LGBT movement for new participants even when there was no campaigning going on and helped participants form a new identity. For many, attending a Gay West event was merely a stepping stone onto the commercial scene, for others the group served as an induction into more politically-aware activism. Gay West kept the movement going at quiet times, allowing political activists to call on a pre-existing network and mobilise support when they saw a political opportunity or threat. In practice, this did not always run smoothly, as in Gay West's failure to react vigorously to Section 28, and most Gay West members remained apolitical. But even when engaged in purely social activities, the public existence of a group like Gay West served as a reminder of the presence of LGBT people in local society, thus fostering cultural change.

Friendship and Community

At the beginning of this work I drew attention to the distinction made by

Ferdinand Tönnies between civil society and community. Most of this work has been about civil society but I now turn to the question of community. Gay West's original name, still used for banking purposes, is Bath Gay Community Organisation. As detailed in Chapter 4, this derives from the decision to split CHE into campaigning and social wings. So far I have generally avoided using the term "gay community". This phrase was widely used in the gay movement in the 1970s and 1980s but gradually fell out of favour in the 1990s and 2000s, largely as a result of the proliferating identities referred to in Chapter 5. Today it is more likely to be used by public bodies in referring to what they perceive as the constituency of LGBT interest groups. As mentioned in the introduction, "community" is one of the few terms in regular use in political discourse which is universally held to have positive connotations. Yet it is a highly controversial concept, with views ranging from sceptics who deny that it really exists to conservative communitarians who invoke it as a backward-looking utopia. For many academic commentators, from Tönnies onwards, community has embodied a strong element of the local and the traditional, as presented in the early studies of small-town life and enclosed working-class groups. More recent writers have seen a much wider scope for community, living in the imagination or spread over cyberspace. While conservative writers see community as inward-looking and sometimes exclusionary, more progressive thinkers have seen its potential for looking outwards and embracing a diversity of groups.

A number of writers have looked at LGBT history in particular localities in terms of commmunity.[641] Where does Gay West stand in this debate? On one level, it fits into the mould of the traditional local social group, one of a myriad of organisations such as the Women's Institute and village bowling clubs, which together make up the local community. Gay West is spatialised, holding events within a defined region where people physically meet and interact with each other in specific locations. But Gay West is also a community of choice, not a community of fate – each and every member has had to make a personal decision to join the group. Gay West is part of what Benedict Anderson terms an "imagined community".[642] On entering a Gay West meeting, the participant enters a liminal space, where the rules of the everyday world are reversed by the knowledge that the majority of the other people there are also gay or lesbian. Particularly in the early days when anti-gay prejudice was widespread and for people just coming out, this sometimes gave Gay West meetings a tinge of utopianism, a forward-looking vision towards a world without homophobia.

Discussion is usually centred on "the gay community" but, as Mike Homfray found when interviewing people in the Liverpool/Manchester area, it would be more accurate to talk in terms of a plurality of communities.[643] As indicated in the course of this work, there are a number of areas in the Bristol/Bath region where LGBT people come into contact with each other, ranging from the cottaging/cruising sites through the commercial scene to the voluntary movement. To the extent that people recognise and acknowledge each other in these areas, they can be seen as networks, if not exactly communities. Many people restrict their activities to just one area, such as cottagers who never set foot in a gay pub or members of voluntary groups who never go cruising. But there is also some overlap, with individuals who engage in more than one area and know people who are not known to each other. Perhaps this is best represented by the classic diagram of partially-overlapping circles. Gay West forms one circle within this array of interlinked networks. There are some people to whom the group has offered little appeal, such as teenagers, drag queens, ethnic minorities and lesbian separatists. There are others for whom it is just a small part of their LGBT life. But for some, it has formed a major part of their existence, at least for some stages of their lives, and in this context it is meaningful to consider the concept of community.

The mechanics by which the group was set up, organised itself and related to the outside world have been described in the previous chapters. These are very much within the conventional mould of associationism and civil society. However, though important, these fail to grasp all the ramifications of the group. Underneath the superstructure of committee meetings and cake recipes, there is a more basic human emotion holding the group together, that of friendship. This has been forcefully brought home to me in the course of the research for this book, as I have been able to contact some of the interviewees thanks to friendship networks which go back nearly forty years in some cases.

Back in the 19th century, Tönnies recognised friendship as a major component of community and one of the leading modern theorists of community, Ray Pahl, has written that friendship may be seen as an increasingly important form of social glue in contemporary society.[644] The link has also been recognised by gay researchers. In a study of gay men in New York City, David Woolwine outlined three sociological concepts of community – imagined community, community as friends and friendship networks and community as local organisations or groups – and found that for his interviewees friendship was the most important form of community.[645] In *Gay Men's Friendships: Invincible Communities*, Peter Nardi set out to to "understand how interpersonal friendships contribute to a political or civic friendship and to the emergence of social movements, gay identities, gay communities, and gay neighborhoods" in the United States.[646]

The findings for Gay West are remarkably similar. When asked what for them is Gay West's most important achievement, the majority of the members interviewed replied that it was putting people in contact and the friendships which the group allowed them to make. In some cases, they found life-long partners and in others it was non-sexual but deep and long-lasting friendships. While some groups may have formed out of pre-existing friendship networks, Gay West's long-established existence means that the group itself has enabled people to make new friendships. This was particularly important for people just coming out or who had become tired of the commercial scene. One such person wrote that, in contrast to the commercial gay scene: "it was the friendliness and openness which impressed me most when I first met people in the group."[647] The group has recently recognised this aspect of its activities when it adopted the slogan "Out for friendship" in place of the earlier "Out for a good time".

Friendship networks are nothing new but in contrast to private friendship networks, Gay West has a public, structured presence, available to all who care to take advantage of it. By providing an open means for LGBT people to meet and relate to each other socially, which has endured over time, a group such as Gay West has made an important contribution towards creating a gay community based on friendship. To those who have found friendship in the group, it has offered the chance of becoming part of a genuinely affirmative community. As another new member, Julian Vagg, who subsequently went on to become an active committee member, wrote:

> I [...] have only recently joined and cannot overstate the benefits I have found in belonging to Gay West. Before 'coming out' my life was an empty void. Lonely and depressed, I hid myself from the world. [...] Underneath I had a fear of homosexuality, making me feel I'd spend the rest of my life fighting my emotions. But then on my twenty third birthday I felt I had to do something and after much hesitation I rang Gay Switchboard. Since then I have not looked back and with my family's support I have begun a new life and the world seems a better place for it. Whether members join to campaign, socialise or both, the underlying importance of being together must never be forgotten. Now that I have friends who know me for what I am, I no longer feel lonely and for the first time in my life I feel content. So all I can say is long live Gay West! And thank you for being my life saver.[648]

Here we have personal agency, identity-formation, community-building and integration with mainstream society on the basis of self-acceptance, bound together by friendship.

10

Conclusion

Lord Kilmuir would undoubtedly have been shocked if he had known that a representative of a "buggery club" would one day be invited to meet the Queen. And yet, there is an irony here because, as Sir David Maxwell Fyfe, he had been the main British prosecutor at the Nuremburg War Crimes Trials, which were largely responsible for launching the modern concept of human rights. Homosexuals were among the victims of the Nazi concentration camps and it has been chiefly the principle of human rights which has underpinned the improvement in LGBT rights and the drive towards equality across Europe. The concept of human rights lay behind much of the agenda of the Policing Initiative, as well as the reforms enacted at national level by the New Labour government between 1997 and 2010. Without the overarching framework of human rights, it is difficult to imagine civil society assuming the importance which it has since the 1980s. Lord Kilmuir left a legacy which might have surprised him.

The preceding chapters have looked in detail at the organisation and activities of one group and the environment in which it operated in one English region. Taken together with its predecessors, Gay West is now one of the oldest LGBT organisations in the country but it is likely that many aspects of its history would find parallels at times in other cities in the UK. Gay West's history can be seen as a microcosm of the LGBT movement in the provinces.

In summary, this book has shown that the LGBT movement has had a continuous presence in the Bristol/Bath area since 1970. For much of that time, it operated below the radar of mainstream society, small in numbers, barely visible even to many LGBT-identified people. Only in periods of crisis, such as the onset of AIDS in the area and the protests against Section 28, or of celebration, like the regular Bristol Gay Festival/ Avon Pride/Pride West events did the general public become aware of an organised LGBT presence trying to make its voice heard in the local public sphere. This pattern follows that suggested by Melucci of submerged or invisible networks of civil society and the temporary mobilisations through which they become publicly visible. The local movement followed a cyclical pattern reflecting national trends, with a period of growth and enthusiasm in the early 1970s, followed by a period of decline in the mid 1970s and limited development in the early 1980s. It began to expand again during the later 1980s, largely because of the impact of AIDS and Section 28, and the number of groups increased during the 1990s and 2000s.

For much of this time, local LGBT activists debated the tension between campaigning and social activities, and generally found it difficult to reconcile the two in one organisation. With the benefit of hindsight, however, this tension can be seen as characteristic of new social movements, with social activities providing the ongoing cultural support through inducting new people and helping them develop a LGBT identity, while campaigning fulfilled the role of a protest movement, seeking political change and alterations to specific areas of public policy. In the Bristol/Bath area, different groups of activists played different roles: Gay West concentrated on social activities and was most successful in the 1980s when there were few political opportunities. The ex-CHE Bristol and other activists with a more interventionist outlook seized the opportunities which increasingly opened up from the late 1980s, working through dedicated organisations to press for political change and to negotiate with public bodies on policy changes in favour of LGBT people. In part this was due to the different temperaments and political outlooks of the individuals concerned but it also reflected the different political cultures of the two cities, Bristol with its tradition of Labour politics and Bath with its long history as a leisure centre.

Gay West drew in its origins on both the reformist and liberationist strands of the gay movement and it continued to find inspiration in the vision of gay liberation, both in its long-term aspiration towards a better society for LGBT people to live in and, more immediately, in its enthusiasm for participating in the annual London pride marches. In its day-to-day practical activities, however, it was firmly rooted in the assimilationist camp. It relied heavily on the traditional structures of British voluntary organisations and paid particular attention to creating space for LGBT people in local civil society. With its emphasis on social activities it frequently ran the risk of falling into conformism but it managed to retain some of the campaigning spirit from its CHE origins. If it failed to rise to the challenge of Section 28, it stuck up for its rights to hold discos and demanded acknowledgment of LGBT views in its dealings with the BCVS.

At the same time, Gay West helped expand the space available to

186

The actor and gay activist, Simon Callow, visited the Rainbow Cafe in April 2009 and was presented with a certificate making him an honorary member of Gay West by the Chairman, Paul Green. Photo: Robert Howes.

openly-gay people beyond the closed circle of public toilets and semi-clandestine pubs. Through its links with other voluntary organisations and its constant search for premises to hold its meetings and discos, the group created new opportunities in the use of space. This expanded space was both physical and moral or social – the group's use of premises frequented by the rest of the population effectively asserted the legitimacy of LGBT activities.

Like all organisations, Gay West faced both outwards and inwards. To most of its members, its most important functions were its social activities and the opportunities for forming friendships which they offered. By maintaining a continuous presence in the public sphere over a long period of time, Gay West offered a gateway, helping people to come out and to develop a LGBT identity, as and when they needed it. In contrast to private friendship networks, which depend on who you know, Gay West was impartial, open in principle to all who wished to avail themselves of it. While some may have found it uncongenial, for others it formed a major part of their social life, leading to deep and long-lasting friendships. In this way, the group helped form a gay community, if not the gay community.

In its forty years of existence, Gay West and its predecessors have seen many changes in the LGBT movement, which has moved from a marginal position on the fringes of society to much closer involvement with the state, both at national and local level. Public funding offers opportunities to carry out activities at a level unimaginable on the basis of voluntary donations and can have a redistributive effect but it also carries the risk of incorporation into the political system and dependence on public spending priorities. Purely voluntary groups have to some extent become marginalised because of the financial limitations on the scale of their operations but they retain the freedom to set their own agendas. It is up to them how they use this freedom.

This conclusion is written in summer 2011, amidst major cuts in public expenditure and much political rhetoric about an increased emphasis on the voluntary sector. It remains to see what the future will hold for organisations such as Gay West and for the broader LGBT movement over the coming years.

Gay West stall at Swindon Pride, August 2011. From l. to r: Colin O'Brian, Michael Reid, Paul Green (Chairman) and Martin Reeves. Photo: Robert Howes.

Abbreviations

Abbreviations used in the endnotes:

ART:	Aled Richards Trust
ASLGPI:	Avon and Somerset Lesbian and Gay Policing Initiative
BC:	Bath Chronicle
BEP:	Bristol Evening Post
BGAG:	Bath Gay Awareness Group
BGG:	Bath Gay Group
BRO:	Bristol Record Office
CBA:	Charlie Beaton Archive
CHE:	Campaign for Homosexual Equality
GLF:	Gay Liberation Front
GMHNA:	Gay Men's Health Network in Avon
GN:	Gay News
GWA:	Gay West Archive
GWCM:	Gay West Committee Meeting Minutes
GWDE:	Gay West Newsletter (which has had various titles over the years: see Chapter 4)
HCA:	Hall Carpenter Archives, London School of Economics
THT:	Terrence Higgins Trust
WDP:	Western Daily Press

Note: where no source is given for internal documentation, it is generally held in Gay West's own archive.

Endnotes

1   Jack Babuscio, *We speak for ourselves: experiences in homosexual counselling* (London: SPCK, 1976); Malcolm Macourt, *How can we help you? Information, advice and counselling for gay men and lesbians* (London: Bedford Square Press, 1989); Tony Walton, ed., *Out of the shadows: how London gay life changed for the better after the Act: a history of the pioneering London gay groups and organisations, 1967–2000* (London: Bona Street Press, 2010).

2   Jeffrey Weeks, *The world we have won : the remaking of erotic and intimate life* (London: Routledge, 2007).

3   Peter Robinson, *The changing world of gay men* (Basingstoke: Palgrave Macmillan, 2008): the research was carried out in Australia but most of it is equally applicable to Britain.

4   GWDE, June 1994.

5   Peter Wildeblood, *Against the law* [1955] (London: Weidenfeld & Nicolson, 1999), p. 1.

6   Johann Hari, 'How party leaders showed me new attitudes to gay rights', *The Independent* (London), 19 March 2005 (Nexis).

7   Adam Lent, *British social movements since 1945: sex, colour, peace and power* (Basingstoke: Palgrave, 2001).

8   Paul Byrne, *Social movements in Britain* (London: Routledge, 1997), p. 165–177.

9   Sidney Tarrow, *Power in movement: social movements and contentious politics*, 2nd. ed., (Cambridge: Cambridge University Press, 1998).

10 John D'Emilio, *Sexual politics, sexual communities: the making of a homosexual minority in the United States, 1940–1970*, 2nd. ed., (Chicago: University of Chicago Press, 1998), p. 262.

11 Alberto Melucci, *Nomads of the present: social movements and individual needs in contemporary society*, ed. by John Keane and Paul Mier (London: Hutchinson Radius, 1989), p. 228.

12 Melucci, *Nomads of the present*, p. 219.

13 Stephen M. Engel, *The unfinished revolution: social movement theory and the gay and lesbian movement* (Cambridge: Cambridge University Press, 2001).

14 Ferdinand Tönnies, *Community and civil society*, ed. by Jose Harris [1887] (Cambridge: Cambridge University Press, 2001).

15 Zygmunt Bauman, *Community: seeking safety in an insecure world* (Cambridge: Polity Press, 2001), p. 1–3.

16 Keally D. McBride, *Collective dreams: political imagination & community* (University Park, Pennsylvania: Pennsylvania State University Press, 2005), p. 1.

17 Miranda Joseph, *Against the romance of community* (Minneapolis: University of Minnesota Press, 2002), p. vii, xxii.

18 Shlomo Avineri and Avner De-Shalit, eds., *Communitarianism and individualism* (Oxford: Oxford University Press, 1992); Gerard Delanty, *Community* (London: Routledge, 2003).

19 Marilyn Friedman, 'Feminism and modern friendship: dislocating the community', in *Communitarianism and individualism*, ed. by Shlomo Avineri and Avner De-Shalit (Oxford: Oxford University Press, 1992), p. 101–119.

20 Joseph, *Against the romance of community*, p. viii.

21 Friedman, 'Feminism and modern friendship', p. 101–119; Adrian Little, *The politics of community: theory and practice* (Edinburgh: Edinburgh University Press, 2002), p. 156–161.

22 Young, Iris Marion, 'The ideal of community and the politics of difference', *Social theory and practice*, 12, 1 (Spring 1986): 1–26.

23 Mike Homfray, *Provincial queens: the gay and lesbian community in the North-West of England* (Oxford: Lang, 2007).

24 Frank Prochaska, *Schools of citizenship: charity and civic virtue* (London: Civitas, 2002), p. 4–5, 18. See also Peter Burnell and Peter Calvert, eds. *Civil society in democratization* (London: Cass, 2004); Nicholas Deakin, *In search of civil society* (Basingstoke: Palgrave, 2001); Michael Edwards, *Civil society* (Cambridge: Polity Press, 2004); Marlies Glasius, David Lewis and Hakan Seckinelgin, eds., *Exploring civil society: political and cultural contexts* (London: Routledge, 2004); Charles Taylor, 'Modes of civil society', *Public culture*, 3, 1 (Fall 1990): 95–118; Michael Walzer, 'The idea of civil society: a path to social reconstruction', *Dissent* (Spring 1991): 293–304.

25 Oscar Vilhena Vieira and A. Scott DuPree, 'Reflections on civil society and human rights', *SUR: International Journal on Human Rights*, 1,1 (1ˢᵗ Semester 2004): 47–65. See also G. B. Madison, *The political economy of civil society and human rights* (London: Routledge, 1998); Lesley C. Hodgson, 'Helping the salmon: the role of civil society in the development of human rights', *JIJIS*, 5 (2005): 11–23.

26 Eric Heinze, *Sexual orientation: a human right: an essay on international human rights law* (Dordrecht: Martinus Nijhoff, 1995).

27 Carol A. B. Warren, *Identity and community in the gay world* (New York: Wiley, 1974); Mary McIntosh, 'The homosexual role', in *The making of the modern homosexual*, ed. by Kenneth Plummer (London: Hutchinson, 1981), p. 30–49; Jeffrey Weeks, 'Questions of identity', in his *Against nature* [1991] (London: Rivers Oram Press, 1995), p. 68–85; Vera Whisman, *Queer by choice: lesbians, gay men, and the politics of identity* (New York: Routledge, 1996); Mark Blasius, ed., *Sexual identities, queer politics* (Princeton, NJ: Princeton University Press, 2001); Christopher Kendall and Wayne Martino, eds., *Gendered outcasts and sexual outlaws: sexual oppression and gender hierarchies in queer men's lives* (New York: Harrington Park Press, 2006); Peter Robinson, *The changing world of gay men* (Basingstoke: Palgrave Macmillan, 2008).

28 Craig Calhoun, 'Civil society and the public sphere', *Public culture*, 5 (1993): 267–280.

29 David Higgs, ed., *Queer sites: gay urban histories since 1600* (London: Routledge,

1999); George Chauncey, *Gay New York: gender, urban culture, and the making of the gay male world, 1890–1940* (New York: Basic Books, 1994); James N. Green, *Beyond Carnival: male homosexuality in twentieth–century Brazil* (Chicago: University of Chicago Press, 1999); Matt Cook, *London and the culture of homosexuality, 1885–1914* (Cambridge: Cambridge University Press, 2003); Matt Houlbrook, *Queer London: perils and pleasures in the sexual metropolis, 1918–1957* (Chicago: University of Chicago Press, 2005).

30 David Bell & Gill Valentine, eds., *Mapping desire: geographies of sexualities* (London: Routledge, 1995); Gordon Brent Ingram, Anne-Marie Bouthillette and Yolanda Retter, eds., *Queers in space: communities, public places, sites of resistance* (Seattle: Bay Press, 1997).

31 Jean L. Cohen and Andrew Arato, *Civil society and political theory* [1992] (Cambridge, Mass.: MIT Press, 1994), p. 346.

32 Patrick Higgins, *Heterosexual dictatorship: male homosexuality in postwar Britain* (London: Fourth Estate, 1996), p. 168–169.

33 James Kirkup, *A poet could not but be gay: some legends of my lost youth* (London: Peter Owen, 1991), p. 19–20.

34 'Incidents at Bath flat: Allegations against photographer: Six men accused', *BC*, 5 Feb. 1942; 'Grave charges at Bath: Six men sent for trial', *BC*, 6 Feb. 1942; 'Sequel to raid on Bath flat', *BC*, 7 March 1942; 'Four years for Angus McBean', *BC*, 9 March 1942; 'Youth named in Angus McBean case: Riddle of death crash in Wiltshire', *BC*, 16 March 1942; Adrian Woodhouse, *Angus McBean: face-maker* (Richmond, Surrey: Alma Books, 2006), p. 184–194. It seems that the authorities were particularly concerned about the security implications of the presence of servicemen, as McBean's flat was not far from the naval intelligence headquarters; if so, this would make the case a precursor of the famous homosexual spy scandals of the 1950s and 1960s, p. 186. The local impact of this case was such that one of my interviewees, who was a young man in Bath at the time, recalled it unprompted seventy years later: Ken Little, interview, 21 Aug. 2009.

35 Higgins, *Heterosexual dictatorship*, p. 124–125, 325.

36 'Vice prosecutions', *Spectator*, 6758, 3 Jan. 1958, p. 18.

37 'Homosexual acts: call to reform law', *Times*, 7 March 1958.

38 HL Deb. 266 (24 May 1965), 649.

39 HL Deb. 266 (24 May 1965), 655; he was presumably speaking about private clubs in London such as the Spartan, Rockingham and Huntsman: see Peter Burton, *Parallel lives* (London: GMP, 1985), p. 14–16.

40 HL Deb. 266 (24 May 1965), 666.

41 Paul Crane, *Gays and the law* (London: Pluto Press, [1982?]), p. 14.

42 'Magazine publishers win appeal in part', *The Times*, 15 June 1972; 'The 1967 confidence trick: law or sexuality: which corrupts?', *GN*, 2 [June 1972], p. 3–4.

43 Roy Walmsley, 'Indecency between males and the Sexual Offences Act 1967', *Criminal Law Review* (July 1978): 400–407; '"Indecency convictions between males" 1931–89', *Capital Gay*, 18 May 1990, p. 11; 'Coleherne gays "near riot"', *GN*, 97 (17–30 June 1976), p. 1–2.

44 Stephen Jeffery-Poulter, *Peers, queers, and Commons: the struggle for gay law reform*

from 1950 to the present (London: Routledge, 1991); David Rayside, *On the fringe: gays and lesbians in politics* (Ithaca, NY: Cornell University Press, 1998), p. 19–101.

45 One of the leading personalities in both *Arena Three* and Kenric was Diana Chapman, who was born in Bristol: *Inventing ourselves: lesbian life stories*, ed. by Hall Carpenter Archives Lesbian Oral History Group (London: Routledge, 1989), p. 45.

46 HCA/CHE/1/1–2: CHE, *Annual accounts & financial report, 1974/75* gives approx. 4,900 subscriptions; a handwritten report in the CHE Bristol minute book says that National CHE once had a peak membership of 5,500: CBA: CHE Bristol Minute book, 1982 AGM, National Convenors' report, 1981/82.

47 Lisa Power, *No bath but plenty of bubbles: an oral history of the Gay Liberation Front, 1970–73* (London: Cassell, 1995).

48 Madge Dresser and Philip Ollerenshaw, eds., *The making of modern Bristol* (Tiverton: Redcliffe Press, 1996); Martin Boddy, John Lovering and Keith Bassett, *Sunbelt city? A study of economic change in Britain's M4 growth corridor* (Oxford: Clarendon Press, 1986); Ian Archer, Spencer Jordan & Keith Ramsey, *Abstract of Bristol historical statistics. Part 2: Unemployment statistics, 1910–1997* (Bristol: Bristol Historical Databases Project, Faculty of Humanities, University of the West of England, 1997).

49 Geoffrey Amey, *City under fire: the Bristol riots and aftermath* (Guildford: Lutterworth Press, 1979).

50 Kieran Kelly and Mike Richardson, 'The shaping of the Bristol labour movement, 1885–1985', in *The making of modern Bristol*, ed. by Dresser and Ollerenshaw, p. 210–236.

51 June Hannam, '"An enlarged sphere of usefulness": the Bristol women's movement, c. 1860–1914', in *The making of modern Bristol*, ed. by Dresser and Ollerenshaw, p. 184–209.

52 Gordon Priest and Pamela Cobb, eds., *The fight for Bristol: planning and the growth of public protest* (Bristol: Bristol Civic Society/Redcliffe Press, 1980); Deborah M. Withers, *Sistershow revisited: feminism in Bristol, 1973–1975* ([Bristol?]: HammerOn Press, 2011).

53 For evidence of homosexuality in the 18th century, see Steve Poole, '"Bringing great shame upon this city": sodomy, the courts and the civic idiom in eighteenth-century Bristol', *Urban history*, 34, 1 (2007): 114–126.

54 Hugh David, *On queer street: a social history of British homosexuality, 1895–1995* (London: HarperCollins, 1997); Matt Houlbrook, *Queer London: perils and pleasures in the sexual metropolis, 1918–1957* (Chicago: University of Chicago Press, 2005).

55 Jeffrey Weeks and Kevin Porter, eds., *Between the Acts: lives of homosexual men, 1885–1967*, 2nd. ed., (London: Rivers Oram Press, 1998).

56 Cottaging was a regular topic of discussion in the early days of the gay movement: see Sebastian Helmore, 'Whited sepulchres', *GN*, 46 (9–22 May 1974), p. 12; Barrie Kenyon, 'Sex, consequences and disgrace', *GN*, 88 (12–25 Feb. 1976), p. 11. The pioneering academic work on the subject, based on research in the United States, is Laud Humphreys, *Tearoom trade: a study of homosexual encounters in public places* [1970] (London: Duckworth, 1974): it was summarised for a British audience in 'The cottage industry', *GN*, 36 (29 Nov.–12 Dec. 1973), p. 9–10; since then there has been more academic research on public sex, such as David Bell, 'Perverse dynamics, sexual

citizenship and the transformation of intimacy', in *Mapping desire: geographies of sexualities*, ed. by David Bell & Gill Valentine (London: Routledge, 1995), p. 304–317; Maurice van Lieshout, 'Leather nights in the woods: locating male homosexuality and sadomasochism in a Dutch highway rest area' in *Queers in space: communities, public places, sites of resistance*, ed. by Gordon Brent Ingram, Anne-Marie Bouthillette and Yolanda Retter (Seattle: Bay Press, 1997), p. 339–355; William L. Leap, ed., *Public sex/gay space* (New York: Columbia University Press, 1999); Dharman Jeyasingham, '"Ladies" and "gentlemen": location, gender and the dynamics of public sex' in *In a queer place: sexuality and belonging in British and European contexts*, ed. by Kate Chedgzoy, Emma Francis, Murray Pratt (Aldershot: Ashgate, 2002), p.73–88.

57   Gerry Nichols, *Clifton and Durdham Downs: a place of public resort and recreation* (Bristol: Bristol Branch of the Historical Association, 2006), p. 20–21.

58   Nichols, *Clifton and Durdham Downs*, p. 21, and discussions in the Policing Initiative (see Chapter 9).

59   'Another moment of madness, Ron?', *The Sun*, 4 March 2003 (Nexis).

60   CBA: ASLGPI, Minutes of meeting at Kingswood Police Station, 1 March 1995.

61   The licensee of the Union pub in Manchester was imprisoned for a year in 1965 for having "outraged public decency" by "exploiting abnormality", although this was probably exceptional: Stephen Whittle, 'Consuming differences: the collaboration of the gay body with the cultural state', in *The margins of the city: gay men's urban lives*, ed. by Stephen Whittle (Aldershot: Arena, 1994), p. 27–41 (p. 32).

62   Peggy Hancock, interview, 6 June 2011, and various conversations.

63   '"Gay" guide angers West publicans', *BEP*, 19 April 1975; 'Pubs angry over gay guide', *GN*, 70 (8–21 May 1975), p. 1; 'No "Hello sailor" at the Ship', *Move*, 8 (May 1975), p. 16–17.

64   Keith Howes & Michael Mason, 'Gay Britain: Bristol', *GN*, 98 (1–14 July 1976), p. 13–14.

65   GWCM, 1 March 1987.

66   *Gay News' gay guide*, 1, 1 (March 1975).

67   *Gay News' gay guide*, 1, 1 (March 1975).

68   Philip Smith, interview, 16 Aug. 2008; Dale Wakefield, interview, 19 Jan. 2010.

69   Peggy Hancock, interview, 6 June 2011.

70   *GN*, 16 [Feb. 1973], p. 16; Howes & Mason, 'Gay Britain: Bristol'; *Move*, 23 (Nov. 1976), p. 1–3; 'Gay club loses music licence', *BEP*, 15 Oct. 1976.

71   *Move*, 7 (April 1975), p. 13–14; Julia Wassell, 'Bristol, "Where women have got it together"', *Sappho*, 4, 5 (1975), p. 29.

72   *Move*, 7 (April 1975), p. 14; Howes & Mason, 'Gay Britain: Bristol'; see an advert for Kings Club with photos of the interior in *GN*, 67 (27 March–9 April 1975), p. 5.

73   Howes & Mason, 'Gay Britain: Bristol'.

74   Howes & Mason, 'Gay Britain: Bristol'; Gay Bristol Festival [programme] 1979; CHE Bristol [Newsletter], 19 (21 April 1981).

75   *Move*, 33 (Dec./Jan. 1977/78), p. 8–9.

76   *Move*, 33 (Dec./Jan. 1977/78), p. 8–9.

77   Peter Burton, 'Spotlight on Bristol and Bath', *GN*, 246 (5–18 Aug. 1982), p. 44.

78   Dale Wakefield, interview, 19 Jan. 2010.

79   Howes & Mason, 'Gay Britain: Bristol'.

80   Philip Smith, interview, 16 Aug. 2008.

81   Berkeley Wilde, interview, 19 March 2010.

82   CHE Bulletin, Dec. 1970, p. 2; CBA: Charlie Beaton, CHE Bristol's anecdotes [1983].
      Unfortunately, I have not been able to interview anyone from the first phase of CHE
      Bristol.

83   CHE Bulletin, Aug., Nov., Dec., 1969; Jan., March, April 1970.

84   CHE Bulletin, Nov. 1971; Jan. 1972.

85   'The loneliest people...', BEP, 22 May 1972.

86   HCA/CHE/7/17: CHE Bristol Main group committee minutes, 27 June 1973; CHE
      Bristol Chewssheet, [July–Aug.] 1973.

87   CHE Bristol Chewssheet, Nov.–Dec. 1973; [Jan.–Feb. 1974]; April–May 1974; July
      1974.

88   Trevor Locke, 'The Campaign for Homosexual Equality: a time for revitalisation',
      CHE Bristol Chewssheet, [July/Aug. 1973].

89   CHE Bristol Chewssheet, April–May 1974.

90   CHE Bristol Chewssheet, [Jan.–Feb. 1974].

91   HCA/CHE/7/17: Read this side now: Views of CHE Bristol: Recognition of new
      groups [Leaflet].

92   'Bristol CHE attacks "Hybrids"', Reading Gay Alliance, Gay Arrow, 11 (8 Nov. 1972).

93   CHE Bristol Chews Letter, Xmas 1972; in contrast, the three members of the Bath
      group who appeared on the programme "enjoyed it immensely and experienced a
      great sense of solidarity with everyone present": BGAG Newsletter, 1 (24 Oct. 1972).

94   HCA/CHE/7/17: The correspondence is in this file.

95   CHE Bristol [Newsletter], 25 (Oct. 1981).

96   CHE Bristol Newsletter, July 1974.

97   HCA/Ephemera 55: University of Bristol Gay Liberation Front newsheet one, 1st
      December 1971; University of Bristol Gay Liberation Front Society, Minutes of the
      inaugural General Meeting held 15 December 1971.

98   HCA/Ephemera 55: Trevor Locke to Ruan Bone, Editor, Lunch Magazine, [Bristol], 5
      Nov. 1972.

99   HCA/Ephemera 56: University of Bristol Union Gay Students Society, Agenda &
      minutes of Gaysoc committee meeting, 17 Oct. 1973.

100   BGAG Newsletter, 4 (27 March 1973); HCA/Ephemera 56: University of Bristol
      Union Gay Students Society Gaysoc News sheet, June 1973.

101   'Three hundred attend gay students conference', GN, 35 (1–28 Nov. 1973), p. 4.

102   HCA/Ephemera 55: Trevor Locke to Ruan Bone, Editor, Lunch Magazine, [Bristol],
      5 Nov. 1972; HCA/Ephemera 56: University of Bristol Union Gay Students Society
      Gaysoc Programme, July/August 1973; Gay Students Society & the C.H.E. Bristol
      Youth Group, Pro-forma letter from Convenor to prospective members.

103   GN, 6 [Sept. 1972], p. 6; BGAG Newsletter, 4 (27 March 1973).

104   HCA/CHE/7/17: Bristol Icebreakers [typescript, June 1974]; Bristol Icebreakers 1st
      report [1974]; CHE Bristol news, June 1974; BGAG Newsletter, Dec. [1974]; CHE
      Bristol Newsletter and diary of events, Aug./Sept. 1974; 'Bristol Icebreakers will
      expand', GN, 54 (12–25 Sept. 1974), p. 24.

105 Edward Cherrie, telephone interview, 5 Feb. 2010.

106 Bristol GLF Newsheet, # 1, Oct.–Nov. [1974]; *Move*, 7 (April 1975), p. 15.

107 'Women's group success', *GN*, 54 (12–25 Sept. 1974), p. 24; 'Gay women join parades', *GN*, 67 (27 March–9 April 1975), p. 5.

108 Dale Wakefield, interview, 19 Jan. 2010.

109 Edward Cherrie, telephone interview, 5 Feb. 2010; Dale Wakefield, interview, 19 Jan. 2010.

110 'Queen Victoria does a Nelson', *GN*, 88 (12–25 Feb. 1976), p. 3; 'Lesbians in Bristol', *GN*, 90 (11–24 March 1976), p. 4; 'Gay girls on the march', *News of the World*, 29 Feb. 1976; BGAG Newsletter, May 1976.

111 Angela Needham, telephone interview, 30 Nov. 2009.

112 'CLAN issues womanfesto', *GN*, 91 (25 March–7 April 1976), p. 4; 'Sapphoscene', *Sappho*, 4, 8 (1976), p. 4.

113 'Picket forms outside "gay" club', *GN*, 105 (21 Oct.–3 Nov. 1976), p. 3; 'Gay club loses music licence', *BEP*, 15 Oct. 1976.

114 Edward Cherrie, telephone interview, 5 Feb. 2010.

115 Nigel Collins, interview, 24 Aug. 2009.

116 *Move*, 3 (Nov. 1974), p. 19; *Move*, 7 (April 1975), p. 14; 'Gay alliance meets in new club', *GN*, 68 (10–23 April 1975), p. 4.

117 'New shop opens', *GN*, 152 (5–18 Oct. 1978), p. 8.

118 Bristol Ref. Library B29354: *Gay Bristol news*, 2 (May 1979).

119 HCA/CHE/7/17: Gay Switchboard, Bristol 712621 [Appeal for support, 19.4.75]; 'Bristol too – wherever next?', *GN*, 64 (13–26 Feb. 1975), p. 2; 'Help!', *GN*, 73 (19 June–2 July 1975), p. 5; Dale Wakefield, interview, 19 Jan. 2010.

120 'Bristol's first', *GN*, 91 (25 March–7 April 1976), p. 3; HCA/CHE/7/17: Bristol Gay Switchboard: 5 years of service, 1975–1980; *Move*, 41 (May 1980), p. 2.

121 'Gays go for a civic HQ', *WDP*, 1 Dec. 1976; 'Homosexuals may take over dispute house,' *BEP*, 1 Dec. 1976; 'Trial run for gay shop', *WDP*, 2 Dec. 1976; 'Social centre can go ahead', *BEP*, 2 Dec. 1976; 'Gay group in bid for cash aid', *BEP*, 21 Dec. 1976; 'A centre for gays', *WDP*, 21 July 1977; 'Plans for Bristol centre', *GN*, 107 (18 Nov.–1 Dec. 1976), p. 2; 'Green light for gay fun palace', *GN*, 109 (16 Dec. 1976–12 Jan. 1977), p. 1; 'Amber light – get ready', *Move*, 24 (Dec. [1976]–Jan. [1977]), p. 15–16; *Move*, 25 (Feb. 1977), p. 1–2.

122 'Gay Centre', *Move*, 40 (Sept. 1979), p. 21–22; Bristol Gay Centre news/newsletter, [Nov. 1981]-Summer 84; BRO, 40765 Bristol Gay Centre, Minutes of the Extraordinary General Meeting, 11 Sept. 1984; Chris Leigh, interview, 4 Aug. 2009; Charlie Beaton, interview, 9 Sept. 2009; Dale Wakefield, interview, 19 Jan. 2010.

123 GWDE, Sept. 1995; Feb. 1996; May 1996; Aug. 1996.

124 Gay Bristol Festival, 16th–31st July [1977] [Programme].

125 Dale Wakefield, interview, 19 Jan. 2010.

126 *Move*, 28 (June 1977), p. 24–28; *Move*, 30 (Sept. 1977), p. 19–21.

127 'Gays given festival go-ahead', *BEP*, 21 Oct. 1977; 'Protest on gays fails', *WDP*, 23 Dec. 1977.

128 'Vicar campaigns against "gay festival"', *Times*, 16 Jan. 1978; 'Brotherly love sermon for gays', *WDP*, 4 July 1978.

129 'It's yes to the festival of gays', *WDP*, 15 March 1978; Gay Bristol Festival, 8–16 July [1978] [Programme]; Charlie Beaton, comments on draft, Aug. 2010.

130 Gay Bristol Festival [programme] 1979 and programmes of later festivals and Pride events.

131 'Now Bristol has a "Gay Church"', *BEP*, 18 Oct. 1975; 'Bristol's latest church', *GN*, 82 (6–19 Nov. 1975), p. 7; Angela Needham, telephone interview, 30 Nov. 2009.

132 '"Gay" church attracts more', *BEP*, 20 Oct. 1975; 'A "gay church" gets order to quit', *WDP*, 4 Nov. 1975; 'Gay church told to quit premises', *BEP*, 4 Nov. 1975; 'Church finds home', *WDP*, 5 Nov. 1975; 'MCC eviction', *GN*, 83 (20 Nov.–3 Dec. 1975), p. 4.

133 Angela Needham, telephone interview, 30 Nov. 2009; Avon Pride 90 Lesbian & Gay Festival [programme]; You will be very welcome! Living Springs Metropolitan Community Church, Bath [flyer distributed at Bristol Pride 2010].

134 This section is based on documents and interviews with Chris Leigh, 4 Aug. 2009, and Charlie Beaton, 9 Sept. 2009.

135 *Bridge: the magazine of the Bristol group of the Campaign for Homosexual Equality*, 1 (September 1977) – 5 (September 1978); a 6th issue was being produced when the mimeograph machine broke down: CBA: CHE Bristol Minute book, Planning meeting of 19 Sept. 1978.

136 CBA: CHE Bristol Minute book: Bristol CHE Report on campaigning activities to the 1980 AGM.

137 CHE Bristol, Planning meetings of 27 Nov. 1979; 18 Dec. 1979; CHE Bristol [Newsletter], 6 (15 Dec. 1979).

138 CHE Bristol [Newsletter], 11 (4 July 1980); 12 (23 July 1980).

139 Ibid., 13 (9 Sept. 1980).

140 Ibid., 11 (4 July 1980); Chris Leigh, interview, 4 Aug. 2009.

141 Ibid., 24 (Sept. 1981).

142 Ibid., 25 (Oct. 1981).

143 Ibid., 24 (Sept. 1981).

144 Chris Leigh, 'Gang of five rules .. OK?', ibid., 25 (Oct. 1981).

145 Ibid., 28 (Feb. 1982).

146 Ibid., 31 (May 1982).

147 Ibid., 25 (Oct. 1981).

148 Ibid., 26 (Nov. 1981); 29 (March 1982).

149 Avonscene event calendar, Jan.–Feb. 1982.

150 CHE Bristol [Newsletter], 27 (Jan. 1982).

151 Bath CHE Newsletter, [Aug.–Oct. 1981].

152 CHE Bristol, Planning meetings of May 1981; 16 June 1981; 21 July 1981; 15 Sept. 1981; 20 Oct. 1981; 15 Dec. 1981.

153 CHE Bristol [Newsletter], 32 (June 1982).

154 Ibid., [Sept.–Nov. 1982].

155 Ibid., 33 (July 1982).

156 Ibid., 34 (Aug. 1982).

157 Ibid., 34 (Aug. 1982).

158 Ibid., 9 (22 April 1980).

159 Ibid., [Sept.–Nov. 1982].

160 CBA: Charlie Beaton, CHE Bristol's anecdotes [1983].

161 CHE Bristol [Newsletter], 10 (24 May 1980); 25 (Oct. 1981).

162 Ibid., 18 (30 March 1981); 29 (March 1982).

163 CHE Bristol, Planning meeting of 16 Nov. 1982.

164 CBA: CHE Bristol Minute book, EGM, 11 Jan. 1983.

165 CBA: Charlie Beaton, CHE Bristol's anecdotes [1983].

166 Chris Leigh, interview, 4 Aug. 2009.

167 Trevor Fawcett, *Bath commercialis'd: shops, trades and market at the 18th-century spa* (Bath: Ruton, 2002).

168 Adam Fergusson, *The sack of Bath: a record and an indictment* (Salisbury: Compton Russell, 1973).

169 Patrick Higgins, *Heterosexual dictatorship: male homosexuality in postwar Britain* (London: Fourth Estate, 1996), p. 186, gives a summary of the case; 'Four Bath youths on "Robbery with violence" charge', *BC*, 23 March 1953; '"Stringent" bail for Bath youths', *BC*, 30 March 1953; 'Bath youths charged', *BC*, 22 April 1953; 'Bath youths accused of blackmail', *BC*, 27 April 1953; '"Blackmail" charge: youths for trial', *BC*, 28 April 1953; '"Form of gangsterism" that did not pay', *BC*, 28 May 1953.

170 Ken Little, interview, 21 Aug. 2009.

171 Fred Pearce, *The critical guide to Bath pubs* (Bristol: Bristol Pub Guides, [1976]), p. 6; *GN*, 38 (17–30 Jan. 1974), p. 21.

172 Steve Cossey, interview, 24 July 2009.

173 '"Don't drive us out of our pub" say gays', *BC*, 1 Jan. 1998.

174 BGAG Newsletter, 2 (31 [sic] Nov. 1972); *GN*, 19 [March 1973], p. 16; BGAG News sheet, [Sept.–Oct. 1973].

175 Pearce, *The critical guide to Bath pubs*, p. 8.

176 BGAG Newsletter, 8 [Dec. 1973].

177 GWCM, 18 Dec. 1988.

178 '"Yes" to gay nightclub', *BEP*, 16 Aug. 1997 (Nexis).

179 'Bath Tap's new image', *BC*, 25 Feb. 2010.

180 Kirsten Elliott & Andrew Swift, *Bath pubs* ([Bath?]: Akeman Press, 2003), p. 120.

181 'Row over new gay pub', *BC*, 30 Dec. 2003; 'City pub reopening as gay bar', *BC*, 13 Feb. 2004; 'Gay bar opens after £75,000 revamp', *BC*, 20 Feb. 2004 (all Nexis).

182 'New owner takes over at award-winning gay bar', *BC*, 25 June 2009. The fact that Bath, with its population of 80,000, has had difficulty in supporting more than one pub for any length of time back ups the suggestion that a population of 50,000 men over 20 are required to support a male or mixed gay venue: see Paul Hindle, 'Gay communities and gay space in the city', in *The margins of the city: gay men's urban lives*, ed. by Stephen Whittle (Aldershot: Arena, 1994), p. 7–25 (p. 8), quoting B.P. Hindle, *Gay space: contact and community*, paper presented to Sexuality and Space Network Conference, London, 1992.

183 BGAG Newsletter, 2 (31 [sic] Nov. 1972); *BC*, 7 Nov. 1972.

184 *Move*, 5 (Jan./Feb. 1975), p. [22]; 17 (April 1976), p. 22.

185 *Move*, 6 (March 1975), p. [24].

186 *Move*, 21 (Sept. 1976), p. 1.

187 BGG Newsletter, [March–May 1980]; 45 (Jan./Feb./March 1981).

188 GWDE, Oct. 1986.

189 GWDE, Oct. 1986; Nov. 1986; Dec.1986/Jan. 1987; GWCM, 9 Nov. 1986: as a token of solidarity, the committee agreed not to cash the cheque for the advertisement which the landlady had placed in the newsletter.

190 GWDE, April 1995.

191 *Come Together*, 7 [July 1971], p. 8.

192 This section is based on a collective interview with three of the founding members, Bob Illingworth, Keith Thomas and Norman Lapper, 13 Dec. 2009.

193 UBA: STU9/26: 'Sympathy needed', *SUL: Journal of Bath Union*, 18 March 1971, p.2.

194 UBA: STU9/27: 'Discussion', *SUL: Journal of Bath Union*, 6 May 1971, p.2.

195 HCA/CHE/7/17: Paul [Temperton], CHE, to Ike Cowen, [Manchester], 11 April 1972.

196 *BC*, 24 July 1972.

197 BGAG Newsletter, 1 (24 Oct. 1972).

198 *GN*, 1 [May 1972], p. 12.

199 BGAG Newsletter, 8 [Dec. 1973].

200 Nigel Collins, interview, 24 Aug. 2009; Chris Leigh, interview, 4 Aug. 2009.

201 The first issue of the BGAG Newsletter is no. 1, dated 24 Oct. 1972.

202 BGAG Newsletter, 3 (25 Jan. 1973); 4 (27 March 1973).

203 Ibid., 15 (Sept. 1974).

204 The Constitution of BGAG as adopted by the E.G.M.s on 17th and 24th October [or November] 1974. The month is overtyped on the stencil and it is not clear which is intended, although it is almost certainly October.

205 Andrew Swift & Kirsten Elliott, *The lost pubs of Bath* (Bath: Akeman Press, 2005), p. 62.

206 '"Preacher" in pub row', *BC*, ca. 1975 [exact date unknown]; 'Cold Bath', *GN*, 84 (4–17 Dec. 1975), p. 5; Angela Needham, telephone interview, 30 Nov. 2009.

207 Bob Illingworth, Keith Thomas and Norman Lapper, interview, 13 Dec. 2009.

208 HCA/CHE/7/17: Bob Illingworth to Paul Temperton, Bath, 17 Aug. 1972; BGAG Newsletter, 2 (31 [sic] Nov. 1972).

209 *Lunch*, 17 (Feb. 1973), p. 14–15.

210 BGAG Newsletter, 2 (31 [sic] Nov. 1972).

211 'Bath porn case JPs rule: This one's not obscene', *BC*, 17 April 1974; 'Obscenity trial: Triumph: No case to answer', *GN*, 45 (26 April–8 May 1974), p. 1.

212 'Fight Censorship now', BGAG Newsletter, 11 (April 1974).

213 'Silent demo against censors', *BC*, 17 April 1974; the demonstrators were not liable to prosecution as they were distributing the newspaper free of charge.

214 Bob Illingworth, Keith Thomas, Norman Lapper, interview, 13 Dec. 2009.

215 'What price innocence?', *GN*, 54 (12–25 Sept. 1974), p. 1; 'With all our love', *GN*, 56 (10–23 Oct. 1974), p. 2; 'Grand total for Bath Fund', *GN*, 58 (7–20 Nov. 1974), p. 2.

216 'Gay News' second obscenity trial', *GN*, 66 (13–26 March 1975), p. 3.

217 BGAG Newsletter, 5 (7 June 1973).

218 Ibid., 15 (Sept. 1974).

219 Ibid., 13 (July 1974).

220 The conference reports are in the following issues of the BGAG Newsletter: Morecambe: 5 (7 June 1973); Malvern: 12 (June 1974); NUS Gay Rights Conference in Sheffield: Nov. 1974; International Gay Rights Conference in Edinburgh: Jan. 1975;

Southampton: July 1976.

221 BGAG Newsletter, 12 (June 1974).

222 Ibid., Dec. 1974.

223 Ibid., March 1976; April 1976.

224 Ibid., Feb. 1975.

225 Ibid., May 1976.

226 'Replies to survey', *BC*, 26 May 1976.

227 BGAG Newsletter, March 1977.

228 Ibid., April 1977.

229 Ibid., June 1977.

230 Ibid., End of '78/Beginning of 1979.

231 Ibid., Jan./Feb. 1979.

232 Ibid., April/May/June 1979.

233 Ibid., March/April 1979.

234 BGG [Newsletter], [Nov. 1979–Jan. 1980].

235 Ibid., [Jan.–March 1980].

236 Bath CHE [Newsletter], [March–April 1981].

237 BGG [Newsletter], 45 (Jan./Feb./March 1981); Roland Gonzalez Attwell, telephone interviews, 28 July 2007; 23 Aug. 2010.

238 Bath CHE [Newsletter], [March–April 1981].

239 Ibid., [March–April 1981]; 'Clergy meets gay fighters', *BC*, 30 Jan. 1981.

240 Bath CHE [Newsletter], [March–April 1981]; July–Aug. 1981; 'Rebuff for gays', *BC*, 10 March 1981.

241 Bath CHE Newsletter, series 3, no. 2 (Jan. & Feb. 1982); 'Anger at Gay News in the library', *WDP*, 31 Oct. 1981; 'Gays get a yes', *BC*, 2 Nov. 1981; HCA/CHE/7/17: Roland N. Attwell to G[ay] N[ews], Bath, 2 Nov. 1981, enclosing Press release 'Gay News in Avon Libraries'.

242 Gillian E. Hanscombe & Andrew Lumsden, *Title fight: the battle for Gay News* (London: Brilliance Books, 1983).

243 BGAG Newsletter, Jan./Feb. 1979; BGG Newsletter, April/May/June 1979; July/Aug./ Sept. [1980]; Bath CHE Newsletter, March–April [1982].

244 Bath CHE Newsletter, May/June 1982.

245 Ibid., Nov.–Dec. 1981; May/June 1982.

246 Stephen Jeffery-Poulter, *Peers, queers, and Commons: the struggle for gay law reform from 1950 to the present* (London: Routledge, 1991); Bath CHE committee meeting, 13 July 1982; Bath CHE Newsletter, May/June 1982.

247 'Gay quiz for councillors', *Bath Herald*, 19 March 1981; 'Candidates answer gays', *ibid.*, 30 April 1981; 'Gays get their reply', *ibid.*, 18 June 1981; 'Classroom "ban" on gays', *ibid.*, 25 June 1981; 'The other side of the fence', *ibid.*, 9 July 1981; there were also some letters from readers, both hostile and supportive, commenting on these articles; Bath CHE Newsletter, May/June 1981.

248 Bath CHE Newsletter, July/Aug. 1981.

249 Ibid., [Aug.–Oct. 1981].

250 Ibid., [Aug./Oct. 1981]; 'Union throws shop steward out', *GN*, 216 (28 May–10 June 1981).

251 Bath CHE Newsletter, series 3, no. 2 (Jan. & Feb. 1982); 'The pink triangle vandals',

BC, 9 Nov. 1981.

252 Bath CHE Newsletter, series 3, no. 2 (Jan. & Feb. 1982).

253 Ibid., May & June 1982.

254 'Tory talk', GN, 75 (17 July–13 Aug. 1975), p. 6.

255 BGAG Newsletter, 11 (April 1974).

256 Angela Needham, telephone interview, 30 Nov. 2009.

257 HCA/CHE/7/17: Bath CHE, Annual report, 1981–2, p. 2.

258 'Talk by Gay Awareness Group', Chippenham News, 10 Feb. 1978; BGAG Newsletter, Oct. 1977; Nov. 1977; Bath CHE Gay Group [Newsletter], Sept–Nov. 1980; Bath CHE Newsletter, Nov.–Dec. 1981.

259 Bath CHE Newsletter, May & June 1982.

260 Stephen Bradford, interview, 6 July 2008; extracts from his diaries, 1978–82, and copies of the leaflets circulated by both sides in his collection.

261 BGG, EGM, 24 Sept. 1981; Bath CHE Newsletter, Nov./Dec. [1981].

262 Constitution of the Bath Group of Campaign for Homosexual Equality, 24 September 1981.

263 Bath CHE Newsletter, Nov.–Dec. [1981].

264 'Split in Bath', GN, 228 (12–25 Nov. 1981), p. 7. The new Bath CHE committee replied contesting many of the claims in the article: 'Growing stronger', GN, 229 (26 Nov.–9 Dec. 1981), p. 20.

265 Move, 21 (Sept. 1976), p. 1, 14.

266 HCA/GCO/4/1: CHE, Report of the Special Commission, August 1980; HCA/GCO/1/1:Yes! Together we can build a gay community [Leaflet, 1982]; HCA/CHE/4/5: 'Two views', CHE, Broadsheet, Sept. 1980; HCA/CHE/4/6: 'CHE and GCO Progress Report', CHE, Broadsheet, Aug. 1982; CHE, Annual reports, 1980–1982; Mike Blackmore, 'Report on the Gay Community Organisation' in Gay West, Annual report and accounts, September 1983; HCA/GCO/1/2: Mike Blackmore, 'How it all began … the GCO story', Community news: the national newsletter of the Gay Community Organisation, 1 (April 1984), p. 4–6.

267 Bath CHE, Extraordinary General Meeting, 16 Sept. 1982; GWDE, Oct. 1982.

268 Bath CHE Committee meeting minutes, 17 Aug. 1982. The name has sometimes been written GayWest as one word but for the sake of consistency I have adopted the spelling Gay West except in quotations.

269 CBA: CHE Bristol Minute book, Planning meetings of 16 Nov. 1982; 14 Dec. 1982; EGM, 11 Jan. 1983 ; GWCM, 16 Nov. 1982; 14 Dec. 1982; Gay West General meeting, 13 Jan. 1983.

270 R.J. Morris, 'Clubs, societies and associations', in The Cambridge social history of Britain, 1750–1950. Volume 3. Social agencies and institutions, ed. by F. M. L. Thompson (Cambridge: Cambridge University Press, 1990), p. 395–443; Martin Gorsky, 'Mutual aid and civil society: friendly societies in nineteenth-century Bristol', Urban History, 25, 3 (Dec. 1988): 302–322; Martin Gorsky, Patterns of philanthropy: charity and society in nineteenth-century Bristol (Woodbridge, Suffolk: Royal Historical Society/Boydell Press, 1999).

271 HCA/GCO/3/1: Bath CHE, Notice of Extraordinary General Meeting, 16th September 1982.

272 Bath CHE, EGM, 16 Sept. 1982.

273 HCA/CHE/7/17: Campaign for Homosexual Equality – Bristol, Constitution, valid from 7 March 1972, dated in mss. 25/10/73; CHE-Bristol [Constitution], 8.12.73, mjt; A matter of great great importance to you all [Leaflet]; CHE Bristol, *Chewssheet Group News Extra*, Nov.–Dec. 1973; CHE Bristol, *Chewssheet*, [Jan.–Feb. 1974].

274 CBA: CHE Bristol Minute book, Planning meetings of 23 Aug. 1977; 24 Jan. 1978; AGM, 18 March 1980; Planning meetings of 24 Sept. 1980; 18 Nov. 1980; Jan. 1981; AGM, 17 March 1981.

275 CBA: Constitution of Campaign for Homosexual Equality, Bristol Group, 17 March 1981.

276 The Constitution of Bath Gay Awareness Group as adopted by the E.G.M.s on 17th and 24th October [or November] 1974. The month is overtyped on the stencil but it is almost certainly October.

277 Constitution of the Bath Group of Campaign for Homosexual Equality, 24th September 1981.

278 Bath Gay Community Organisation Constitution, 16th September 1982; Gay West, General Meeting, 13 Jan. 1983.

279 It is not possible to give an exact figure as for some years in the 1990s only first names were given.

280 The membership figures are based on those given in Gay West committee meeting minutes, AGMs and annual reports. Membership figures were published at some periods in the newsletter, particularly from mid-1986 to early 1994. These figures are slightly different, probably because of different ways of counting renewals, but show the same trends.

281 CHE Bulletin, Jan. 1972.

282 CHE Bristol, *Chewssheet*, [Jan.–Feb. 1974].

283 CHE Bristol Group [Newsletter], 10 (24 May 1980); 25 (Oct. 1981).

284 Ibid., 18 (30 March 1981); 29 (March 1982); CBA: Charlie Beaton, CHE Bristol's anecdotes [1983].

285 Bath Gay Group AGM, 22 May 1980; Bath Gay Group CHE Annual report, May 1981; Bath CHE Annual report, 1981–2.

286 Gay West Annual report & accounts, Sept. 1983.

287 John Pritchett, interview, 3 June 2007.

288 GWDE, Sept.–Oct. 2001; Sept. 2002–March 2003; John Bescoby, interview, 20 July 2007.

289 This is a quite different pattern from the predominance of a new middle class based on education and public sector employment found by Paul Byrne and can perhaps be explained by the fact that the incidence of homosexuality cuts across all social classes; see Paul Byrne, *Social movements in Britain* (London: Routledge, 1997), p. 63.

290 Ernie Everest, interview, 31 March 2008.

291 GWCM, 5 Dec. 1994.

292 Gay West AGM, 5 Sept. 1998.

293 Gay West Membership Secretary to author, email, 5 Sept. 2010.

294 GWDE, June 1996.

295 GWCM, 10 Feb. 1985.

296 *BC*, 16 May 1981; 26 March 1982; 1 Oct. 1982; *Chippenham News and Wiltshire Times*, March 1981.

297 CHE Bristol, *Chewssheet*, Autumn 1973.

298 *Bridge: the magazine of the Bristol group of the Campaign for Homosexual Equality*, 1 (September 1977) – 5 (September 1978); a 6th issue was being produced when the mimeograph machine broke down: CBA: CHE Bristol Minute book, Planning meeting of 19 Sept. 1978.

299 The earliest issue of the new series which I have been able to find is no. 6 of 15 December 1979.

300 The last issue I have found is not dated but covers Sept.–Nov. 1982 and there is a reference in the minutes to delaying the November 1982 newsletter to cover December: CBA: CHE Bristol Minute book, Planning meeting of 19 Oct. 1982.

301 Bath CHE committee meeting, 22 June 1982.

302 GWDE, May 2000; Sept. 2001.

303 GWCM, 11 March 2002; 10 April 2002.

304 Bath CHE Committee meeting, 13 July 1982.

305 Bath CHE/Gay West, *Gaylink*, 1 [Aug. 1982], 2 (Oct. 1982), 3 (Xmas 1982) and 4 (Spring 1983).

306 John Pritchett, interview, 3 June 2007.

307 Bath CHE Committee meeting, 2 Dec. 1981; Bath CHE Newsletter, Series 3, no. 2, Jan./Feb. 1982; Roland Gonzalez-Attwell, telephone interview, 28 July 2007.

308 GWCM, 14 Dec. 1982: it was listed among the January events simply as "Coffee @ BCVS" with no other comment; GWDE, Jan. 1983.

309 GWDE, Jan. 1984.

310 Lisa Duggan, 'Making it perfectly queer', in *Sex wars: sexual dissent and political culture*, ed. by Lisa Duggan and Nan D. Hunter (New York: Routledge, 1995), p. 155–172.

311 Sarah. F. Green, *Urban Amazons: lesbian feminism and beyond in the gender, sexuality and identity battles of London* (Basingstoke: Macmillan, 1997); Janet Dixon, 'Separatism: a look back in anger', in *Radical records: thirty years of lesbian and gay history, 1957–1987*, ed. by Bob Cant & Susan Hemmings (London: Routledge, 1988), p. 69–84.

312 Ian Lucas, *Outrage! An oral history* (London: Cassell, 1998).

313 Lesbian Line published a newsletter entitled *Lines* in 1987.

314 *The Bristol radical lesbian feminist magazine*, 1–2 (Sept.–Nov. 1986).

315 GWDE, March 1992; Berkeley Wilde, interview, 19 March 2010.

316 John Pritchett, interview, 3 June 2007.

317 Bath Gay Awareness Group Newsletter, Dec. [1974].

318 S. Roberts, 'Bisexuality: myth and mystery', GWDE, June 1999.

319 GWDE, Oct. 1990.

320 GWDE, Nov. 1985.

321 Gay West AGM, 20 Sept. 1984; GWCM, 11 Oct. 1984; see also John Bescoby's letter to the Southampton GCO, 13 Sept. 1984 in HCA/GCO/4/1.

322 GWDE, March 1983; Feb. 1985.

323 GWCM, 16 Dec. 1990; 17 Feb. 1991; 12 Jan. 1992; Ernie Everest, comments on draft text, Oct. 2010.

324 Avonscene event calendar, Jan.–Feb. 1982.

325 GWDE, Feb. 1983.

326 BRO, 40765: Bristol Gay Centre, Minutes of the Member's Meeting held on 17 Jan. 1984 refers to the winding -up of Avonscene.

327 GWDE, May 1985, Feb 1990. The same contact name, Alwyn, appeared in the *Gay News* listings for, consecutively, CHE Bristol, Avonscene and Amicus.

328 Chris Brown, interview, 15 March 2010.

329 GWCM, 18 Feb. 1990; 21 July 1991; 25 Aug. 1991; 17 Nov. 1991.

330 GWDE, Oct. 1990.

331 GWDE, April 1998; Sept.–Oct. 2001; Sept. 2002–March 2003.

332 GMG Southwest Newsletter, March–April 2010.

333 GWCM, 28 June 1987; *Observer*, 25 June 1989.

334 GWCM, 21 May 1989; 18 March 1990. The Gay West committee thought the coach might not be filled and Lesbian Line declined to underwrite any potential loss.

335 GWDE, Sept. 1986.

336 GWDE, Aug. 1988.

337 Paul Green, conversation, 10 April 2010.

338 GWDE, June 1991.

339 GWDE, March 1988.

340 Diesel Balaam, interview, 26 July 2008; Diesel Balaam to author, email, 27 July 2008.

341 GWDE, June 1992.

342 GWDE, July 1992.

343 GWDE, Oct. 1990.

344 GWDE, June 1987.

345 GWDE, Aug. 1987.

346 GWDE, Aug. 1989; Nov. 1990.

347 GWDE, July 1991.

348 GWDE, Aug. 1991.

349 GWDE, Aug. 1995.

350 GWDE, March 2000.

351 GWDE, April 2000.

352 GWDE, May 2000.

353 CHE Bristol, *Chewssheet*, March 1973.

354 GWDE, July 1986.

355 GWCM, 17 March 1991.

356 'Gay not isolated', *Bath & Keynsham Advertiser*, 27 April 1990; GWDE, June, July, Aug., Sept. 1990.

357 Peter Robinson, *The changing world of gay men* (Basingstoke: Palgrave Macmillan, 2008). See also Anthony R. D'Augelli, Charlotte J. Patterson, eds., *Lesbian, gay, and bisexual identities over the lifespan: psychological perspectives* (New York: Oxford University Press, 1995); Douglas Kimmel, Tara Rose, and Steven David, eds., *Lesbian, gay, bisexual, and transgender aging: research and clinical perspectives* (New York: Columbia University Press, 2006).

358 GWCM, 18 Oct. 1992.

359 GWCM, 5 Dec. 1994.

360 GWCM, 4 Jan. 1995; 8 Feb. 1995.

361 Gay West Constitution, 15 Sept. 1997.

362 GWDE, Dec. 1993/Jan. 1994.

363 GWDE, Oct. 1989.

364 David Rayside, *On the fringe: gays and lesbians in politics* (Ithaca, NY: Cornell University Press, 1998), p. 11–12.

365 Stephen M. Engel, *The unfinished revolution: social movement theory and the gay and lesbian movement* (Cambridge: Cambridge University Press, 2001), p. 9.

366 Matthew Waites, *The age of consent: young people, sexuality and citizenship* [2005] (Basingstoke: Palgrave Macmillan, 2009), p.133–157.

367 Campaign Secretary's reports in Bath CHE *Annual Report*, 1981–2; Gay West *Annual Report and Accounts*, September 1983; General Secretary's Report 1982.

368 'Gays stage protest on advert ban', *BC*, 3 March 1983; 'Postcard protest', *BC*, 7 March 1983.

369 Bristol Gay Festival, 8–16 June 1985 [Programme]; Lesbian Line produced a newsletter entitled *Lines: Bristol Lesbian Line Newsletter*, Sept. 1987.

370 *The Bristol radical lesbian feminist magazine*, 1–2 (Sept.–Nov. 1986).

371 CBA: Chris Leigh, *Results of questionnaire to candidates standing in Avon County Council elections, 7ᵗʰ May 1981*, Bristol: C.H.E. Bristol, 19 May 1981 (mimeograph); CHE Bristol Minute book, Planning meeting of May 1981.

372 Donald Branch, interview, 4 Aug. 2009.

373 Charlie Beaton, interviews, 9 Sept. 2009; 2 May 2010.

374 'Benn in gay plea', *WDP*, 28 Jan. 1981.

375 'Call to battle for gay rights', *BEP*, 11 June 1986; 'MP in battle against prejudice: Dawn attacks gay bashers in new campaign', *BEP*, 20 March 2000.

376 Donald Branch, interview, 4 Aug. 2009.

377 Charlie Beaton, interview, 9 Sept. 2009.

378 Peter Purton, *Sodom, Gomorrah and the New Jerusalem: Labour and lesbian and gay rights, from Edward Carpenter to today* (London: Labour Campaign for Lesbian and Gay Rights, 2006).

379 CBA: Labour Party conference 1985 agenda, p. 26, attached to Minutes of LCLGR meeting, 4 March 1986.

380 'My terror, by gay Labour man', *BEP*, 4 Oct. 1985; 'Homosexuality law: delegates back gays on age of consent', *Times*, 5 Oct. 1985; 'Unions back plea for teen gay sex', *WDP*, 5 Oct. 1985; 'Homosexual age of consent "should be 16"', *Guardian*, 5 Oct. 1985; 'Victory for gay rights resolution', *Labour weekly*, 11 Oct. 1985; 'We won! Historic decision at party conference', *Capital Gay*, 11 Oct. 1985, p. 1, 3.

381 '"Yes, I'm gay" says the Liberals' man in Bath', *BC*, 4 March 1980; 'Why Mr. Atack is not defensive', *BC*, 6 March 1980; 'Gay Lib: call for new vote', *BC*, 11 March 1980; 'Gay Lib's speech on liberty gets ovation', *BC*, 13 March 1980; 'Wardle: "I'll not work for Steve Atack"', *BC*, 18 March 1980; 'Bath's Liberal candidate quits', *BC*, 22 Oct. 1980; *Gay News*, 204 (27 Nov.–10 Dec. 1980), p. 2.

382 Bath Gay Group Newsletter, 3 (25 Jan. 1973).

383 Ibid., [May–July 1980].

384 Bath CHE Newsletter, Nov.–Dec. [1980].

385 Sue Coffey, 'Gay quiz for councillors', *Bath Herald*, 19 March 1981; Ray Wardle, 'Family life backbone of the nation', *ibid.*, 26 March 1981; David England, Roland

Attwell, 'A fact of life', *ibid.*, 2 April 1981; D.M. Heard, 'Queer-bashing – even in Bath', *ibid.*, 9 April 1981.

386 en.wikipedia.org/wiki/Stephen_Williams_(politician), accessed 17/06/2011; Williams was re-elected with a larger majority in 2010.

387 en.wikipedia.org/wiki/Robert_Hayward, accessed 15/06/2010.

388 'Gays in war on Tories', *BC*, 24 Oct. 1981.

389 'Students to ballot on Tory "joke" book', *BC*, 28 Oct. 1981; 'Setback for gays and feminists', *BC*, 30 Oct. 1981.

390 'Tory agent takes gay post', *BC*, 14 Nov. 1986.

391 'Tories back Patten agent in gay job', *BEP*, 18 Nov. 1986; 'Tory disquiet over Bob's gay post', *WDP*, 18 Nov. 1986; 'Top Tory backs agent's gay campaign', *WDP*, 19 Nov. 1986.

392 'Tory agent is gay club chief', *Daily Telegraph*, 19 Nov. 1986; 'Tory agent in gay row', *Daily Express*, 19 Nov. 1986; 'Top Tory runs club for gays', *The Sun*, 19 Nov. 1986.

393 'Brigadier in storm over a gay Tory', *Sunday Express*, 21 Dec. 1986.

394 GWCM, 9 & 30 Nov. 1986.

395 Bob Osborne, interview, 6 July 2008.

396 Alexandra Chasin, *Selling out: the gay and lesbian movement goes to market* (New York: Palgrave, 2000); for a Marxist view, see Nicola Field, *Over the rainbow: money, class and homophobia* (London: Pluto Press, 1995).

397 Authors cited in Mario Diani, 'The concept of social movement', in *Civil societies and social movements, domestic, transnational, global*, ed. by Ronnie D. Lipschutz (Aldershot: Ashgate, 2006), p. 129–153 (p. 140).

398 Bath Gay Awareness Group Newsletter, 8 [Dec. 1973].

399 One of the entertainments was to watch theatre-goers come in for a quick drink. After getting their drinks from the bar, they began to look around and then the penny dropped. Most drank up quickly and left.

400 GWCM, 26 April 1987.

401 GWCM, 6 July 1995; 8 April 1998; GWDE, March 1998; May 1998.

402 GWCM, 12 Nov. 1997.

403 GWCM, 10 Dec. 1997.

404 '"Don't drive us out of our pub" say gays', *BC*, 1 Jan.1998.

405 GWDE, May 1998.

406 GWCM, 9 or 30 Sept. 2002.

407 GWDE, Jan. 1985.

408 GWDE, Nov. 1991.

409 GWDE, Jan. 1985.

410 GWDE, Sept./Oct. 1985.

411 Roland Gonzalez Attwell, telephone interviews, 28 July 2007; 23 Aug. 2010.

412 Bath Gay Group/Bath CHE News letter, 45 (Jan./Feb./March 1981); Bath CHE/Bath Gay Group [Newsletter, March–April 1981]; Bath Gay Group CHE Annual report, year ending May 1981; 'Clergy meets gay fighters', *BC*, 30 Jan. 1981; 'Spotlight on help for gays', *BC*, 2 March 1981. The venue for the meeting with the clergy was subject to confirmation and the reports do not mention the actual location, so I cannot confirm that this was indeed the first use; the building was certainly used for the CHE

Regional Conference: Bath Gay Group/CHE Annual report, May 1980–May 1981.

413 GWDE, Nov. 1984.

414 GWCM, 9 Dec. 1984; 18 Dec. 1988.

415 GWCM, 24 July 1988.

416 'Homosexuality and the voluntary sector', *BCVS Newsletter*, May 1989, p. 11–28; GWCM, 21 May 1989; Diesel Balaam, 'Campaigning', GWDE, June 1989; Diesel Balaam, interview, 26 July 2008.

417 GWCM, 10 Nov. 1985; Steve Cossey, interview, 24 July 2009.

418 GWCM, 11 Oct. 1984; 5 Nov. 1984; GWDE, Dec. 1989/Jan. 1990.

419 'Angry charge of the gay brigade', *BC*, 1 Feb. 1985.

420 GWCM, [23] June 1994; 'Gay times on the TV soaps', *BC*, 23 June 1994.

421 GWCM, 17 Nov. 1991; 10 May 1995; 8 Aug. 1995; 20 Sept. 1995; 4 Oct. 1995; 13 Dec. 1995; 5 March 1996; 10 April 1996; GWDE, Dec.1991/Jan. 1992.

422 Ernie Everest, comments on draft text, Oct. 2010.

423 Bath CHE, General Secretary's report, 1982.

424 GWDE, Jan. 1985.

425 '"Gay" cancer? Or mass media scare? A report from Canada's "Body Politic"', *GN*, 228 (12–25 Nov. 1981), p. 21.

426 Virginia Berridge, *AIDS in the UK: the making of policy, 1981–1994* (Oxford: Oxford University Press, 1996).

427 Philip Gatter, *Identity and sexuality: AIDS in Britain in the 1990s* (London: Cassell, 1999).

428 'AIDS: how a simple touch can ease the suffering', *BC*, 27 Jan. 1986.

429 GWDE, March 1986.

430 'Four hit by killer disease', *BC*, 28 Jan. 1985.

431 CBA: Social services funding for the Aled Richards Trust (ART) [June 1989].

432 Gay West, General Meeting, 13 Jan. 1983.

433 GWDE, July 1983; Feb. 1984; May 1985; July 1985.

434 GWDE, March 1985; April 1985; March 1986; April 1986.

435 'Four hit by killer disease', *BC*, 28 Jan. 1985.

436 'Angry charge of the gay brigade', *BC*, 1 Feb. 1985.

437 'It's gay plague! Story of a new terror', *BC*, 8 Feb. 1985.

438 'AIDS: official advice', *BC*, 13 Feb. 1985.

439 GWDE, March 1985.

440 CBA: Gay Men's Health Network in Avon [hereafter GMHNA], Notes of meeting held 20 Feb. 1985.

441 CBA: GMHNA, Notes of meeting held 6 March; 21 March; 14 April; 22 May; 27 June; 7 Aug.; 9 Sept.; 29 Oct.; 12 Nov.; 10 Dec. 1985; 14 Jan.; 11 Feb. 1986.

442 CBA: GMHNA, Press releases, 7 March 1985; 23 March 1985.

443 CBA: GMHNA, Agenda for 14 April 1985.

444 GWCM, 10 March 1985; CBA: Paul Cannon, BBC television reporter, to Charlie Beaton, Bristol, [March 1985?] + Charlie Beaton's mss draft reply, 10.4.85.

445 Charlie Beaton, interview, 9 Sept. 2009; Chris Leigh to author, comments on draft, 22 Aug. 2010.

446 CBA: GMHNA, Notes of meetings held 27 June 1995; 7 Aug. 1985.

447 CBA: A new Trust to help people with A.I.D.S. [fundraising leaflet, Nov. 1985].

448 CBA: The Constitution of the Aled Richards Trust.

449 CBA: Dr. Martin R.F. Reynolds, Chief Medical Adviser, SWRHA, Bristol, to C. Beaton, 4 Feb. 1986.

450 CBA: Charlie Beaton to W.K. Mitchell, Bristol, 9 April 1986; ART, Press release, 16 April 1986; 'Charity sets up AIDS help line', *WDP*, 17 April 1986; 'Help on the line for Aids victims', *BEP*, 17 April 1986.

451 CBA: Estimate attached to Charlie Beaton to Sarah Marks, Bristol Council for Voluntary Service, 27 Oct. 1985.

452 Aled Richards Trust, *Annual report*, 1987–88, p. 2–3; CBA: ART Trust Management Committee, Report to TMC from Development Group, Funding application to District Health Authorities, 24.I.90.

453 CBA: Aled Richards Trust: Special Management Committee Meeting, Wednesday 28 January [1987]; Aled Richards Trust, *Broadsheet*, Feb. 1987.

454 GWCM, 27 March 1988; 17 April 1988. The Bath group was initially unsure of its status and was firmly told that it was a subcommittee under the control of the Bristol office: CBA: Aled Richards Trust, Bath to Aled Richards Trust, Bristol, Trust Management Committee, 31.3.89; Aled Richards Trust, Development Sub-committee held 13 April 1989, Services in Bath.

455 CBA: Social services funding for the Aled Richards Trust (ART) [June 1989]; Aled Richards Trust, *Broadsheet*, June–July 1989.

456 Aled Richards Trust, *News*, Dec. 1989.

457 Aled Richards Trust, *Annual report*, 1998–99, p. 24.

458 Adam Lent, *British social movements since 1945: sex, colour, peace and power* (Basingstoke: Palgrave, 2001).

459 CBA: Charlie Beaton to the Secretary, Bristol Gay Switchboard, 27 Oct. 1985.

460 Jeffrey Weeks et al., 'Community responses to HIV and AIDS: the "de-gaying" and "re-gaying" of AIDS', in *Sexual cultures: communities, values and intimacy*, ed. by Jeffrey Weeks and Janet Holland (Basingstoke: Macmillan, 1996), p. 161–179.

461 Flyer inserted in GWDE, March 1992.

462 GWDE, March 1992.

463 GWDE, July 1998.

464 GWDE, Feb. 1996; July 1998.

465 GWCM, 27 April 2004.

466 Aled Richards Trust Gay Men's Project, *Report to the community*, Edition One, July 1998.

467 Terrence Higgins Trust West, Gay Men's Team, *Report to the community*, June 2000.

468 Aled Richards Trust, *Broadsheet*, June–July 1989; GWDE, June 1992.

469 There was a sauna called the Gemini in West Street in the mid 1970s.

470 GWCM, 10 Aug. 1986; 4 Jan. 1987; 26 June 1988; GWDE, March 1987.

471 Aled Richards Trust, *Broadsheet*, June–July 1989; Aled Richards Trust (Bath group), [Newsletter, Sept.–Oct. 1989].

472 GWDE, June 1994.

473 Stewart Lansley, Sue Goss and Christian Wolmar, *Councils in conflict: the rise and fall of the Municipal Left* (Basingstoke: Macmillan, 1989), p. 160–174; Davina Cooper, *Sexing the city: lesbian and gay politics within the activist state* (London: Rivers Oram Press, 1994).

474 House of Commons Parliamentary Papers Online, 1987/88 Bill 65 Local Government.

475 The clause changed its number during its passage through Parliament but after passing was usually referred to as Section 28 of the Local Government Act 1988.

476 GWDE, Feb. 1988; March 1988; April 1988.

477 'Lesbians in £200 grant rumpus', *BEP*, 11 March 1988; 'Homosexuals' protest posters torn down: Banners anger of city gays', *BEP*, 8 April 1988; 'Gay outrage as city hits protest', *WDP*, 9 April 1988.

478 '"Pupils getting advice on gays"', *BEP*, 10 March 1988; 'The storm over that Clause 29: School probed on gay papers', *BEP*, 11 March 1988; Charlie Beaton, interview, 9 Sept. 2009.

479 GWCM, 24 Jan. 1988.

480 GWDE, Feb. 1988.

481 GWDE, March 1988.

482 GWDE, April 1988.

483 GWDE, Feb. 1988.

484 GWDE, May 1988.

485 GWDE, June 1988.

486 GWDE, July 1988.

487 GWCM, 28 June 1987; Gay West AGM, 9 Sept. 1987.

488 Bob Osborne, interview, 6 July 2008.

489 GWCM, 22 May 1988.

490 GWDE, July 1988.

491 GWDE, July 1988.

492 GWDE, May 1988.

493 Gay West Campaign Secretary's report, 14 Oct. 1988–7 Jan. 1989; GWCM, 20 Nov. 1988.

494 'Head bans "gay" play', *BEP*, 26 Oct. 1988; 'Trapped by "Clause 28"', *Stage and Television Today*, 3 Nov. 1988.

495 'Our concern at "gay" article', *BEP*, 3 Nov. 1988; 'Young watch "banned" play', *BC*, 1 Nov. 1988.

496 GWDE, June 1989.

497 GWDE, Christmas double issue 88–89.

498 GWDE, April 1992.

499 GWDE, March 1994.

500 GWDE, April 1994.

501 GWDE, June 1994.

502 GWDE, June 1997.

503 Anya Palmer, 'Lesbian and gay rights campaigning: a report from the coalface', in *A simple matter of justice? Theorizing lesbian and gay politics*, ed. by Angelia R. Wilson (London: Cassell, 1995), p. 32–50.

504 Ian Lucas, *Outrage! An oral history* (London: Cassell, 1998).

505 Geoffrey Evans, 'In search of tolerance', in *British social attitudes: the 19th report*, ed. by Alison Park et al. (London: Sage Publications, 2002), p. 213–229.

506 David Rayside, *On the fringe: gays and lesbians in politics* (Ithaca, NY: Cornell University Press, 1998); Peter Purton, *Sodom, Gomorrah and the New Jerusalem:*

Labour and lesbian and gay rights, from Edward Carpenter to today (London: Labour Campaign for Lesbian and Gay Rights, 2006).

507 Melvyn Read, David Marsh and David Richards, 'Why did they do it? Voting on homosexuality and capital punishment in the House of Commons', *Parliamentary affairs*, 47, 3 (July 1994): 374–386; David Smith, 'The anatomy of a campaign', and Anya Palmer, 'Lesbian and gay rights campaigning: a report from the coalface', in *A simple matter of justice?* ed. by Wilson, p. 10–31, 32–50; Derek McGhee, *Homosexuality, law and resistance* (London: Routledge, 2001); Matthew Waites, *The age of consent: young people, sexuality and citizenship* [2005] (Basingstoke: Palgrave Macmillan, 2009).

508 Labour is protecting, extending and defending LGBT rights [leaflet distributed at 2009 London Pride].

509 For an outsider's view of the area at this time, see Paul Burston, *Queens' country* (London: Little, Brown, 1998), chap. 7 'A cottage in the country: Somerset', p. 149–178.

510 John Hesketh, interview, 26 Nov. 2010.

511 GWDE, Sept. 1997.

512 GWDE, May 1999; Sept. 1999.

513 'Bristol set to create village atmosphere', *Pink Paper*, 910 (5 Oct. 2006), p. 10; Paul Hindle, 'Gay communities and gay space in the city' and Stephen Whittle, 'Consuming differences: the collaboration of the gay body with the cultural state', both in *The margins of the city: gay men's urban lives*, ed. by Stephen Whittle (Aldershot: Arena, 1994), p. 7–25, 27–41; Stephen Quilley, 'Constructing Manchester's "New Urban Village": gay space in the entrepreneurial city', in *Queers in space: communities, public places, sites of resistance*, ed. by Gordon Brent Ingram, Anne-Marie Bouthillette and Yolanda Retter (Seattle: Bay Press, 1997), p. 275–292.

514 Berkeley generally used his first name or Berkeley B. at this time but is now known as Berkeley Wilde.

515 'If enough of us act, we can create change; Profile: Gay campaigner Berkeley Burchell talks to Keith Bradford about why he at last feels at home in the city of his birth', *BEP*, 17 Feb. 2000 (Nexis); Berkeley Wilde, interview, 19 March 2010.

516 GWDE, March 1992; June 1992.

517 GWDE, Jan./Feb. 1993; March 1993.

518 GWDE, Nov. 1993; Berkeley Wilde, interview, 19 March 2010.

519 Pride West programmes, 1994; 1995; 1996; GWDE, Dec. 1995/Jan. 1996.

520 'Bristol struts its stuff', *Pink Paper*, 906 (10 Aug. 2006), p. 3.

521 'Gay first as mayor opens Pride festival', *Pink Paper*, 381 (2 June 1995), p. 6; 'Festival first for gays in the West', *BEP*, 5 June 1995.

522 Pride Bristol programme 2010.

523 www.pridewest.co.uk.

524 Aled Richards Trust, *Annual report*, 1998–1999, p. 24–25.

525 Aled Richards Trust, Gay Men's Project, *Report to the Community*, Edition One, July 1998; Terrence Higgins Trust West, Gay Men's Team, *Report to the community*, June 2000.

526 David Abbott and Joyce Howarth, *Secret loves, hidden lives? Exploring issues for*

people with learning difficulties who are gay, lesbian or bisexual (Bristol: Policy Press, 2005).

527 Charlie Beaton, interviews, 9 Sept. 2009; 2 May 2010.

528 Chris Leigh, interview, 4 Aug. 2009.

529 'Bigoted view of city cash for gays', *BEP*, 26 Nov. 1986; 'Attack on gay grant by Tories is a flop', *BEP*, 14 Oct. 1987; 'Stop the prejudice and help gay groups', *BEP*, 14 Oct. 1987; 'Lesbians in £200 grant rumpus', *BEP*, 11 Mar. 1988; 'Outrage at bid to hold "gay courses" for council', *WDP*, 23 June 1988; 'Council backs "gay bias" courses', *WDP*, 29 June 1988.

530 'Fury over £1,000 help for lesbians', *The Sport*, 15 Aug. 1991.

531 'Councillor in "dirty tricks" row over lesbian group', *Pink Paper*, 369 (10 March 1995), p. 2.

532 GWDE, May 1995.

533 GWDE, Oct. 1995.

534 GWDE, March 1995; Aug. 1996.

535 GWDE, July 1998.

536 *Second best value: lesbian, gay and bisexual life in Bristol* (Bristol: Bristol LGB Forum, 1999).

537 *Compact between the lesbian, gay and bisexual community and Bristol City Council* (Bristol: LGB Forum, 2000).

538 *A guide to lesbian, gay and bisexual life in Bristol* (Bristol: Bristol City Council, [2004]).

539 Bristol LGB Forum website, www.bristol-lgb-forum.org.uk, accessed 15/02/10.

540 HCA/Ephemera 53: letters and flyers relating to the BLGYG in 1985–86; GWDE, Oct. 1986.

541 GWDE, Feb. 1992.

542 GWDE, Sept. 1995.

543 'Gay barbecues to burn Lottery cash', *Daily Mail*, 20 June 1996: www.thefreelibrary.com, accessed 21/06/10; Berkeley Wilde, interview, 19 March 2010.

544 GWDE, June 1998.

545 Freedom Youth website, www.freedomyouth.co.uk/intro.htm, accessed 21/06/10.

546 GWDE, Oct. 1996.

547 GWDE, July 1998; Nov. 1998.

548 GWDE, Aug. 1996; Oct. 1996.

549 Craig Denney, *History of the lesbian, gay, bisexual & transgender community in South Gloucestershire since 1995: a personal history* (Gay History Month 2007), www.southglos.gov.uk, accessed 28/06/10.

550 GWDE, June 1997.

551 Denney, *History of the lesbian, gay, bisexual & transgender community in South Gloucestershire*.

552 www.sglgbf.org.uk/young_people.htm#PTABOUT, accessed 26/07/10.

553 GWDE, Dec. 1995/Jan. 1996.

554 GWDE, May 1998; June 2010; www.bristolfamiliesandfriends.org.uk/aboutus.htm, accessed 21/06/10.

555 GWDE, Feb. 1992; Manuel Gosano to author, 24 and 25 Aug. 2010, emails.

556 www.singoutbristol.com, accessed 27/07/10.

557 GWDE, Dec. 2002/Jan. 2003.

558 GWDE, Nov. 1996; June 2010; www.bisonsrfc.co.uk, accessed 12/12/10; www.bristolpanthers.co.uk/about.html, accessed 21/06/10; www.cycleoutbristol.ning. com, accessed 27/07/10.

559 *The University of Bristol LGBTsoc handbook '09/10.*

560 GWDE, Dec. 1995/Jan. 1996.

561 GWDE, May 1991.

562 Sid Roberts, interview, 21 July 2009.

563 GWDE, Dec. 1993/Jan. 1994.

564 Gay West AGM, 5 Sept. 1998.

565 GWCM, 22 July 1997.

566 GWCM, 7 Jan. 1998; 8 April 1998; 6 May 1998.

567 GWCM, 8 July 1998; GWDE, Aug. 1998.

568 GWDE, July 1999.

569 GWDE, Sept 2000.

570 GWDE, Dec. 2000/Jan. 2001.

571 BGAG Newsletter, 2 (31 [sic] Nov. 1972).

572 'Legal status for gay relationships: council backing: bid to stamp out discrimination', *BC*, 22 Feb. 2002 (Nexis); GWDE, April 2002; May 2002.

573 GWCM, 19 Jan. 2006.

574 GWCM, 10 April 2002; 20 May 2002; GWDE, June 2002.

575 'Church honours gay support group', *BC*, 30 June 2007 (Nexis); 'Church honours gay support group', *BC*, 21 July 2007 (Nexis).

576 Paul Green, interview, 2 Aug. 2008.

577 BGAG Newsletter, [Sept. 1973]; Series 2, no. 2 [Nov.–Dec. 1973]; 8 [Dec. 1973].

578 Ibid., End of '78/Beginning of 1979; Jan./Feb. 1979; BGG Newsletter, June/July 1979; Aug./Sept. 1979.

579 Bath CHE Newsletter, Nov.–Dec. [1981].

580 Ibid., [Aug.–Oct. 1981]; Series 3, no. 2, Jan./Feb. 1982.

581 Bath CHE Diary of events, May 1982; Bath CHE committee meeting, 17 May 1982.

582 GWDE, April 1983; June 1983.

583 John Pritchett, interview, 3 June 2007.

584 GWDE, Oct. 1984.

585 GWCM, 10 Feb. 1985.

586 GWCM, 12 April 1985.

587 GWCM, 7 July 1985.

588 GWCM, 15 July 1990; 21 Oct. 1990; 16 Dec. 1990; 20 Jan. 1991; 17 Feb. 1991; 'Angry gays blast bid to block disco', *BC*, 23 Nov. 1990; 'Gay disco at sport centre is approved', *BC*, 29 Nov. 1990.

589 GWCM, 4 May 1986.

590 GWDE, Sept. 1987.

591 GWDE, Sept. 1988.

592 '"Don't drive us out of our pub" say gays', *BC*, 1 Jan. 1998.

593 Bristol CHE, *Chewssheet*, [March–April 1974]; 'Censorship', Bristol CHE, *Chewssheet*

Supplement, [April–June 1974].

594   BGAG Newsletter, 2 (31 [sic] November 1972).

595   GWDE, July 1990.

596   GWDE, Nov. 1990.

597   'Cruiser's guide to cottaging', Gay West, *Gaylink*, 3 (Xmas 82), p. 12, 14.

598   GWDE, Oct. 1988.

599   Martin Grant, 'Nasty tales,' *Lunch*, 19 (April 1973), p. 16–18.

600   'Police rushed in', *BC*, 6 April 1977.

601   'Man denies indecency charge', *BEP*, 24 Feb. 1982.

602   'Astounded', *BC*, 12 Sept. 1979.

603   Bath CHE Newsletter, [March–April 1981].

604   CBA: The police in cottages [Leaflet]; CHE Bristol Minute book, Planning meetings of
       13 July 1982; 21 Sept. 1982; 19 Oct. 1982; 16 Nov. 1982.

605   'Outcry over men of vice: picnic site sex scandal', *BEP*, 9 July 1983; 'Call to clear
       up "picnic vice spot"', *WDP*, 11 July 1983; CBA: Portway picnic, 3 pm, Sunday 7th
       August [Leaflet];'"Men of vice" go picnicking', *Capital Gay*, 108 (19 Aug. 1983), p. 3.

606   'Vice police trap gay sex pests', *BEP*, 4 July 1986; 'Police arrest men in swoop on West
       picnic spot', *WDP*, 5 July 1986; CBA: Report of the meeting on entrapment held on
       19th August 1986 with Superintendent Tweedie; Keith Houghton to Superintendent
       Tweedie, Bristol, 4 Oct. 1986.

607   HCA/Ephemera 56: University of Bristol Union Gay Students Society, News sheet 3
       (12 May 1973).

608   CBA: CHE Bristol Minute book, Planning Meeting on 24 Oct 1978.

609   Bath CHE Newsletter, May & June 1982; GWCM, 16 Nov. 1982.

610   GWDE, May 1990.

611   Nick Tilley, 'Modern approaches to policing: community, problem-oriented and
       intelligence-led', in *Handbook of policing*, ed. by Tim Newburn (Cullompton, Devon:
       Willan Publishing, 2008), p. 373–403.

612   LAGPA, *Annual report*, 1993.

613   Her Majesty's Inspectorate of Constabulary, *Winning the race: policing plural
       communities: HMIC thematic inspection report on police community and race
       relations 1996/97*, p. 42–43; Her Majesty's Inspectorate of Constabulary, *Winning
       the race: policing plural communities revisited: a follow-up to the thematic inspection
       report on police community and race relations 1998/99*, p. 28.

614   CBA: ASLGPI, Briefing notes, Section 7, Significant dates [1998].

615   CBA: The constitution of the Avon and Somerset Lesbian and Gay Policing Initiative,
       to be proposed 22 Sept. 1998.

616   GWA: New police liaison group with lesbian and gay communities: News release,
       17 Feb. 1995; CBA: Sgt. M Thompson, Community Affairs Unit, Avon & Somerset
       Constabulary, to Charlie Beaton, Portishead, 24 Feb. 1995; ASLGPI, Minutes of
       meeting, 14 March 1995.

617   CBA: ASLGPI, Minutes of meeting held at Kingswood Police Station, 1 March 1995.

618   'Police patrol call on "gay sex" toilet block', *BEP*, 3 June 1995.

619   CBA: B Berkeley to Bristol City Council Health & Environmental Services Committee,
       Bristol, 6 June 1995.

620 CBA: ASLGPI, Notes of the meeting held 8 July 1996.

621 CBA: Policing public sex environments (PSE's), Feb. 1998.

622 CBA: Avon and Somerset Constabulary, Policing Public Sex Environments (PSE's), with covering mss. note dated 25/9/98.

623 CBA: Charlie Beaton to Nigel Burbidge, email, no date, commenting on 1001 Force procedural guide 3930 Homophobic incidents, fax copy dated 9 Oct. 1998; 1001 Force procedural guide 3930 Homophobic incidents, HAHQ Force Executive, produced 15 Jan. 1999; Avon and Somerset Constabulary policy: Homophobic incidents 52QP–1133–03, Effective commencement date 9 Oct. 2001.

624 'Fire crew fined for "gay slur"', BEP, 3 Oct. 2007 (Nexis); 'Fire service conference on gay issues', BEP, 9 Oct. 2007 (Nexis); 'Death threat for fire chief after gay sex fine row', BEP, 12 Oct. 2007 (Nexis).

625 Manuel Gosano, interview, 11 April 2008. Under the 1967 Act, sexual activity in saunas was illegal because it was not in private; in the 1970s and 1980s, there were police raids on saunas and they generally had a reputation as dangerous places where customers risked arrest: Paul Crane, Gays and the law (London: Pluto Press, [1982?]), p. 35.

626 'Dad found dying in park toilets', Weston & Worle News, 8 Oct. 1998.

627 Derek McGhee, 'Community safety and lesbian, gay, bisexual and transgender communities' in Community safety: critical perspectives on policy and practice, ed. by Peter Squires (Bristol: Policy Press, 2006), p. 35–51.

628 CBA: M. J. Thompson, Lesbian and gay men issues [ca. 1997].

629 CBA: Notes of meeting with ACC T Grange and ASLGPI, 1 May 1997.

630 Berkeley Wilde, interview, 19 March 2010.

631 CBA: Charlie Beaton to Francis Wilkinson, Bristol, 17 March 1997; Alan McQuillan to Charlie Beaton, Cwmbran, 25 March 1997; ASLGPI, Achievements 1994 to 1997: Briefing Notes, Section 5 [1998].

632 CBA: ASLGPI, Notes of Extra-ordinary Meeting held on 18 Nov. 1999; ASLGPI HQ Policy Liaison meeting, 14 March 2000.

633 CBA: Email from Sal, 20/10/99.

634 'New police post for the vulnerable', BC, 24 Feb. 2000.

635 CBA: Action Against Homophobic Hate Crime Avon & Somerset, Notes of the meeting, 4 Aug. 2004; Charlie Beaton to Steve Cossey, email, 10 May 2005.

636 GWDE, Aug. 1996.

637 GWCM, 7 Aug. 1996.

638 www.avonandsomerset.police.uk/diversity, accessed 27/06/2010.

639 The Policing Initiative also had positive results for some of the individuals involved. For example, the night-club owner, John Hesketh, later became the equalities officer for South Gloucestershire Council and attributes his change of career to the experience he gained with the Initiative: John Hesketh, interview, 26 Nov. 2010.

640 Jürgen Habermas, Between facts and norms: contributions to a discourse theory of law and democracy [1996] (Cambridge: Polity Press, 2008), p. 372.

641 John D'Emilio, Sexual politics, sexual communities: the making of a homosexual minority in the United States, 1940–1970, 2nd ed., (Chicago: University of Chicago Press, 1998); Emma Healey and Angela Mason, eds., Stonewall 25 : the making of the

lesbian and gay community in Britain (London: Virago Press, 1994).

642 Benedict Anderson, *Imagined communities: reflections on the origin and spread of nationalism*, rev. ed., (London: Verso, 2003).

643 Mike Homfray, *Provincial queens: the gay and lesbian community in the North-West of England* (Oxford: Lang, 2007), p. 189–195.

644 Ferdinand Tönnies, *Community and civil society*, ed. by Jose Harris [1887] (Cambridge: Cambridge University Press, 2001), p. 29; Ray Pahl, *On friendship* (Cambridge: Polity Press, 2000), p. 1.

645 David Woolwine, 'Community in gay male experience and moral discourse', in *Gay community survival in the new millennium*, ed. by Michael R. Botnick (New York: Haworth Press, 2000), p. 5–37.

646 Peter M. Nardi, *Gay men's friendships: invincible communities* (Chicago: University of Chicago Press, 1999), p. 189.

647 GWDE, Dec. 1982.

648 GWDE, Christmas double issue 1988–89.

Bibliography

Abbott, David, and Joyce Howarth. *Secret Loves, Hidden Lives? Exploring Issues for People with Learning Difficulties Who Are Gay, Lesbian or Bisexual*. Bristol: Policy Press, 2005.

Amey, Geoffrey. *City under Fire: The Bristol Riots and Aftermath*. Guildford: Lutterworth Press, 1979.

Anderson, Benedict. *Imagined Communities: Reflections on the Origin and Spread of Nationalism*. Rev. ed. London: Verso, 2003.

Anstey, Christopher. *The New Bath Guide*. Bath, 1809.

Archer, Ian, Spencer Jordan, and Keith Ramsey. *Abstract of Bristol Historical Statistics. Part 2: Unemployment Statistics, 1910–1997*. Bristol: Bristol Historical Databases Project, Faculty of Humanities, University of the West of England, 1997.

Avineri, Shlomo, and Avner De-Shalit, eds. *Communitarianism and Individualism*. Oxford: Oxford University Press, 1992.

Babuscio, Jack. *We Speak for Ourselves: Experiences in Homosexual Counselling*. London: SPCK, 1976.

Bauman, Zygmunt. *Community: Seeking Safety in an Insecure World*. Cambridge: Polity Press, 2001.

Bell, Barbara. *Just Take Your Frock Off: A Lesbian Life*. Ed. by Brighton Ourstory Project. Brighton: Ourstory Books, 1999.

Bell, David, and Gill Valentine, eds. *Mapping Desire: Geographies of Sexualities*. London: Routledge, 1995.

Berger, Raymond M. *Gay and Gray: The Older Homosexual Man*. 2nd. ed. New York: Harrington Park Press, 1996.

Bergling, Tim. *Reeling in the Years: Gay Men's Perspectives on Age and Ageism*. New York: Southern Tier Editions/Harrington Park Press, 2004.

Berridge, Virginia. *AIDS in the UK: The Making of Policy, 1981–1994*. Oxford: Oxford University Press, 1996.

Blasius, Mark, ed. *Sexual Identities, Queer Politics*. Princeton: Princeton University Press, 2001.

Boddy, Martin, John Lovering, and Keith Bassett. *Sunbelt City? A Study of Economic Change in Britain's M4 Growth Corridor*. Oxford: Clarendon Press, 1986.

Botnick, Michael R., ed. *Gay Community Survival in the New Millennium*. New York: Haworth Press, 2000.

Brook, Lindsay. "The Public's Response to AIDS." *British Social Attitudes: The 5th Report*. Eds. Roger Jowell, Sharon Witherspoon and Lindsay Brook. Aldershot: Gower, 1988, p. 71–91.

Burnell, Peter, and Peter Calvert, eds. *Civil Society in Democratization*. London: Frank Cass, 2004.

Burston, Peter. *Queens' Country*. London: Little, Brown, 1998.

Burton, Peter. *Parallel Lives*. London: GMP, 1985.

Byrne, Paul. *Social Movements in Britain*. London: Routledge, 1997.

Calhoun, Craig, ed. *Habermas and the Public Sphere*. Cambridge, Mass.: MIT Press, 1992.

——. "Civil Society and the Public Sphere." *Public Culture* 5 (1993): 267–80.

Cant, Bob, ed. *Footsteps & Witnesses: Lesbian and Gay Lifestories from Scotland*. New expanded ed. Edinburgh: Word Power Books, 2008.

Cant, Bob, and Susan Hemmings, eds. *Radical Records: Thirty Years of Lesbian and Gay History, 1957–1987*. London: Routledge, 1988.

Chasin, Alexandra. *Selling Out: The Gay and Lesbian Movement Goes to Market*. New York: Palgrave, 2000.

Chauncey, George. *Gay New York: Gender, Urban Culture, and the Making of the Gay Male World, 1890–1940*. New York: Basic Books, 1994.

Chedgzoy, Kate, Emma Francis, and Murray Pratt, eds. *In a Queer Place: Sexuality and Belonging in British and European Contexts*. Aldershot: Ashgate, 2002.

Clarke, Eric O. *Virtuous Vice: Homoeroticism and the Public Sphere*. Durham, NC: Duke University Press, 2000.

Clements, Phil. *Policing a Diverse Society*. Oxford: Oxford University Press, 2006.

Cohen, Jean L., and Andrew Arato. *Civil Society and Political Theory*. Cambridge, Mass.: MIT Press, 1994.

Cook, Matt. *London and the Culture of Homosexuality, 1885–1914*. Cambridge: Cambridge University Press, 2003.

——, ed. *A Gay History of Britain: Love and Sex between Men since the Middle Ages*. Oxford: Greenwood World Publishing, 2007.

Cooper, Davina. *Sexing the City: Lesbian and Gay Politics within the*

Activist State. London: Rivers Oram Press, 1994.

Crane, Paul. *Gays and the Law*. London: Pluto Press, [1982?].

D'Augelli, Anthony R., and Charlotte J. Patterson, eds. *Lesbian, Gay, and Bisexual Identities over the Lifespan: Psychological Perspectives*. New York: Oxford University Press, 1995.

D'Emilio, John. *Sexual Politics, Sexual Communities: The Making of a Homosexual Minority in the United States, 1940–1970*. 2nd. ed. Chicago: University of Chicago Press, 1998.

David, Hugh. *On Queer Street: A Social History of British Homosexuality, 1895–1995*. London: HarperCollins, 1997.

Deakin, Nicholas. *In Search of Civil Society*. Basingstoke: Palgrave, 2001.

Delanty, Gerard. *Community*. Reprint ed. London: Routledge, 2005.

Dresser, Madge, and Philip Ollerenshaw, eds. *The Making of Modern Bristol*. Tiverton: Redcliffe Press, 1996.

Duggan, Lisa, and Nan D. Hunter, eds. *Sex Wars: Sexual Dissent and Political Culture*. New York: Routledge, 1995.

Edwards, Michael. *Civil Society*. Cambridge: Polity Press, 2004.

Ehrenberg, John. *Civil Society: The Critical History of an Idea*. New York: New York University Press, 1999.

Elliott, Kirsten, and Andrew Swift. *Bath Pubs*. [Bath?]: Akeman Press, 2003.

Engel, Stephen M. *The Unfinished Revolution: Social Movement Theory and the Gay and Lesbian Movement*. Cambridge: Cambridge University Press, 2001.

Evans, David T. *Sexual Citizenship: The Material Construction of Sexualities*. London: Routledge, 1993.

Evans, Geoffrey. "In Search of Tolerance." *British Social Attitudes: The 19th Report*. Ed. Alison Park [et al.]. London: Sage/National Centre for Social Research, 2002, p. 213–29.

Fawcett, Trevor. *Bath Commercialis'd: Shops, Trades and Market at the 18th-Century Spa*. Bath: Ruton, 2002.

Fergusson, Adam. *The Sack of Bath: A Record and an Indictment*. Salisbury: Compton Russell, 1973.

Field, Nicola. *Over the Rainbow: Money, Class and Homophobia*. London: Pluto Press, 1995.

Ford, Theresa, and Karen Birch. *Bath: The Golden Years; from the Archives of the Bath Chronicle*. Tiverton: Halsgrove/Bath Chronicle, 2003.

Gatter, Philip. *Identity and Sexuality: AIDS in Britain in the 1990s*. London: Cassell, 1999.

Gay Left Collective, ed. *Homosexuality: Power & Politics*. London: Allison and Busby, 1980.

Glasius, Marlies, David Lewis, and Hakan Seckinelgin, eds. *Exploring Civil Society: Political and Cultural Contexts*. London: Routledge, 2004.

Goldstein, Richard. *Homocons: The Rise of the Gay Right*. London: Verso, 2003.

Gorsky, Martin. "Mutual Aid and Civil Society: Friendly Societies in Nineteenth-Century Bristol." *Urban History* 25.3 (1998): 302–22.

——. *Patterns of Philanthropy: Charity and Society in Nineteenth-Century Bristol*. Woodbridge, Suffolk: The Royal Historical Society/ The Boydell Press, 1999.

Green, James N. *Beyond Carnival: Male Homosexuality in Twentieth-Century Brazil*. Chicago: University of Chicago Press, 1999.

Green, Sarah F. *Urban Amazons: Lesbian Feminism and Beyond in the Gender, Sexuality and Identity Battles of London*. Basingstoke: Macmillan, 1997.

Grey, Antony. *Quest for Justice: Towards Homosexual Emancipation*. London: Sinclair-Stevenson, 1992.

——. *Speaking Out: Writings on Sex, Law, Politics and Society, 1954– 1995*. London: Cassell, 1997.

Habermas, Jürgen. "Further Reflections on the Public Sphere." *Habermas and the Public Sphere*. Ed. Craig Calhoun. Cambridge, Mass.: MIT Press, 1992, p. 421–61.

——. *Between Facts and Norms: Contributions to a Discourse Theory of Law and Democracy*. Cambridge: Polity Press, 2008.

——. *The Structural Transformation of the Public Sphere: An Enquiry into a Category of Bourgeois Society*. Cambridge: Polity Press, 2009.

Hagemann, Karen, Sonya Michel, and Gunilla Budde, eds. *Civil Society and Gender Justice: Historical and Comparative Perspectives*. Oxford: Berghahn Books, 2008.

Hall Carpenter Archives Gay Men's Oral History Group, ed. *Walking after Midnight: Gay Men's Life Stories*. London: Routledge, 1989.

Hall Carpenter Archives Lesbian Oral History Group, ed. *Inventing Ourselves: Lesbian Life Stories*. London: Routledge, 1989.

Hamer, Emily. *Britannia's Glory: A History of Twentieth-Century Lesbians*. London: Cassell, 1996.

Hanscombe, Gillian E., and Andrew Lumsden. *Title Fight: The Battle for Gay News*. London: Brilliance Books, 1983.

Harding, Stephen. "Trends in Permissiveness." *British Social Attitudes: The 5th Report*. Eds. Roger Jowell, Sharon Witherspoon and Lindsay Brook. Aldershot: Gower, 1988, p. 35–51.

Healey, Emma, and Angela Mason, eds. *Stonewall 25: The Making of the*

Lesbian and Gay Community in Britain. London: Virago Press, 1994.

Heinze, Eric. *Sexual Orientation: A Human Right: An Essay on International Human Rights Law.* Dordrecht: Martinus Nijhoff Publishers, 1995.

Herdt, Gilbert, ed. *Gay Culture in America: Essays from the Field.* Boston, Mass.: Beacon Press, 1992.

Higgins, Patrick. *Heterosexual Dictatorship: Male Homosexuality in Postwar Britain.* London: Fourth Estate, 1996.

Higgs, David. *Queer Sites: Gay Urban Histories since 1600.* London: Routledge, 1999.

Hodgson, Lesley C. "Helping the Salmon: The Role of Civil Society in the Development of Human Rights." *JIJIS* 5 (2005): 11–23.

Homfray, Mike. *Provincial Queens: The Gay and Lesbian Community in the North-West of England.* Oxford: Peter Lang, 2007.

Horsfall, Allan. "Wolfenden in the Wilderness." *New Left Review* I.12 (1961): 29–31.

Houlbrook, Matt. *Queer London: Perils and Pleasures in the Sexual Metropolis, 1918–1957.* Chicago: University of Chicago Press, 2005.

Humphreys, Laud. *Tearoom Trade: A Study of Homosexual Encounters in Public Places.* Reprint ed. London: Duckworth, 1974.

Ingram, Gordon Brent, Anne-Marie Bouthillette, and Yolanda Retter, eds. *Queers in Space: Communities, Public Places, Sites of Resistance.* Seattle: Bay Press, 1997.

Jeffery-Poulter, Stephen. *Peers, Queers, and Commons: The Struggle for Gay Law Reform from 1950 to the Present.* London: Routledge, 1991.

Jordan, Spencer, Keith Ramsey, and Matthew Woollard. *Abstract of Bristol Historical Statistics. Part 3: Political Representation and Bristol's Elections, 1700–1997.* Bristol: Bristol Historical Databases Project, Faculty of Humanities, University of the West of England, 1997.

Joseph, Miranda. *Against the Romance of Community.* Minneapolis: University of Minnesota Press, 2002.

Kendall, Christopher, and Wayne Martino, eds. *Gendered Outcasts and Sexual Outlaws: Sexual Oppression and Gender Hierarchies in Queer Men's Lives.* New York: Harrington Park Press, 2006.

Kimmel, Douglas, Tara Rose, and Steven David, eds. *Lesbian, Gay, Bisexual, and Transgender Aging: Research and Clinical Perspectives.* New York: Columbia University Press, 2006.

Kirkup, James. *A Poet Could Not but Be Gay: Some Legends of My Lost Youth.* London: Peter Owen, 1991.

Lansley, Stewart, Sue Goss, and Christian Wolmar. *Councils in Crisis: The*

Rise and Fall of the Municipal Left. Basingstoke: Macmillan, 1989.

Leap, William L., ed. *Public Sex/Gay Space*. New York: Columbia University Press, 1999.

Leishman, Frank, Barry Loveday and Stephen P. Savage, eds. *Core Issues in Policing*. 2nd. ed. Harlow: Pearson Education, 2000.

Lent, Adam. *British Social Movements since 1945: Sex, Colour, Peace and Power*. Basingstoke: Palgrave, 2001.

Lipschutz, Ronnie D., ed. *Civil Societies and Social Movements: Domestic, Transnational, Global*. Aldershot: Ashgate, 2006.

Little, Adrian. *The Politics of Community: Theory and Practice*. Edinburgh: Edinburgh University Press, 2002.

Lucas, Ian. *Outrage! An Oral History*. London: Cassell, 1998.

Macourt, Malcolm. *How Can We Help You? Information, Advice and Counselling for Gay Men and Lesbians*. London: Bedford Square Press, 1989.

Madison, G. B. *The Political Economy of Civil Society and Human Rights*. London: Routledge, 1998.

Marshall, Peter. *The Prevalence of Convictions for Sexual Offending*. [London]: Home Office Research and Statistics Directorate, 1997.

McBride, Keally D. *Collective Dreams: Political Imagination & Community*. University Park, Pennsylvania: Pennsylvania State University Press, 2005.

McGhee, Derek. *Homosexuality, Law and Resistance*. London: Routledge, 2001.

Melucci, Alberto. *Nomads of the Present: Social Movements and Individual Needs in Contemporary Society*. Ed. by John Keane and Paul Mier. London: Hutchinson Radius, 1989.

Morris, R. J. "Clubs, Societies and Associations." *The Cambridge Social History of Britain, 1750–1950. Volume 3. Social Agencies and Institutions*. Ed. F. M. L. Thompson. Cambridge: Cambridge University Press, 1990, p. 395–443.

Mort, Frank, and Lynda Nead, eds. *Sexual Geographies* (New Formations; 37). London: Lawrence & Wishart, 1999.

Nardi, Peter M. *Gay Men's Friendships: Invincible Communities*. Chicago: University of Chicago Press, 1999.

Nichols, Gerry. *Clifton and Durdham Downs: A Place of Public Resort and Recreation*. Bristol: Bristol Branch of the Historical Association, 2006.

Pahl, Ray. *On Friendship*. Cambridge: Polity Press, 2000.

Pearce, Fred. *The Critical Guide to Bath Pubs*. Bristol: Bristol Pub Guides, [1976?].

Phelan, Shane. *Sexual Strangers: Gays, Lesbians, and Dilemmas of Citizenship*. Philadelphia: Temple University Press, 2001.

Plummer, Kenneth, ed. *The Making of the Modern Homosexual*. London: Hutchinson, 1981.

Poole, Steve. "'Bringing Great Shame upon this City': Sodomy, the Courts and the Civic Idiom in Eighteenth-Century Bristol." *Urban History* 34.1 (2007): 114–126.

Power, Lisa. *No Bath but Plenty of Bubbles: An Oral History of the Gay Liberation Front, 1970–73*. London: Cassell, 1995.

Priest, Gordon, and Pamela Cobb, eds. *The Fight for Bristol: Planning and the Growth of Public Protest*. Bristol: Bristol Civic Society and the Redcliffe Press, 1980.

Prochaska, Frank. *Schools of Citizenship: Charity and Civic Virtue*. London: Civitas, 2002.

Purdue, Derrick, Mario Diani, and Isobel Lindsay. "Civic Networks in Bristol and Glasgow." *Community Development Journal* 39.3 (2004): 277–88.

Purton, Peter. *Sodom, Gomorrah and the New Jerusalem: Labour and Lesbian and Gay Rights, from Edward Carpenter to Today*. London: Labour Campaign for Lesbian and Gay Rights, 2006.

Rayside, David. *On the Fringe: Gays and Lesbians in Politics*. Ithaca, NY: Cornell University Press, 1998.

Read, Melvyn, David Marsh, and David Richards. "Why Did They Do It? Voting on Homosexuality and Capital Punishment in the House of Commons." *Parliamentary Affairs* 47.3 (July 1994): 374–86.

Richards, Peter G. "Homosexuality." *Parliament and Conscience*. Ed. Peter G. Richards. London: George Allen & Unwin, 1970, p. 63–84.

Rimmerman, Craig A. *From Identity to Politics: The Lesbian and Gay Movements in the United States*. Philadelphia: Temple University Press, 2002.

Robinson, Lucy. *Gay Men and the Left in Post-War Britain: How the Personal Got Political*. Manchester: Manchester University Press, 2007.

Robinson, Paul. *Queer Wars: The New Gay Right and Its Critics*. Chicago: University of Chicago Press, 2005.

Robinson, Peter. *The Changing World of Gay Men*. Basingstoke: Palgrave Macmillan, 2008.

Segal, Lynne, ed. *New Sexual Agendas*. Basingstoke: Macmillan, 1997.

Smith, Anna Marie. *New Right Discourse on Race and Sexuality*. Cambridge: Cambridge University Press, 1994.

Squires, Peter, ed. *Community Safety: Critical Perspectives on Policy and*

Practice. Bristol: Policy Press, 2006.

Sullivan, Andrew. *Virtually Normal: An Argument about Homosexuality*. London: Picador, 1995.

Swift, Andrew, and Kirsten Elliott. *The Lost Pubs of Bath*. [Bath?]: Akeman Press, 2005.

Tarrow, Sidney. *Power in Movement: Social Movements and Contentious Politics*. 2nd. ed. Cambridge: Cambridge University Press, 1998.

Taylor, Charles. "Modes of Civil Society." *Public Culture* 3.1 (1990): 95–118.

Tilley, Nick. "Modern Approaches to Policing: Community, Problem-Oriented and Intelligence-Led." *Handbook of Policing*. Ed. Tim Newburn. 2nd. ed. Cullompton: Willan Publishing, 2008, p. 373–403.

Tobin, Ann. "Lesbianism and the Labour Party: The GLC Experience." *Feminist Review* 34 (1990): 56–66.

Tönnies, Ferdinand. *Community and Civil Society*. Ed. by Jose Harris. Cambridge: Cambridge University Press, 2001.

Troiden, Richard R. *Gay and Lesbian Identity: A Sociological Analysis*. New York: General Hall, 1988.

Turner, Mark W. *Backward Glances: Cruising the Queer Streets of New York and London*. London: Reaktion Books, 2003.

Vieira, Oscar Vilhena, and A. Scott DuPree. "Reflections on Civil Society and Human Rights." *SUR: International Journal on Human Rights* 1.1 (2004): 47–65.

Waites, Matthew. *The Age of Consent: Young People, Sexuality and Citizenship*. Basingstoke: Palgrave Macmillan, 2009.

Walmsley, Roy. "Indecency between Males and the Sexual Offences Act 1967." *Criminal Law Review* (July 1978): 400–07.

Walton, Tony, ed. *Out of the Shadows : How London Gay Life Changed for the Better after the Act: A History of the Pioneering London Gay Groups and Organisations, 1967–2000*. London: Bona Street Press, 2010.

Walzer, Michael. "The Idea of Civil Society: A Path to Social Reconstruction." *Dissent* (Spring 1991): 293–304.

Warner, Michael, ed. *Fear of a Queer Planet: Queer Politics and Social Theory*. Minneapolis: University of Minnesota Press, 1993.

Warren, Carol A. B. *Identity and Community in the Gay World*. New York: John Wiley & Sons, 1974.

Weeks, Jeffrey. *Coming Out: Homosexual Politics in Britain from the Nineteenth Century to the Present*. Rev. ed. London: Quartet Books, 1990.

——. *Against Nature: Essays on History, Sexuality and Identity.* London: Rivers Oram Press, 1995.

——. *Making Sexual History.* Cambridge: Polity Press, 2000.

——. *The World We Have Won: The Remaking of Erotic and Intimate Life.* London: Routledge, 2007.

Weeks, Jeffrey, and Janet Holland, eds. *Sexual Cultures: Communities, Values and Intimacy.* Basingstoke: Macmillan, 1996.

Weeks, Jeffrey, and Kevin Porter, eds. *Between the Acts: Lives of Homosexual Men, 1885–1967.* 2nd. ed. London: Rivers Oram Press, 1998.

Wellings, Kaye, and Jane Wadsworth. "AIDS and the Moral Climate." *British Social Attitudes: The 7th Report.* Eds. Roger Jowell, Sharon Witherspoon and Lindsay Brook. Aldershot: Gower, 1990, p. 109–26.

Whisman, Vera. *Queer by Choice: Lesbians, Gay Men, and the Politics of Identity.* New York: Routledge, 1995.

Whittle, Stephen, ed. *The Margins of the City: Gay Men's Urban Lives.* Aldershot: Arena, 1994.

Wildebood, Peter. *Against the Law.* London: Weidenfeld and Nicolson, 1999.

Wilson, Angelia R., ed. *A Simple Matter of Justice? Theorizing Lesbian and Gay Politics.* London: Cassell, 1995.

Withers, Deborah M. *Sistershow Revisited: Feminism in Bristol, 1973–1975.* [Bristol?]: HammerOn Press, 2011.

Woodhouse, Adrian. *Angus Mcbean: Face-Maker.* Richmond, Surrey: Alma Books, 2006.

Young, Iris Marion. "The Ideal of Community and the Politics of Difference." *Social Theory and Practice* 12.1 (1986): 1–26.

Lightning Source UK Ltd.
Milton Keynes UK
UKOW040658191011

180569UK00001B/2/P

9 781906 236755